Jean Murray

please review

on amazon.co.uk

or share it's name
on your face book page

available on
amazon

Jean Murray left school at age 16 to become a hairdresser. Her love for education brought her to St Peter's College in Dunboyne in 2003/4 where she completed a fulltime PLC course in Business Studies. She received distinctions in each of her seven modules including media studies. A lover of reading, Jean had always wanted to write her own book and began to write notes over the years until she finally started writing in September 2013! She is married to Anthony and they have three children, Anthony Jr 24, Sarah 18 and Yasmin aged 9.

Her beloved mother is still alive at age 72, and she has five sisters: Olive 47, Herself 46, Josie 45, Sharon 44, Eleanor 42 and Christine 41 and 14 nieces and nephews on her side. She loves her huge extended family on Anthony's side also!

15/3/17

I'd like to dedicate my book to my dad Christopher Sutton, 1942 – 2006 for without his pain, I would never have been able to write this book. For my mam Marie Kelly Sutton, who although it pained her, supported me all the way.

(My brother-in-law who passed away) Myles Graham.

I would like to thank Yasmin's team of helpers, Andrea Magennis Dyslexia tutor; Also, Emir Crowley for Occupational Therapy, Catherine Clinton for Maths and English Resource and OT in school, and the dedicated team of Special needs assistants and teachers at Rathbeggan National School. Not forgetting Margaret in the office, for all the plasters and tissues to comfort Yasmin's falls!'

I would like to thank Danyelle Dominguez for the beautiful cover photo of Yasmin. Danyelle is the photographer that took lots of lovely pictures of the children at Yasmin's cousin Amanda's wedding in Texas in 2012.

I would like to acknowledge the passing of dear family and friends during my journey of writing this book.

Val Murray
Peter Murray
Joey Hanway
Thomas Shaw

Jean Murray

MY BEAUTIFUL FLOWER

AUSTIN MACAULEY
PUBLISHERS LTD.

A CIP catalogue record for this title is available from the British Library.

ISBN 9781849637138

www.austinmacauley.com

First Published (2015)
Austin Macauley Publishers Ltd.
25 Canada Square
Canary Wharf
London
E14 5LB

Printed and bound in Great Britain

Acknowledgments

I'd like to thank my sister in law, Marcy Murray, English Literature Lecturer in Florida, for her guidance.

I'd like to thank my dear friends, Caroline, Teresa and Lorraine for being there to share my tears and laughter; also Jacinta, Pauline Christine and Martha Dowling , for being great fun girls!

I'd like to thank my husband's loyal crew for their hard work, dedication and support throughout this recession; John Tormey, Paul O Conner, Patrick Doyle, Derek Ward, Tony Hawkins, Billy Murray, Anthony Murray Jr, John Murray Jr. and Christine Turner, for keeping all things going in the office.

The Hanway's for being good friends throughout.

Aunty Josie for feeding her boys. The McMahon's. The O Reilly's. All of my aunties, uncles and cousins.

Stephanie, Catherine and Ursula and the rest of my Finbar GAA Club girlfriends for treasured memories.

I'd like to thank Rosena, Caroline, Ciara, Ray, Sue and Mark and my 'Wysteria Lane' neighbours, Catherine, Taunya, Bernie , Lorna, Sharon, Brenda, Suzanne, Cairosa and Emma for my new memories.

I'd like to thank Josie Shaw for telling me to keep going, it wasn't finished.

I'd like to thank my Ma, my sisters, Olive, Josie, Sharon, Eleanor and Christine for putting up with all of my tantrums throughout our lives.

I'd like to thank Pauline and Deco and Derek for all of their help and all of my brothers in law, all of my sisters in law and all of our nieces and nephews, for all their love.

I'd like to thank my husband Anto, my son Anthony, his future wife Sally and my daughter Sarah for all their support and encouragement. For the constant loyalty of my dogs, Skye, Storm and Sully and our dearly missed, Pongo, Buster and Buffy.

I would like to acknowledge Bob and Noeleen Grace and their family, who will always hold a special place in my heart.

I would like to also thank, Hayley, Gemma, Vinh and Rob from the Austin Macauley team. For saying yes to my story and for guiding me through it.

I would like to take this opportunity to thank all of you who have bought my book and are reading it right now!

I would also like to thank Steven Hawking for being an amazing example of a human being.

Most of all, I would like to thank God for giving me a second chance and for sending me his gift of Yasmin.

My Beautiful flower!

Contents

Introduction

Yasmin is a great one for talking in the car. Ever since she could talk, she would babble away in her little car seat. In her early years of life, I would take the opportunity to think about all my problems while driving, not listening to Yasmin. I was in my own world, thinking of my woes. If I had of known to just focus on listening then, I would have saved myself a lot of heartache and trouble.

I had been through quite a lot in my life and even when I was in my early 30's, I thought that I should write a book. It could be funny! Looking back, I probably felt a bit sorry for myself. I also had a lot of things to say about the world we live in and I knew a book was a great way to have my say!

I kept putting it off though, making excuses. When I had my much adored last child Yasmin, now aged 9, I was very busy. Yasmin had a lot of difficulties. She had a delayed mental development, which meant she was a baby for a lot more years than the average child. My biggest fear was that Yasmin couldn't be educated. I loved reading and when I started to research Yasmin's difficulties, I was aghast to find that Yasmin may never read beyond the age of a 5 year old. It broke my heart to discover that she wouldn't be able to participate in sports at any level. I couldn't accept that and I took on the task to make sure that Yasmin had every opportunity to be educated, in her literacy, numerical, emotional and physical needs. I could see that Yasmin found it really difficult and it pained me, but she never gave up.

She amazed me from the very start!

I started to really listen to Yasmin then. She was so special! Plentiful with her love and laughter. Through her strength and stamina, she inspired me to write my book.

To not just try to do it! To actually do it!

Initially my book was going to be about growing up in tough times in Cabra. There were also lots of funny things I could write about my husband and his family, but as I started to write, it became about my personal struggles with myself and the difficulties I encountered in life and as a parent. I was side by side with Yasmin's struggles trying to learn to read, to write, to fit in with her friends. As I looked at my little girl working so hard to overcome her difficulties, I began to work harder on myself. I had to be better for her. I wanted to write about Yasmin, to share with you her difficulties and her strengths. I wanted to share with you my difficulties with depression.

I had listened to the radio over the last few years and there was a lot of coverage about depression.

It's fairly new in Ireland for people to talk about their emotions and they were very cautious, both the interviewer and the interviewee. I wanted to go into a lot more detail, partly because as a woman I think we are more vocal and also the confusion as to why people commit suicide. Their families are left behind to carry the burden of guilt.

My depression had a huge effect on my husband, my children and my other family members and I had to learn to live with it peacefully.

I would never have worked on my own difficulties had I not witnessed Yasmin's determination to succeed because she loved me so much and wanted to please me.

I am so proud of her.

As a child growing up in the 1970's male dominated Ireland, I struggled with my dad's alcoholism and the tolerance of our system that allowed the Irish man to behave as badly as they wanted to. In a world that wasn't encouraged to talk about emotions or fears, I repressed my feelings, which was the start of my losing myself. I struggled through puberty and had early signs of depression. I struggled as a parent, I struggled with relationships and I struggled with God. I blamed others.

It led me to an inevitable breakdown. I wasn't looking at myself and accepting my own responsibility for the mistakes and the choices I had made in my life. I had become a victim. I had allowed myself to become a victim.

So, after all the years of counselling and taking advise from others on how to do it right. Something wasn't right. I thought back to my counselling sessions. I was always saying, 'he did, she did.' I knew that I was at fault in some way, but I just didn't know where. I was confused, cloudy, emotional, focused on the wrong problem each time.

I wanted help. I wanted to change. I wanted to be happy. The counselling wasn't enough. It hadn't worked completely. I was still a failure. I wasn't happy inside. I could blame only myself.

I had to finally listen to myself and dissect the feelings in my head. Then I started to hear God. His advice. His direction.

And when I looked at my beautiful Yasmin then, I realised that she was a gift from God.

He had sent Yasmin to me to help me. God had sent me a child who needed me to be a different me. Calm, focused, patient, quiet, loving, accepting and encouraging. And all of a sudden, I was grateful!

When I looked at the beautiful sky and clouds, I realised they were also gifts and I was grateful. Then I was grateful for all the other beautiful creations from God. There were so many beautiful things around me that I was so grateful for. Now I started to see clearly.

And only then did my life start to change.

As I finally let go of the resentments of the past 45 years, I could finally rejoice in each new day of life.
My gratitude for the gifts that I have received in life, family and friends, health, beautiful children and the beautiful Earth we live on. I am blessed.

When I started to listen to Yasmin I realized that she had a lot of important things to say too! I acknowledge her. In having a better relationship with my last child, it's also helped me in my relationships with my older children, now young adults. Now, after a car journey, I dash into the house to write down the things that Yasmin talks about, because sometimes they're so funny, sometimes so cute, sometimes she's trying to figure things out!

Yasmin is My Beautiful Flower!

1

My Beautiful Flower

I see my beautiful child,
not with a disability.
She wants to dance
She wants to sing
She likes being pretty.

I see my beautiful child,
She wants to run
She wants to swim
She wants to show jump competitively!

I don't see her disability.
I let her dance
I let her run
I let her sing
I let her swim
I'll let her show jump competitively!

She works so hard,
She likes to please,
I don't see her disability!

Some don't see what I see.
What a loss for them,
because if they looked at this beautiful child,
They would learn God's wishes.

This poem is about my little girl Yasmin. I wrote it after an upsetting plane journey to France in June 2013, when a French woman spoke rudely about my little girl in French, not realising I understood what she said.

When I started to look back over my life as I began to write notes for my book a couple of years ago, I realized my life was crazy. It was chaotic. It was busy. I couldn't have stayed at that pace for long.

I was able to keep up that hectic pace as a young woman in my 20's. I could work, have my house spotless, do sports, drink, take Anthony to his sports, wash and dry our clothes, be a wife.

My body looked similar to the woman in her 20's, yet my mind was different.

Why did it decide to change now? Take a stand! Say no! I can't do it anymore!

It certainly slowed me down, big time. What did I have to do to get my mind going again? Would it be easy? No. It was going to be difficult. I had to discover everything that I had forgotten about myself to make it work again. I have learned a lot and I would like to share these words with others and maybe prevent any one person from feeling the pain that I have felt and the loneliness that I have experienced.

I am not better and I am not cured, but I am trying. I think honesty is very important to oneself.

My words go deep and personal into my innermost thoughts, but I don't think it would have worked if it didn't. People are playing the game of life. We are all performing in our roles as worker, Mother, Father, Wife, Husband and so on. We look at others playing their role in what seems to be happier or better than ours. We then judge them by appearances, making us feel better than them or maybe making us feel worse off than them, causing us to resent them. We don't really know what's going on for these people, but I can assure you, everybody has their fair share of problems. I'm pretty sure most people want to live life to the best of their ability.

There are a few bad people, but where did they come from? Can we really ever change society so that the bad ones are gone for good?

In a fantasy world, if all of the children came from ordinary happy homes and had all of their educational, physical and emotional needs met, would society change?

I think it would.

At the very least, everyone would be equally educated and have higher self-esteem. Having low self-esteem gives people a negative view of themselves causing self-hatred and secrecy. There's an old age tradition among the Irish people; Tell people nothing!

I think it's time we got rid of that tradition and started a new one. Tell people everything! Take the taboo away. Talking about our problems will take the stigma of shame away. We are all the same. We are all human beings. Our bodies all work the same way, regardless of colour or creed.

I have finally accepted that I am not perfect, but I am grateful for who I am now. I'm not striving for perfection, just happiness. As a young woman, I wanted to be perfect. I whipped myself for making mistakes.

I don't blame God for putting me through anguish and pain. I heard a saying once that God will only give you what you can handle. I take comfort in those words delighted that I won't be crushed in a crumbling building or lost in caves! My claustrophobic fear! I do believe that on our road of life, we are given two paths, an easy one and a hard one. I remember choosing the hard path and letting the easy one go. At the time, I didn't think I deserved straight forward happiness. I didn't value myself. I deserved misery. I also think the hard path will teach you what you didn't learn in your childhood years, so maybe there is the reason I took it.

I think the Devil is present in weak people and can enter our lives at any moment. I think our challenge in life is to shake him off, to walk in the footsteps of respect, compassion and kindness. I know we are capable of doing it.

I believe life is a learning place. We have to learn how to live. Some of us take a long time to learn. Some of us might not be lucky enough to learn before we die.

This is not about preaching to people that I know better than they. I don't.

I know my life was very painful before I started to realize what life was really about. I started counselling sessions when I was 22 years old. The reason being that I suffered severe Post Natal depression after I had my first son and I had no idea of what it was. My depression was so severe because I was already carrying around depression since I was 11 years old. Of course I never knew what was wrong with me so I wore a mask and on the outside I had this happy go lucky attitude.

I cried a lot in those sessions over the years. I didn't know what was wrong with me, why I was so angry. I didn't know what life was about then. Although a new word at the time, I suspected I had the new word doing the rounds at that time, Post Natal depression.

My doctor wisely suggested self-help groups to find out why I was depressed rather than start me on the early road of anti-depressants at that young age. It was the best advice to receive. When I went to Al Anon, a self-help group for families of alcoholics, it turned my life around for the better and then I started on my road to discovery of myself. It was a long road, but worth it.

When I had Yasmin, I was forced to slow down to her pace and only then did I really start to learn.

Open your eyes and see the beauty that surrounds you. Focus on the beauty. Focus on the smile of your child, that's the only thing that's important in life. What greater gift than the love of a child?

But, you also have to love yourself.

When we were growing up, we were taught that it was a sin to love yourself. That came from our catholic religion. That was the road to disaster for the Irish people right there. We had to put ourselves last. We couldn't be vain, we couldn't say we were good at anything. We couldn't compliment ourselves for a kind act. That kind of thinking does a lot of damage to us human beings.

As owners of a construction company, myself and my husband have had our own huge financial challenges since the recession hit Ireland in January 2007. Having a child with difficulties that needed to have various assessments cost us a small fortune, which we were happy to pay for. Yasmin was our responsibility. We would give her every educational chance possible regardless of the cost, but mortgages and bills have to be paid. Groceries have to be bought. Santa has to come.

I began to worry.

Also, having a child with huge needs put a real strain on our marriage. I found it difficult to meet my husband's needs.

I had no needs of my own. My needs were making sure everybody was ok and that everything was organised.

I was used to putting my needs last, but now I was worn down. It didn't bother me when I was younger. Then through my 30's and 40's I guess I felt I was getting worse at life instead of better and I began to feel very unimportant. It had a huge effect on my self-esteem. I began to doubt myself. I wasn't sure if I was doing anything right as a mother. In the early years of Yasmin, I knew I was doing things wrong. I began to hate myself. I was in a bad place emotionally.

As a young woman, I was ambitious. I yearned for success in my career. Now, all I wanted was to be successful in my relationships with my children.

I realised , the joy of seeing my children's achievements because of the difference I make as a Mother is the positive energy I breathe every day. I am important. I make a difference. I had to start believing this..

Yasmin was born with a disability called Dyspraxia, which is a muscular disability, which simply explained means delayed mental and muscle development.

It also affected her eye tracking muscles, affecting her ability to read in sequence. Basically, all her gross motor skills and all her fine motor skills, sensory difficulties, comprehension difficulties, anxiety and learning difficulties which I will go into in a lot more detail later on.

As a baby of 10 and 12 months when some babies are nearly walking at this stage, Yasmin had no balance. She had difficulty in sitting and would just topple over, often hurting her head seriously.

But Yasmin's excitement for life, the love she spreads and the beautiful smile she gives me every morning, saying, "I love you Mammy, you're the best Mammy in the whole wide world", has been the force behind my fight with depression. She has brought me closer to God, and through Yasmin, God is teaching me love, gratitude, patience, compassion, sympathy, strength, courage, value for life, and self-happiness.

I learned in these nine years, what I hadn't learned in my first 37 years of life.

When each one of my three children was born, I was amazed by my capacity to love and cherish. I had never felt anything like it before.

The depth of my love was endless. I would do anything for my children, I knew that for sure. Each child would teach me about life, if I listened carefully. They would show me the way.

My story is about the life I was born into. Situations that formed and moulded me into the person I became, that I may not have become, had my spirit been nurtured and encouraged to grow.

Being constantly criticized and controlled as a child by my father led me to be secretive and defensive throughout my life with no confidence. I never trusted anyone enough to ask for help often leading me into dangerous situations.

I struggled with the pain of life from age 11, causing eating disorders and suicide thoughts.

I witnessed my dad changing through alcoholism, from a good man into the Devil himself. Taking advantage of the fact that men had the power to abuse their women in 1970 Ireland.

I resented the fact that other women and my mother had to live under this regiment of control.

Through my own dysfunctions, I ran into a life of challenges with my own alcoholic husband. I struggled with my emotions, raising my children with a Dad they loved but the difficulty of the unreliability of a husband who made excuses each time he was late or missed a family event, or passed out at the Christmas dinner .

I needed to go back to the beginning to see where my parents came from to discover why their two different lives, both born into poverty led to such different personalities. Dad holding on to bitterness and resentment. Mam, accepting, kind and always forgiving. How both of their personalities had affected their children.

Raised as a Catholic child, God was very present in in our lives. School was very much like, 'What would God think about that?' I struggled with God and the Catholic Church. I used to say, 'Where are you God?' Women and children suffered terrible violence, abuse and poverty in Cabra where I grew up. And God never helped.

I knew the Devil existed as I met him twice in my life. He had possessed my dad's mind for ten long years in 1977. He was evil, mean, ugly and torturous. He spat venom. He wouldn't leave my dad's body. My dad wasn't strong enough to banish him.

The second time was even more horrific, when he gazed through my husband's eyes. as I banished him from my home.

I'll remember forever the shock I felt at that moment when I saw the Devil again.

It amazes me even now, that the Devil was so obviously visible during those years and I couldn't see God at all.

I thought I'd write about my struggles through the 2007 recession as a Mother this time and as a Wife, trying to support my husband in his struggles with his construction company.

And as a Woman, struggling to find my path in life.

Difficult times cause disturbances in the normal mental attitude.

I started to behave just like my father , with my beautiful children. I was aware of my bad behaviour though and I was in agony. I knew I didn't want to continue it. Thankfully, a subconscious force of Good coming from somewhere guided me, pushed me on, forced me to change. I learned to admit when I was wrong, to accept my responsibility and permanently change. It wasn't an easy task.

This book is not about blame or judgement. My father was a good man. He did his best. He was weak and he allowed the Devil to take him over. Through his mistakes, I am cautious of making the same, so through his pain, I have learned.

It's my path of self-discovery. I needed to understand my mind. I needed to work it out. How did this once tough toddler with lots of confidence get depression? How did my mind get sick? I had to look back at my beginning and follow the path. I needed to learn about my parents and their parenting skills. I needed to learn how to do things differently.

I needed to change the circle of abuse.

Giving every child, especially from poorer areas, a complete education is their only path from dysfunction. It's imperative to meet the educational, emotional and physical needs of each child, so that there will be a different outcome to their lives.
Of course, our government has known this for a long time. They are the only force who can help the poverty stricken. They can make sure each child's educational needs are met through more welfare nurses, teachers and special needs assistants. Surely they realise that in the long run it will pay off, with less suicides alone!

My daughter Yasmin's amazing struggle, her stamina, climbing over each hurdle, growing in spirit, teaching me, guiding me has been my inspiration . Through experiencing Yasmin's difficulties, I have found help for myself.

Having to completely slow down and hear and feel Yasmin's needs has given me huge respect for her and every child.

Yasmin was teaching me and I was starting to listen.

When she is in pain, I have to comfort her, a hundred times a day, learning that I needed to comfort myself. When she found it too hard to learn, she had to keep trying. Showing me not to give up, to keep trying in life.

When she willingly goes to all her extra help sessions, she puts her trust in me that this is a good thing.

She will be able to succeed in life.

She showed me trust and support.

My Beautiful Flower Yasmin. My gift from god.

Truly delivered by the angels.

Children who come from poverty backgrounds with dysfunctions such as, illiteracy, alcoholism, drugs, violence, go on to have mental problems, go into crime, become violent and murderers themselves. They become sex offenders after receiving sexual abuse and inevitably some commit suicide because life is just too painful.

Those of us who survive have a message to spread.

Jean age 45, 2012 Breakdown

I can't do this God! It's too hard!

I'm no good at it anyway. Why did you choose me for this life?

I was so angry one day as I was running around trying to be the perfect person. I was screaming at God in my car as I was speeding down a motorway. 'Fuck you! I fucking hate you! I hate you! I hate myself! I hate myself! If anyone had heard me they would have surely sent me off to a mental house.

I blamed God for putting me in this life. I hated myself so much because I couldn't do it. My husband disliked me and it seemed like my two older children did too.

I was so sad and weary. I wanted it to end.

God take me please. Take me out of this life, I'm making a mess of it. My mind was in pain.

'You have to live with your mind,
The pain that you cause,
The guilt that you carry,
For not being good enough. For not being a better person.
They would be better off without you.
But your child needs you!
How to do this?
How to carry on?
Go out and try enjoy the nature of life, maybe it will help.
It will distract you at least.'

Why is life so hard?
'The pain, emotional pain,
feelings of uselessness, feelings of failure, running through my veins.
The nausea in my tummy,
I can't escape.
I can't function.
How can I be a Mother?'

I can't walk out on them, leave them with blame or guilt.
Alone.
I can't take them with me.
Please don't pity me. That's not what I want.
You can't make the pain go away. I have to find the way myself.
Bite the bullet Jean!
Who am I? Where did I go?

On the 1st of December 2012, I was very ill. After finishing taking anti-depressants 18 months previously, I thought I'd try the natural approach with vitamins B5, 6 and 12. I was doing well at first, reading self-help books and using breathing exercises to relax, but it didn't last.

In the last nine months of that period, I was barely functioning. I was having panic attacks. I found it so hard to perform my duties as a Mother and a Wife when I was feeling so sick inside. It's hard to describe. It's like a huge sadness, but it's a deadness. I felt weary, useless, hopeless. I had no interest in myself, barely cleaning myself; I didn't care how I looked. I felt ugly anyway. I had no interest in food, I drank coffee and ate chocolate. I was aware that eating nutritional food was important for depression. I was doing the best I could.

I really wanted to go to bed and bury myself, with no responsibilities, but my children needed me. Yasmin may have to be bathed, the huge task of cleansing her when everything hurt. I wanted to be there for her to comfort her, to teach her that it was unacceptable to behave angrily when things hurt. I wanted to remind her to breathe through her pain. Dinners had to be cooked. House had to be maintained. But I was so tired.

I didn't understand. I tried and tried so hard in my life. All my life. Working hard on myself. Trying so hard to do things right, and it was useless. I was useless.

I couldn't answer my phone, I was afraid to look at text messages, I didn't want to see what people were saying to me, even if it was a greeting. I used to delete messages without looking. I didn't want to see people or talk to them. I'd shop in a shopping centre rather than my local shops, anonymously running in and out.

In the early years of my depression I appeared normal to people. I was always good at putting on the happy face and hiding what was on the inside. As I got older my face looked sick. I avoided looking at people or even looking in the mirror. I could see my depression.

I was ashamed.

I wrote two letters. I sent one to my Solicitor and one to my sister in law, Pauline Murray, Yasmin's Godmother. I can honestly tell you, I had no plan for suicide. In fact, I was so scared of dying and leaving Yasmin, with nobody able to take care of her like I do, that I would never in my right mind have taken my own life and left my kids.

I knew it would destroy them. But I was scared. I was terrified I was going to die suddenly. I had to do something.

One morning I woke up and without logic, I had to write these letters. I wasn't crying while I was writing them, it wasn't a case of me feeling sorry for myself. I was studiously putting down all of Yasmin's therapies and exercises, days and times for everything, her activities and her nutrition. My reasoning to myself was 'if I were to die suddenly'. I wanted to make sure there was a plan for Yasmin that would be followed. I posted them straight away.

To my Solicitor, I wrote him this also, but that if I died, any money I had was to pay for all Yasmin's needs. That was my will.

I know I must've terrified them both. Suicide was rampant at the time, with the recession. I'm pretty sure you'd have to plan suicide, but what if you didn't? What if it was just something that just snapped in your brain? Lots of people believe that.

But I didn't know. I knew the brain was powerful, it was controlling all this. I was afraid of what else it could do. I knew I needed to go back on my anti-depressant, but I was too ill to go to the doctor …

I asked a friend for some of her medication, as she was on the same dose as me, just to get me feeling a bit well, so I could go and talk to a doctor. I didn't want to arrive at the Doctor's surgery looking an emotional wreck with everybody staring at me, feeling sorry for me.

The medication didn't kick in as quickly as usual and I was still feeling quite ill ten days later when I finally went to see my Doctor in Co. Meath. I thought maybe it was time I see a Psychiatrist, to sort out my mind for me. I wasn't holding out much hope of help, as I'd spent 25 years of my life trying to shake the self-hatred from my bones with various self-help groups and counselling sessions.

I hadn't been this bad before though.

I looked awful. I felt physically ill, I was tired and unmotivated. I had no interest in my appearance. I wasn't sleeping well. On the outside I was barely functioning. On the inside I was dead.

The doctor suggested I change my chaotic lifestyle, and continue with my self-help and exercise. She asked me was I eating well, of course I said yes. Good nutrition is vital for people suffering with depression. I was vaguely aware that I hadn't been eating well.

Two weeks later I mentally started to feel a bit better but I also felt weak, frail.

Depression is a mental illness, some believe it's caused by a lack of serotonin in the brain. Serotonin is a neurotransmitter. It relays messages from one area of the brain to another. Of our 40 million brain cells most are influenced by serotonin; Brain cells are related to mood, sexual desire and function, appetite, sleep, memory and learning, temperature regulation and some social behaviour..

Tom Cruise was not wrong when he said depression is a state of mind and that it doesn't need medication to overcome it. But if serotonin has such an effect on our senses, it would be really hard to lift ourselves out of the debts of our depression, that's why replacing our brain with the missing chemical helps people feel better. Left untreated, the chemical imbalance of depression affects all of the other organs too. As an influential man, Tom was wrong to suggest that people didn't need medication.

Typically, most people neglect their emotional state for a long time, by which time they would be feeling physically ill too.

That's what happened to me.

I hobbled through Christmas. I find Christmas hard. The month of December is a hectic time; cleaning the house, putting up the decorations, shopping, paying the bills, buying presents, trying to meet friends for lunch or dinner. The financial strain is difficult for everybody in this recessional time.

Still meeting my Yasmin's emotional, physical and educational needs throughout this month with all her other needs leaves me with little energy for anything else, but this is my priority. I was trying to keep up with her excitement for Christmas and for Santa and all the things she wanted to do to make it perfect, baking, wrapping presents, writing cards. Poor pet, I was trying to smile each time: I was trying to be happy. Isn't she amazing?

I normally go to all the Christmas parties and meet with all the girl friends, but I didn't want to see anybody or talk to anybody. I couldn't make polite conversation, I didn't want to be rude either, I just couldn't talk. I wasn't my usual bubbly self with my sisters either. I didn't feel connected with them. I couldn't put on the face. I just couldn't get into it. I was concerned, could I ever be happy again, or was this the new me? Dull and reclusive. I was so tired and had no energy. I was concentrating really hard, trying not to let my girls see me like this, but I'm sure they did.

I vaguely remember another Christmas when I hadn't been diagnosed with depression as I hadn't had Yasmin at that time. Sarah was 8 and Anthony was 14 and I could barely smile at them on that Christmas morning. I was in such bad form, as I was tired and cranky. How I must have tainted their little hearts, and I was mean and nasty to their dad.

This Christmas morning, I focused all my attention on my children. It didn't matter if I didn't get to visit everybody on this Christmas Day. It didn't matter if I didn't cook 3 or 4 family dinners over the Christmas season. I didn't have the energy. I could only do for my children. Santa came to Yasmin and Sarah and Anthony. (Santa has to come to all the adults in the family too, for Yasmin's sake) I don't know how I shopped for Santa that December month, but I wasn't overly worried this year about the presents on the Santa lists. I was saying to myself, 'My children are nourished and warm, my bills are paid and my family are healthy today: Thank you God'. It gave me a comfort. I was saying the important words to the girls of the real meaning of Christmas; Sharing and caring.

I was walking the dogs. I needed to do that for me as much as the dogs, to see the beauty of life.

My son Anthony was home for Christmas and dinner was lovely. Anthony stayed with us the whole Christmas Day. It was lovely. I was beginning to feel gratitude.

It was actually the middle of January 2013, when the anti-depressants finally kicked in that I started to feel mentally well, a bit able to cope.

It was strange, this time was different. Yasmin was 8 now, I had been on antidepressants on and off since Yasmin was 7 weeks old. I always felt better soon after taking the tablets, this time, it took longer and I didn't bounce back. I wasn't full of the joys of life.

During that period in my life, it was difficult to take care of myself, and showering was a huge effort, I had no interest in my appearance. I was able to get out of bed every day and function for my family. I cleaned the house and washed the clothes. I walked the dogs and I cooked the dinners. I ran the kids around to their activities and I sat with Yasmin doing her homework. I was aware I wasn't feeling the zest for life. I just had to keep trying.

Yasmin woke me up every morning about 6.30am, and called me from her bedroom, Mammy? Mammy? She only wanted me; I had to go into her and hug her and kiss her, and get into bed beside her for a few minutes and give her a cuddle. She would tell me about her funny dreams and she would ask me if I had any funny dreams and I would have to try to think of something funny and it was really hard because I couldn't laugh. Then she'd say, 'Come on Mammy, it's time to get up!'.

Myself and my Husband call her 'The Gift'.

Jean born 1967

I know as a child, I was feisty. My earliest memory was when I was about 20 months.

My dad was Christy, he was 26 years old and my mam was Maire, she was 27 years old. I had an older sister, called Olive. She was 10 months older than me; we were called Irish twins because we were born within one year. We lived in Cabra with my dad's mother, Granny Sutton.

This particular sunny morning, we were at the table having breakfast, my dad had great manners as was standard in those days, the table was always laid out with a lovely lace tablecloth and we sat at the table for our meals.

I didn't want my porridge, and I said "No! No!" as I turned the bowl upside down spilling porridge over the lovely table cloth. I remember my mam and dad and granny hiding their smiles.

This was a small action, but it showed I was strong willed and stubborn, and I was going to be trouble!

I remember one day when I was four years old, my sister Olive wouldn't let me play with her and Caroline, our friend. I was so mad, I shouted out through the front window, 'Fuck Off Caroline Herbert, I don't want that blue skirt you gave me anyway!' I was caught by my mam and slapped hard and grounded for a week.

When I was seven, my sister Josie told a tale on me to my dad and got me grounded for another week, I was so mad at her, I threw a boot at her. She just happened to be standing at the front window and it went right through it. I spent a lot of time grounded!

I remember my dad was quite strict on us six girls, which wasn't unusual for those times. If we were bold we got slapped with the belt across our bottoms. Our clothes would still be on, but nevertheless it still stung! I began to be cautious of what I told my dad as I didn't want to get punished or given out to. I began to be non-trusting at age seven.

I was quite a tomboy in those days. My dad had been collecting some bricks to build an extension to our house, it was seven years later when the extension was actually built!

As a child, I liked to walk on those bricks, dancing across them, pretending I was in a castle. One day I missed my step and fell head first into the bricks. I was in awful pain, but I didn't make a fuss in case I was kept in. I think I broke my collar bone that day, there's still a lump on it!

There it began - my personality. I was tough, I didn't need nor want attention because I was afraid of what it would bring. I decided things for myself in my own mind. I wouldn't look for advice or take it if it was offered to me. This would carry me through life. It would also get me into lots of dangerous situations.

I was my own worst enemy.

Granny Sutton 1900 - 1973

Granny was a stern faced woman, made of tough stuff. She was born in 1900 as Molly Tynan in Grenville street tenements, Dublin.

She was a tall woman at 6ft 2in, had piercing blue eyes and curly black hair.

Grenville Street tenement was barely habitable for the rats that ran up and down the stairs between little Molly's shoeless feet in 1911.

She shared a house with 70 strangers, as well as her parents and siblings. The cold, the damp, the starvation was nothing new to Molly Tinan. There was one germ-filled toilet to serve everybody in the house. No clean running water to drink, never mind to wash. Poor children like Molly had no school to go to and children were treated rough.. Girls were the lower class of the lower class, they had to clean and cook for their brothers and fathers who brought home the food and the girls often married young at 16 years of age to escape their families. With alcohol abuse rampant, many children in the tenements were beaten and abused. Lice crawled in their hairs and bodies.

The Irish who could scrape together the sea fare, were leaving in their droves to emigrate to America and Australia for dreams of food and work. We know that thousands of those poor women and children and men never reached their destinations alive.

Ireland was under English rule since 1494. Many English and Scottish families were sent to Ireland to receive estates as rewards from King Henry VIII, displacing many Irish wealthy families. Dublin and the eastern side of Ireland had begun to lose its own native Irish language.

Over the next few hundred years, the Irish people suffered. In 1910 Ireland there was the very rich and the very poor and Molly Tinan was very poor and very resentful towards the English. Her family and many more had wanted independence from England. They felt they were treated badly under English rule, never having a chance of escaping poverty and starvation, or receiving education and proper jobs. They began to set up groups to fight their cause.

Ireland had never really recovered from The Great Famine in 1845, caused by a potato blight. Most of the poor Irish people relied on potatoes for their nutrition, so in the 7 years of the blight it had wiped out 25% of the population through death. It is thought to have claimed the lives of 1 million Irish people; a further 1 million emigrated from the Irish shores.

Those who survived were the strongest.

Those who survived were the meanest.

The people formed groups called Sinn Fein and The Irish Republican Brotherhood, which was led by Patrick Pearse in early 1900. He was a strong young man, with a strong belief in freedom.

Molly was a skinny tall gangly girl, but she was only a woman. She could only be a firm supporter of The Brotherhood instead of fighting up front with the men. She and many other young Irish women did everything to help their men's fight for freedom. They hid weapons and even men who were wanted for treason. She put herself in grave danger numerous times. Molly was only 14 when World War 1, was declared. She had already endured fourteen hard years of poverty, starvation, violence and abuse. It was shaping her personality. She hadn't seen much happiness..

The majority of young Irish men as well as the English armed forces were taken from Ireland and sent to fight the Germans on the French front line.

While they were gone, The Brotherhood plotted The 1916 Rebellion, thinking it was their best chance while England was fighting the war.

On Easter Sunday 1916, The Brotherhood took control of the GPO, General Post Office, Dublin. My Dad had told me that Molly listened on a neighbour's radio, where all the civilians were hiding indoors, keeping shelter from the inevitable war. Patrick Pearse read The Irish Proclamation of Independence, from the steps of The GPO, O'Connell Street.

There were jubilant cries throughout the city. The people of Ireland thought this was their time for freedom at last.

When the rebellion began, it lasted just a week. Britain had their army of men with their vast supply of weapons. They destroyed most of Dublin city, and reclaimed it easily.

Hundreds of Irish people were killed, including the 14 leaders of the uprising who were executed along with Patrick Pearse.

Molly's heart was broken. Many of the young men Molly would have grown up with in Dublin city were killed. She could see no positive future. Molly became very negative.

A constant tirade of negativity in one's life will lead to a depressive state. She would carry that through raising her children.

A lot of countries have gone through their poverty and wars also. Black people have suffered extremely in this world and the Jews and many other races and creeds.

Ireland had hundreds of years of poverty, war and abuse. It's hard to understand how these people continue to get up and fight for their life.

They only had God. They had a strong belief in God. They prayed for his help. I don't believe God ignored their cries, by not preventing poverty and wars. Poor countries were still in the early days of education. There was no value for life. Human beings were easily replaced. It was a metamorphosis of change. Each individual has to learn within himself how to grow in life.

The next few years that followed the 1916 rebellion were full of blood and destruction and poverty in Dublin.

More young men lost their lives in the fight for Irish Freedom such as Kevin Barry aged 18, a member of the IRA, The Irish Republican Army and Michael Collins for his assistance in setting up The Irish Free State.

A third of Dublin's huge population lived in the city centre tenement slums, where Granny lived. That's 25,000 families, 250,000 people.

The overcrowding, squalor, inadequate sanitation conditions and poor diet caused Dublin to have the highest infant death rates in Europe. These conditions were reported throughout Europe.

The tenement houses were once-great Georgian houses owned by generations of Lawyers, were now abandoned when the wealthy moved to the suburbs away from the city. The Dublin Corporation took over the dwellings and let them out to the poor people for a low rent. One family of 13 or 20 people could only have one room in a tenement. The Corporation didn't do their job in providing safe dwellings for people and let the buildings become dilapidated because of the overcrowding. On average there were 835 people living in 15 houses.

This contrasted with the elite world of middle-class Dublin, living in riches in the suburbs well away from the city streets and slums and the living corpses of the poor.

This was the only accommodation offered to the poor families of Dublin in 1925, when Granny brought her first son Brendan home to Sherif street tenements, Dublin. (Uncle Brendan is still alive at 89 years old and the last remaining son)

Molly was 25, when she had finally given in to marriage to James Sutton the year before, to receive her own room in a tenement. James was a quiet man who also came from the tenements and worked on the docks. He worked long and hard for little pay.

The rent was one and six pence a week paid to The Dublin Corporation, for a room in a tenement. There was plenty of sickness in those tenement houses, as they were filthy, damp and dilapidated.

There were no washing facilities, no toilets, no cooking facilities. Women had to tread up and down stairs all day for their cooking and washing needs.

Granny's second son Noel died when he was two years of age. He had a fall down the stairs and cut his leg. There were no plasters or ointments in those days and infections were quick to develop. It had caused Tuberculosis.

Tuberculosis was an infectious disease affecting the lungs, but could gain entry through an open wound and travel to the lungs. It was rampant among the poor in 1925. Granny was broken hearted, although it was very common for young children to die, it didn't ease the pain. Fear set in Granny. Fear prevents you from being free. Fear causes people to be controlling. She became very cautious, instilling negativities and fears in the rest of her boys. This alone had a devastating effect on Dad. I believe that Granny suffered with depression at this point and coupled with her negativity, it affected her parenting skills and had a different effect on each of her boys.

It seemed to me that Dad picked up her negativity, her fears and depression and when you add stress into your life, it all becomes a dangerous mix.

Granny Sutton had four more boys after that, Tom, John, Joseph and Christopher.

It was hard raising five boys, and although Granddad worked hard, a man couldn't feed his family on his pay. Morale was low.

Granny was tough on her boys. She raised them hard. It was important to her that they had good manners. She lashed out in anger when they were bold. She would never have known that she was ignoring their emotional needs. She was a hard worker herself, constantly scrubbing her little room and her boy's clothes. She performed her duties as a mother and a wife. As Catholic's, the Sutton boys had to go to mass every Sunday and went to school only until they could read and write. The Christian Brothers were vicious with the boys who misbehaved in the smallest way. Dad and his brothers remembered being hit with canes from the brothers. They left school to get jobs, as young as 10 years old.

Her last son Christopher was born in 1942.

Being the last son, my dad's other brothers thought that Christy was more spoiled than the others, because there was a little bit more money in the home from the older brothers working. Looking at how my dad behaved when angry, I do believe he might have got away with a lot of bad behaviour when he was a child. Meaning, if he was demanding or bold, maybe Granny found herself giving him a good hiding sometimes and then just giving in at other times. Dad may have appeared bold and spoiled and out of control, but more than likely, Granny, struggling with her depression was giving him confusing parental messages. Having very unstable emotional needs met as a child left Dad insecure and needy as a man.

World War 2 was causing more devastation and poverty all over Europe. Many Irish men joined the British Army, for secure wages, and some never returned from the war.

Ireland became an independent state in 1949, and now had to look after its own nation in dilapidated tenements with thousands and thousands of people needing welfare.

Dublin Corporation had to address the social housing needs of their people, and start building houses, north and west of the city. They had a huge task at hand.

Molly moved around the Dublin tenements regularly because of filthy dilapidated conditions and sickness. She stayed in Summer hill, Mount Joy square, Sherif Street, North wall, until at last receiving a house in Cabra west in 1953. Having a home of her own for the first time in her hard life!

Although Granny was 6ft 2in, she appeared old and frail when we met her. She had a sad face. She was about 71 then, not really old these days.

Initially, my mam and dad lived in a flat in Ballymun, where three of us children were born, Olive, myself and Josie. Granny wasn't too well at that time and because Dad was the youngest of his brothers and he had the youngest children, it was easier for him and Mam to move in with Granny and take care of her in Cabra.

Granny sat in her chair by the fire most of the time. We had to be very good when Granny was in bed.

Olive was five at the time, and Olive was a lovable little girl with brown curly hair and blue eyes and freckles who giggled a lot, she spread her happiness around, it was easy for Granny to find joy in Olive, and she looked like Granny too!

I was an independent four year old, I was cute enough with almost black curly hair and green eyes. I liked to play by myself and I didn't like attention. I was more serious. I was nice to Granny and she was nice to me, but I didn't need her to do anything for me, as I could do it by myself! (I haven't changed much) so we got along grand.

But our sister, Josephine, who was just three years old then, with beautiful blue eyes and blond curly hair, needed a little bit more attention than Olive or I.

Granny used to slap her away from her chair and call her 'a little rip'. I obviously noticed that Granny did this, quite venomously too. We underestimate what our children take in at a very young age!

Mam or Dad was never in the room when Granny did this to Josie. I looked at Granny and wondered why she was being mean. Josie was obviously trying to play with Granny, but Granny didn't want to play with her. Josie kept running towards Granny, taunting her, and Granny pushed her away.

Josie told me later on that she always felt rejected by Granny. It made her feel sad, and hated. This was the start of Josie's low self-esteem for all of her life.

My Dad Christy 1942 - 2006

I remember my dad being a good dad when I was little. We had some very happy times.

He was quite attractive, tall and broad; he'd carry three of us at a time on his back every night going to bed.! He had black hair, lovely blue eyes. I imagine, when the neighbours of Carnlough Road saw Christy bringing home a wife from Loughlinstown, they were quite deflated, as he might have been considered a good catch.

Dad had a good job as a butcher in Buckley's Abattoir, a Slaughterhouse, in Camden Street. He was a good worker, and very honest.

Children came every year for Mam and Dad, their 6th and last child Christine was born in 1973. Mam had lost a couple of boy babies in pregnancy and I do remember my dad being devastated.

Dad was doing well in work, He had his mates in work, he'd go for 'a pint' after work every Thursday. As a young married woman, Mam wasn't too happy about Dad staying out drinking after work. She feels this is where Dad's problems started.

Summers were good, Dad would clean out his butcher's van and pile all our friends and us, into the van to go to the beach. Ma would have a picnic, and we'd all sing on the way there, and sunburnt and happy, we'd all sing on the way back.

He would always say, "Go and get little Karen Duggan", she was our little friend next door who died when she was 11 years old of Cystic Fibrosis. She was a beautiful little girl with brown eyes and a fiery spirit.

Dad always threw a Halloween party for all our friends. He loved games and held bite the apple blindfolded and with hands tied. We buried our face in a basin of water to retrieve precious 20p and 50p. He'd then tell us ghost stories and giggle when none of us could sleep.

Dad loved Christmas time, he loved the visiting, he loved the board games played at Christmas, he loved his six girls, aged from seven to one, playing with their toys. He loved music, Ma said he sold his guitar and record collection to buy her engagement ring!

We'd sing Christmas carols around the tree.

All the neighbours sent their turkeys and hams to Dad to bone and roll them. He liked doing things like that for his old neighbours.

Dad loved a fresh Christmas tree, and one Christmas, he brought this huge massive thing in, it didn't resemble a Christmas tree, it had no top, but he said it was indeed a Christmas tree, and Dad proceeded to try to get it into the sitting room. It was the funniest thing! It had to be nailed to the wall with butchers string tied around it.

He and Ma would share a smile at it every time they looked at it.

On the icy days of winter, Dad would take us up to the canal and we'd skate across it in just our shoes.

Mam and Dad used to go out to dinner dances, and Mam had fancy dresses and fake jewellery. We used to dress up in Ma's jewels and dresses.

Mam had beautiful auburn coloured hair, brown eyes and freckled skin, and she was a lovely Mammy. I was especially close to my mam. I loved her so much. When I was seven, I bought her a present from my own money, a box of matches for three pence for her smokes.

After that Christmas of 1973 things changed for Dad and he would never be the same again. His Mother died first and Dad was left with feelings of guilt and shame. When he was drunk, he would slag dead granny off, blaming her for him being a bad son!

Shortly after, his brother Joseph died of a massive heart attack aged just 35. Although Joe lived in England with his wife Lily and their three daughters, Dad and Joe were really close, with only a couple of years between them.

Dad was truly broken hearted and started to drink more and more to block out the pain. He was gambling then and he started making mistakes. He was losing all his week's wages.

Ma had to take all us girls into Buckley's Butcher's on Camden Street every Thursday to get his wages from him before he drank and gambled it all away. There were Thursdays she wouldn't get into town and he promised to bring home the money, but when he arrived home on those nights about 10.30pm, his pockets were empty and his belly was full of drink and he was ready to fight.

In 1977 just before the recession came out of the blue and hit like a bolt of lightning, Dad made a wrong decision. He took a managerial position at the new 'International Meat Packers' place, Lower Grand Canal Street, Dublin, promising better money. The Meat Packing Company was a new method in selling meat. It could package meat in various quantities and distribute it all over Europe. Preparing meat faster, and therefore making it more affordable and the company could make huge profits.

Ten weeks later, The Meat Packing Company closed down. I'll never forget Dad's shocked face when he came home to Mam and told her, nor the worried look on my mam's face.

Dad was out of work for over 10 years after that. For a 35 year old proud Irishman, this was to destroy him. I remember my dad saying he'd be considered too old for employment once he reached 40. Men that age rarely got permanent work, as there were hundreds of young men in their 20s who were considered first.

Soon after he lost his job, his best friend Liam O'Brien died suddenly that year of a massive heart attack age 35. Dad was lost.

The 70's and 80s were hard, but Buckley's Butchers were fond of Dad and they sent him a package of meat every Friday. Dad was really on hard times at this point with 6 children and a wife to feed.

One Friday he brought home the meat and he found a mouse in the frozen part of the bag that the meat was in, not actually the little bags that enclosed the meat. He went back into Buckley's and said the mouse was in the meat.

He claimed them for 500 pounds. God knows he needed it to pay rent and bills and debt he had acquired, but he never went back to Buckley's for his meat again.

I remember Dad's face. He was full of shame.

At this point Dad was angry all the time. The anger was to grow into a huge self-hatred: Hatred for everything and everybody. It caused terrifying outbursts, uncontrolled destruction of our house, our windows and our furniture. Terrifying threats with knives to our Mam and us, physical violence, mental abuse: Fear. He didn't care what he said or what he did.

One Christmas, we were just seated for our Christmas dinner. Dad loved the table all set out and one of us had to say

Grace before meals. Dad had spent the morning at Bertie Monaghan's house down the road. Whiskey drinking together.

Dad was quite drunk at the table. We were all walking on eggshells. He didn't like the salt seller on the table and started to moan at Ma. He wasn't getting satisfaction from any of us, as we were ignoring the row, so he up turned the Christmas table, throwing the dinner everywhere, before we ate a bite. Then he went ballistic, blaming Ma. Screaming at us all, throwing plates and glasses. My poor Ma was devastated, all her hard work ruined.

My dad was a huge man. He was at least six foot five inches tall and he was really broad. He actually looked like a male gorilla after his home was invaded. He stood up tall and wide with his arms outstretched, to prevent us running past him and then he'd roar really loudly. This Christmas dinner was one memory that stayed with all of my sisters. The following years were worse.

The Devil had entered our home.

In the late 1970s and early 80s, there was a notorious crowd of teenage boys getting a name for themselves in robbing cars and racing them up and down the streets of Cabra. It was in all the newspapers at the time. The streets weren't safe. It was causing havoc and fear for all the older people and young mothers with children. The police couldn't catch them and eventually they found the cars burnt out and empty on the side roads of Cabra. To be honest, it was great to see some excitement going on outside of our house for a change. We loved to watch the robbed cars from our gardens. Until one wintry Saturday night, the robbed cars were racing up and down Carnlough Road, with the police in hot pursuit.

My dad was unusually not in one of his alcohol fuel rages that night, and heard them speeding past our house. He ran out roaring like a bear. From the garden, Dad picked up one of the railway sleepers he used for his plant beds, he raised it over his head, his arms straight. It weighed about 30 stone.

The cars were speeding up the road in our direction. Dad ran into the road and threw it at the oncoming car, just missing it, causing the car to screech to a halt in a spin.

I remember Dad looked like 'The Incredible Hulk' in a fury. The young lads in the cars got such a fright and jumped from the cars and ran, abandoning the robbed cars. They never came back up our road again.

The word got around Cabra that Dad was a crazed madman, not to be messed with. If he got into conversation in the pubs, it would always end up in an argument. Dad always thought he was right about a subject. I would hear him argue with himself the next morning over the words he said in the pub. He began to sit on his own in the pub, it was easier than getting into a fight and he was the only one that kept getting barred!

Ironically, Dad gained a certain amount of respect that night for stopping the speeding cars.

Jean The breakdown 2012

The lead up to my 'collapse' started in April 2012 when I had my first big panic attack. I had no idea what was happening. I dropped Yasmin to school one Thursday morning, I stopped in Dunshaughlin to put petrol in the car, as it was empty and I knew I wouldn't get too far. I felt a tingling or a numb sensation in my lower legs as I was filling the tank, and then it went away. I thought 'that was strange' and went on to Blanchardstown to get my shopping.

I always went into Butlers first to get my Cappuccino. As soon as I ordered my coffee, the numbness spread through me, I was so scared; I didn't know what was happening.

I knew enough to sit down beside a woman, I forget her name but I'll never forget her kindness. I told her something was happening and I needed some help. I remember the lovely young staff running around getting me help, and calling an ambulance.

The coffee shop was packed of course on that Thursday morning, and I was vaguely aware, that I should be mortified. I looked a mess, and I was crying.

I thought I was having a stroke, and asked the lady to get me an aspirin. I was holding her hand tightly as the waves of darkness was coming through me, telling her I couldn't die yet, my little girl needed me.

There were three foreign girls unaware of what was going on with me, and they were trying to squeeze in behind where I was sitting. One of them noticed I wasn't well, and she was trying to get me to put my head between my knees. I just remember a friend of mine telling me of how staying upright and still, would be important if you were having a stroke. There I was, holding this lady's hand, terrified of moving an inch, waiting for an aspirin, and saying to myself, 'Is that girl crazy? Can't she see I'm obviously having a stroke?

I do smile at the memory of my madness.

I was carted off to Blanchardstown Hospital in an ambulance. The ambulance man was really kind, and asked me did I ever suffer with my nerves. I said no, as I never thought I suffered with my nerves. I remembered as a child there were people who suffered with their nerves, but it never dawned on me that nerves and depression were the same.

At the hospital, I was met with sympathetic staff.

They knew! and I still didn't know! I am slow to cop on to things.

During the recession, the nurses were so used to people coming through the casualty department with symptoms of heart attacks that were actually anxiety attacks.

I had all the usual tests done for a person having a heart attack. They gave me an ECG, Electrocardiogram, to monitor the electric waves in my heart, to see if it was beating normally. They also took blood to check for missing oxygen levels.

Despite the staff shortages, the only negative thing I'll say about Blanchardstown hospital is that the X-ray system is very barbaric.

After the nurses realized I wasn't having a heart attack, the next procedure was to X-ray my chest to see if I had another injury causing the pain.

I was sent down to a corridor where other men and women were waiting for X-rays. A guy comes along and tells us to take off our bras, or boxers or knickers for whatever area we were having X Rayed. We could use the little cubicles facing us; he's speaking randomly to all of us. So we're all sitting there with our bits covered by ill-fitting gowns, then each individual is called into the X-ray room by a big scruffy looking male, who could be working for the Dublin Corporation for all you knew as he wasn't wearing hospital scrubs. He asks me when I last menstruated and he proceeds to count my days.

I was feeling really embarrassed, vulnerable.

I'm 45, I'm not pregnant for God's sake!

I didn't get this, I have private health insurance, isn't there a better, more dignified way to have an X-Ray?

On another return a couple of weeks later, with a pain in my chest this time, the nurse sent me to X-ray again, with the same system. At this point, I kind of knew it wasn't my heart, so I left without an X-ray, and went home.

Later in the day 'Nurse Crachet' from 'One Flew Over The Cuckoo nest'' phoned me angrily and said 'How dare I leave without telling them!'

Didn't she read my record? Surely it was obvious that I was suffering with anxiety at the very least? It was costing me a fortune in hospital visits and ambulances that I couldn't afford at the time; I wasn't going there for a coffee! I obviously wasn't in my right mind or I would have stayed!

Shouting at me wouldn't help…

Unfortunately, Nurse Crachet wasn't limited to Blanchardstown Hospital. I felt during the Celtic Tiger, came a new generation of young people who could afford to be sent to College to be Doctors or Nurses, purely based on their academics and wealth, not their compassion for people.

Since the time I had Yasmin, I spent a lot of time at the Doctor's office or casualty department at Temple Street Children's Hospital, Dublin. Yasmin suffered lots of sinus problems, regular high temperatures and whooping cough.

This month of March in 2011 was a particular difficult month. Yasmin had a bad dose that lasted the whole month. There were lots of sleepless nights as Yasmin woke vomiting also with high temperatures. I had been to the Doctor a couple of times and we were on our second antibiotic. On one Tuesday morning, I took her to casualty in Temple Street Hospital because I was really worried and Yasmin wasn't well at all. Yasmin gets very frustrated and panics when she's ill. It takes all my energy to sooth her and comfort her. She needs a lot of reassurance. After a brief examination, I received an unfamiliar and strong antibiotic from a young Doctor to give Yasmin. When Friday morning came and Yasmin was no better, she now had constant diarrhoea and had blood in her poo and I was really concerned about that.

I phoned the VHI Nurse helpline for assistance at 6am, and the nurse advised me to take Yasmin to casualty again, as she wasn't happy with Yasmin's condition.

I arrived into casualty before 7am. While I was waiting in the waiting area, I noticed that a child had been sick everywhere. The Mom had cleaned up the area and cleaning staff were called. I couldn't help but notice that when the cleaning girl arrived, she sprayed just a solution and cleaned the area with wipes. No bucket of hot water with disinfectant, and there lingered a bad smell in the air…

I was called into see the nurse to give Yasmin's information. I had a sterile sample of Yasmin's pooh, and I explained there was blood in in and I wanted to give in the sample. The nurse looked aghast and snapped, 'We don't take in samples anymore, put that in the bin!' I felt like a bold child. Yasmin was upset and unwell. The nurse proceeded to type and asked me why I was there. I looked and felt dishevelled. I hadn't slept a full night sleep for nearly a month at this point. I was recalling the events since I was in casualty on the Tuesday, and Nurse Crachet snapped at me again, 'I don't want to know what happened on Tuesday, I only want this morning's details!

This is where I felt I was being judged on my appearance, as I wasn't washed and had put an old pair of Jeans and runners on, rushing to the hospital. I'm not one for dolling myself up when a child is vomiting all over you. I looked like a Ma from Dublin city. I am a Ma from Dublin city! But like the Ma's from Dublin city, I can also dress up really well.

As I consider myself to deal with all professionals with respect, something wasn't right here.

I said to Nurse Crachet, 'I'm not happy with your behaviour. I'm here today on Friday morning as I obviously feel my child has got worse since Tuesday morning, when I was here with you. Don't judge me on appearances this morning. I am a Tax Payer. I've just paid another 100 euro to see you this morning!'

I really empathize with any Mother who has no option but to be on social welfare. They are treated differently in our society.

Nurse Crachet was about 29 years old. She was tall, slim, blonde and attractive. But she was mean and she had no compassion that morning. She then brought us straight in to see a Doctor, after warning them, there was a crabby Mother coming in.

A young, 29 to 30 year-old African Doctor came over to us. She was pretty and had modern braids in her hair. She read Yasmin's file. Yasmin was laying on the bed with a high temperature and vomiting. The doctor didn't touch Yasmin to examine her.

The Doctor proceeded to say that Yasmin had a virus, and that it would take its course.

I asked, 'So, I should stop giving Yasmin the antibiotic the other doctor gave me on Tuesday? If it's a virus?'

She wasn't sure.

She called over the male doctor who had seen Yasmin on Tuesday. He was Irish, posh accent, tall, attractive, 30 something or under. He didn't touch Yasmin to examine her. He said, 'Yeah, it's a virus, it'll just have to take its course, keep giving her the antibiotic anyway'.

I asked what about the poo sample with the blood in it, and he said without examining it, that it probably was nothing.

I wasn't convinced. I said, 'Look, her temperature is really high again'. The African doctor said, 'Just keep giving her Calpol to keep it under control'.

I was crying at this point. I felt confused, ignored. Was I imagining things? They didn't give my little girl Calpol or a bag to get sick in, as I left the Casualty Department that morning in Temple street children's hospital. I was too frail to ask for some. Didn't they want to help my beautiful daughter? I felt I had let Yasmin down as I left the hospital.

I was obviously in a depressed state myself. The least they could do was to perform a duty of care to my child. The hospital wasn't busy that morning. It wasn't about staff shortages at that time.

I had to stop the car a couple of times on my way home to Ratoath, County Meath, to help my little girl as she was vomiting and vomiting.

When I got home, I gave her Calpol and then Nurofen to get the temperature down. I called the hospital to complain, where a lovely man called Joe assisted me, and told me to write a letter of complaint in, and I did. I received a meek apology from the doctor's team a few weeks later.

I am a fully paid member of VHI. I pay my Taxes. I was treated like I was a nobody.

This was how the Irish people were treated in The Celtic Tiger years. Something had changed with the Irish people. Everyone was mean spirited. Nobody wanted to help anybody. I was probably guilty of that bit myself at times. I had to look at my own self and my behaviour to others in my own conscience. Hopefully Miss Cratchet has too!

Had all the nice people left the country?

I couldn't catch my breath. I didn't know it was a panic attack. I was surprised to realize I was suffering panic attacks. I had heard about panic attacks from others before, but I couldn't believe when they were happening to me. I was always so strong, never sick.

My panic attacks came in the guise of having a stroke. A numb feeling spread through me. Other people's attacks come in the form of a heart attack or struggling to breathe.

Why didn't the doctor in the hospital refer me to a psychiatrist? Or to somebody who could help me?

That seems to be the failure in our health service, "It's not my department, we only deal in heart attacks here, it's not your heart, so off you go".

A person could be limping in with a broken leg, but if it's not the fracture clinic, they won't help you.

So, also, I never pursued help or the cause of my panic attacks and just continued on. I was trying to keep these panic attacks to myself, and not tell my husband or my family. I just don't like the fuss.

And inevitably, I was going to get worse.

2

Anto

Anthony was born in 1962. He was the last of 12 children born to Maureen County and Peter 'Pader' Murray.

Maureen came from a large family of 13 children born originally in the tenements in Dublin city. Her Mother Biddy County was housed in St Attracta Road in the early 1940's.

In Dublin, there's a huge sense of knowing everyone. The reason being, that everyone started off in the tenements, so they knew each other already by the time they moved into Cabra and other settlements. There was a great unity among the people. That's what tourists found attractive about the Irish people. Irish people were friendly. We were helpful until we became selfish during the Celtic Tiger.

Biddy raised a really quiet family. They were kind and very unobtrusive. Maureen was an attractive young woman with green eyes and strawberry blond hair. She was a softly spoken and gentle woman. She met Peter, who was tall with dark hair. He worked as a truck driver delivering cattle to the docks. Madly in love, they married when Maureen was 25.

Maureen had her first child, Mary when she was 26 years old. Mary was her only girl, then came John and 10 more boys after that. Peter, Billy, Valentine, Emanuel, Fergus, Pascal, Joseph, Declan, Derek and Anthony.

Maureen's precious little girl Mary died when she was 18 months old.

Mary was constantly congested in the nose and ears and she suffered a lot of infections with high temperatures. On this occasion, the doctor called an ambulance to take her to hospital. In those days, in 1947, the parents still weren't allowed to go with their child to hospital, and it left the parents feeling suspicious and untrusting of the hospital system. Maureen's little Marie, as she was called, was crying hysterically when they took her from her mammy.

Maureen was also really upset and Pader tried to console her, telling her Marie would be home soon. Marie never came home. She died in hospital without her mammy, undergoing a simple procedure to unblock the fluid in her airways.

Maureen and Pader never really found out what happened to Marie in hospital and Maureen was never to get over her loss.

Many families suffered in the same way and this is why Irish people became untrusting and suspicious of the hospital system. People in authority took advantage of their power in those days.

Maureen suffered with her nerves after that, known as depression today, but nobody knew much about that at the time and she just got on with it. It left her frail and weak.

Anthony remembers his early years being happy. He was a quiet lad and not as tough as the 10 brothers older than him, playfully bashing each other.

Anthony loved his Da, but Pader worked long hours driving a cattle truck and Anthony didn't see much of him.

When Anthony was 5 years of age, Pader brought him out with him to pick up a big heifer of a cow. Anthony had never seen real cows before and he was terrified. His Da asked him to stand beside the back of the truck and watch as the cow climbed in. But Anthony was a tiny lad, and the cow was enormous! Anthony got such a fright that he ran off and he kept running on the road home, until his Da finally caught up with him.

His Da roared at him for being bold and Anthony felt he disappointed his Da. He wasn't a big brave lad like his brothers. Anthony didn't know his dad too well. Pader was a cattle truck driver. He had to be up in the early hours of the morning to deliver a load to the docks. He and his mates would go off to the early house pubs for a few pints then before continuing his day's work. He finished his day's work with a couple of pints in Downey's pub on Dowth avenue Cabra.

Anthony remembers his dad as always singing and happy. He wasn't angry or aggressive in drink. Anthony's mother was always happy to see her husband home and would sing along with him.

Like all the Irishmen of the time, Pader ruled the house and Maureen knew the conditions of marriage in those days. It was a blessing that Pader was a happy chap, but he still had the freedom to do as he wanted and have his needs met by his wife waiting for him at home. If any of the boys got out of hand Pader took charge of the discipline.

On one occasion, one of the boy's had robbed a half crown. Pader was furious. He lined all the boys up and he had his belt in his hand. "Who took it?" He shouted. Nobody gave in, and everybody felt the pain of the buckle on the belt, all except Anthony. His Da thought he was too little for a good belting.

That didn't help his recognition in the family, the other boys slagged him for being a pet. As it turned out, one of the brothers did take the half crown. He was the charmer of the family with a name and a set of smouldering eyes to match, Valentine. Val as the boys called him was a divil. He was always taking the boys clothes or a few bob, and then ran before they caught up with him.

That didn't just happen in the Murray family. There is a saying in Ireland, 'First up, Best dressed!'

The neighbours had great sympathy with Maureen, with all those boys and not one girl to help.

When Anthony was six years old, his dad got sick.. Pader had never been sick a day in his life but as the days turned into weeks with the flu not seeming to leave him and there was an unsightly infection in his leg. He had to go to hospital to get checked out. The hospital kept him in as he was very ill. Within the week, Pader had died. Maureen was shocked. "What could he possibly die of?" she asked. "He only went in with the flu!" She never found out what he died of exactly. I'm guessing it was TB., Maura was inconsolable with still eight boys at home to rear, now by herself.

Pader was aged 51.

Maureen laid her husband's coffin in the sitting room of her house for the wake, where everybody came to pay their respect. The house was full and everybody was having a few drinks. There was soon song and laughter among the crowd. It was a great wake. Maureen lifted Anthony up to kiss his dad goodbye, but Anthony was crying hysterically as he was terrified. He didn't want to do it. He told me later that the fear stayed with him for a long time. He just kept thinking, 'My dad's dead forever and ever!' He had nightmares for years about what death was. Also, Ireland being a story telling nation, there were plenty of ghost stories about after the dad had died. The older brothers would tease the younger ones about ghosts and 'Banshees'. Anthony was terrified going to sleep.

Maureen had to get on with her life as best she could without her husband. She struggled financially and received help from The Vincent De Paul Society, for which she was very grateful. They provided shoes and clothes for her young boys and gave them holidays in Sunshine House, Balbriggan. This was a state run facility for disadvantaged boys, which there were many of in 1970 Ireland.

The boys loved going to Sunshine House as they had loads of food and as it was right beside the beach they had loads of freedom. The older boys at home, Pascal and Joe, used to pretend they were under 16 also, to be taken to Sunshine House too. They would have to meet up at Connolly Station, Dublin, where there were hundreds of other boys waiting to go off on the train to their holidays. There was great fun in Sunshine House with all the boys. There were gangs of lads from Cabra that the Murray's knew too. It took an army of Christian Brothers to keep this gang in control. There were strict rules and they had to be followed.

Anto remembers one incident with one of the Keogh brothers. They were eating their dinner and one of the boys robbed a sausage from his brother Terry's plate and licked it! Thinking he was safe enough to put it back on his plate till he was ready to devour it. Terry went to grab it back with his fork. While his brother was trying to save his sausage with his own hand, Terry spiked his hand with the fork instead of the sausage. There was blood everywhere! And then a riot, as Terry's brother wanted to kill him!

Maureen delighted in these holidays for the boys as it gave her a much needed break. Soon, she had to go to work to feed her family as there was just never enough food for her growing boys. She found a job with her sister Nan as a silver service waitress at the RDS venue in Ballsbridge, South Dublin. The kids were soon delighted with the leftover cakes and meats from the events that Maureen was able to bring home to her sons. Nan and Maureen were very popular in the RDS for their kind nature and hard work.

Maureen's oldest son John was a handsome young man. He was 22 when his Da had died. He had been off in Borneo fighting the war. He came home to help his Ma cope. But John was a character of a chap. He had a great sense of humour and loved going out on the town partying.

He wasn't long back from Borneo when he went missing for three days. None of the lads were too worried about this as he was a grown man.

Then one of the lads had heard that a young man was brought into the Richmond Hospital, down Stony Batter way. They heard he didn't know who he was.

Maureen thought she should go down and check it out. She brought young Anthony with her. When she arrived at the hospital, the doctor told her that they had discovered it was her son John Murray.

She walked nervously into the intensive care unit and screamed in fright when she saw her son. His head was so swollen and shaved of hair. He was missing teeth and he was paralyzed completely on the right hand side, his face drooped sideways.

Maureen screamed and screamed, 'That's not my son!

John slurred from the bed, 'Ma, it's me, John, it's me, John!'

Anthony ran from the hospital, while the doctor's tried to calm Maureen. He found his older brother Pascal. Anthony was very scared of his mother's reactions to difficult situations.

This new trauma sent Maureen into her own world. She was admitted to St Brendan's mental hospital, Grange Gorman for months to help her breakdown. It was always referred to as Grange Gorman because of its gloomy exterior. Maureen had always struggled with her nerves since she lost her baby girl. The effect of not dealing with her emotions over the years had finally sent her brain into a shutdown mode. She was heavily sedated and medicated in a hope to find something that would bring Maureen back. It took months.

During Anthony's very young years, he had no discipline. Not a bold boy anyway, but now, he could do what he wanted without any corrections or consequences. This would give him problems in his future.

The boy's took John home from the hospital and took on the task of doing his physiotherapy.

They couldn't accept that John was an invalid and neither could John. They strapped sand bags to his paralyzed arm and leg and made him drag himself from wall to wall.

John shouted at them in frustration at times, 'If I get hold of yis little bastard's I'll kill yis!'

The boys said, 'Yeah, go on then!'

You know, John laughs about those happy memories today. His personality got him through his life. He didn't take himself too seriously. If he was worried about how he looked in life, he didn't show it. I always thought of him as a brave man.

The boy's got him up walking and able to take care of himself again! Soon, he was cycling everywhere, which he found much easier. He's only recently given up the bike at age 66, finally finding it too difficult.

John eventually went and looked for work. He applied to the Dublin Corporation as a street cleaner. He almost had the job, but he had to sign the contract with his right hand, his paralyzed one. They wouldn't accept a left hand!

He could just about do an X sign for a signature, which was perfectly acceptable in those days! His excuse was, 'I can't read or write!'

He got the job and was well known all over the North side of the city, for his hearty laugh and helpfulness. He only retired one year ago at age 66.

Maureen came home from hospital, but she was never the same again. The medication and the shock treatment had changed Maureen. She was sad most of the time now.

She started to rely on Anthony a lot more. He was the youngest and he was at home a lot more than the others. Anthony was now 11 years old and he didn't want to stay in with his mother. She scared him as she sat by the fire and talked to the flames.

It was almost a blessing that Maureen wasn't in her right frame of mind when her other son Peter aged 18 was run over by a truck while he was on a bicycle. Peter was seriously injured. The handle bar of the bike had penetrated his stomach. His pelvis and legs were smashed. He had no helmet on, so he suffered head injuries and smashed teeth. He was in hospital for almost a year.

Unfortunately for him though, just before his accident, he had received news that he had won a scholarship place for Trinity College, Dublin. Maureen was broken hearted for Peter.

That was the start of Peter's downward spiral into depression that he and his wife Betty fought through for years. Peter died tragically at age 60, in 2008.

Anthony felt the pressure of his mother's illness and didn't want to be at home with her. He ran out at every opportunity. He carried guilt with him all through his life for thinking he wasn't a good son.

Tragedy was never too far away for the Murrays as one evening, when Anthony was about 13 years old, he arrived home to find his house was on fire. They didn't have much, but everything was destroyed. All the boys were arriving home to witness their burning house. Being young strong men, they were running around trying to gather buckets of water from the neighbour's.

Through the chaos of the firemen trying to put the fire out and the crowds gathering to view the fire, Joseph, Pascal and John Murray were trying to get back into the house to retrieve their money they had saved in their mattresses and the attic! The house was burning down fast. They had hundreds of pounds stashed. Anthony and Derek were trying to comfort their hysterical mother.

The firemen would not let the young men near their burning house.

I asked John recently, 'Why didn't you put your money in the bank?'

He said, 'I didn't trust banks!'

All of their money was burnt in the fire!

The 11 brothers were a close bunch. They were all moved around to various relatives until the Dublin corporation could fix their home. Through it all, the boys kept their sense of humour.

I was very fond of John when I met him. I admired his strength and his laughter, but sometimes I was annoyed with him. He had two children from his first relationship, Lisa and John, that I felt John could have done more for. Their mother had taken Lisa and John away, when they were only 4 and 8 years old.

She moved to Ballymun where she received a flat from the Dublin Corporation. Ballymun was built in the 1960's to house the thousands of families from the Dublin city tenements. It consisted of large blocks of flats. It was similar to the H blocks prison in the north of Ireland, only much taller. Initially, it was an attractive dwellings, but it was soon to attract crime and drugs.

Lisa and John came regular to visit Cabra on the bus by themselves at that young age, as their mammy developed alcoholism.

All the Murray family watched out for Lisa and John, doing as much as they could for them, but it was hard with their own work and family commitments. John felt he couldn't do much because he was working fulltime and he had the paralysis

I noticed that Lisa and young John's physical needs weren't being met. I reported the situation to the social care system and was ignored.

Lisa came into our home most weekends and she returned home to her mother during the week. What we didn't know then was that Lisa's mother's male friend was abusing Lisa since she was six years of age. Lisa couldn't tell us, how could she put what was happening to her into words? She was a baby.

Lisa and John both received bullying threats and violence while growing up in Ballymun. Lisa was eventually attacked with a knife and injured.

We were all outraged. I called the social worker's again. I was ignored and they refused to move Lisa into care. My husband went to Ballymun to stop the violence himself as the police could do nothing. I wanted to take Lisa into my home, but I had taken Catherine in, Val's daughter and she was still struggling to settle after her own mam had died. She wasn't too fond of Lisa either and I was worried about upsetting her. I also had my own two kids Anthony eight and Sarah two at the time and Anto was in extreme stages of alcoholism and I had a full time job! I was busy.

Lisa backed off from us for a couple of years after that and we didn't hear much from her. We had no idea that she was suffering sexual abuse. Things got worse for Lisa and eventually at 15 years of age she sat in the police station and begged the police to take her into care. She told them she had been sexually abused at home since she was 6 years of age. The system was reluctant to take Lisa into care as she was nearly 16. When a child reaches 16 in Ireland, they are technically an adult and the state would have no moral responsibility for her, or financial responsibility. That was in 2002, the height of the Celtic Tiger when the government was doing very well financially. I'm pretty sure our system is failing thousands of children like Lisa.

A couple of years ago, Lisa now 27 years of age, took her abuser to court. He was found guilty of 52 counts of abuse. He was sent to jail for seven years.

Lisa is an amazing young woman. Through adversity, she put herself through college and has since received a degree in higher education.. She has her dad's sense of humour and lightness for life and is able to laugh.

Young John grew up to be a good hard working young man. At 30 now, he has a great wife Debra, and two beautiful children, Sarah and Reece. As a young boy, he had his own struggles with learning difficulties in school with no help.

He and his young wife hold no grudges towards his parents. They include them in their family occasions and help them as much as they can. Selflessly.

I remember when Lisa and John were children, and feeling self-righteous, I had a big row with their dad John. I Judged him and blamed him solely for his children's difficulties. Whether I felt right or not, I had no right to assume I knew everything about another person's life. There is always a bigger picture. We were all responsible for those children and if I let the social workers put me off from helping them, that was my fault. And I'm sorry I did.

Going back to the fire; Maureen died shortly after that, she was 51 years of age. She had a massive brain bleed and died quickly.

The older boys did their best to have some control in the house, but the younger ones were always starving. They took milk from doorways and bread from the bread van. They didn't go to school every day. Mrs Gorman, their next door neighbour had her fridge out in her back porch. The boys would sneak in there each night and steal her food, scoffing it in their beds, laughing their heads off. They were out of control. The social services wanted to take Anthony and Derek into homes, but their older brothers Billy and Peter took them into their married homes till they got jobs at 14 and they returned home.

Work gave Anthony some stability but it also gave him money to drink. He started drinking strong alcohol at that young age and started him on his road to alcoholism. Alcohol made the pain go away and Anthony never had to face his issues.

The boys had no sisters, but they had a huge extended family of female cousins from Maureen's sisters to look out for them. There was Sadie's daughters, Celine, Eta, Therese, Marie and two brothers, Liam and Derek. They lived close to the Murray boys and they were all like sisters and brothers instead of cousins. When they all got together, there was huge laughter heard for miles.

The girls had suffered their own tragedy when their mother Sadie fell down the stairs on her seventh pregnancy and she and the unborn baby later died. She was only 35 years old.

Sadie had been a doting Mother and loved her children. They were all still very young and felt a huge loss of their mother. Their father was selfish and not a good replacement for their mother. He soon married again and added another seven children to his brood. Most of Sadie's children went to New York seeking a new life, when they became of age.

When it was Celine's turn to go, she had saved up all her money and booked her flight to New York. She boarded her plane and was looking forward to her new life in New York. That was until she got off the plane in Montreal Canada!

That was the chaos and organisation of international flights in those days in Ireland. It really was a mad country!

Having no money to book another flight, Celine's sister Eta drove up from New York and picked her up.

They still laugh about the story today!

There were Sheila's daughter's Joanie and Christina and son Tony. Joanie and Chris also had the gift of laughter. Joanie and Chris were raised with the Granny County in Cabra beside all the other cousins when their parents, Sheila and Leo O Reilly had gone to England to find work in 1960. Tony was a very late addition to the sisters and came along when Christina was getting engaged at age 22 years old.

Sadly Sheila developed cancer after having Tony and battled it for 14 years till she died at age 57 years.

Leo was devastated at the loss of his soul mate, but he was a good man and he reared Tony well, with the help of Christina and Joanie.

Granny Biddy County was deeply saddened by the loss of her three young daughters. Anto had said, 'it was like she just gave up the fight of life and died of a broken heart.' Her young daughter Josie never married and she was aunty to all the extended family that came her way. She made ice pops for all the delighted children on her street and fed all the Murray boys.

All these cousins watched out for each other as best they could with their young age.

Through their own tragedies and pitfalls through life, they remain close to each other, giving support when they can.

One of Sadie's children, Liam, because of the loss of a loving Mother and his emotional needs not being met, has chosen alcoholism. He now lives homeless on the streets of New York. His bed is under the Brooklyn Bridge. He is 51 years old. Even in the freezing cold winters, he sleeps under that bridge. He says he loves it and has a great view of the city! He doesn't know how to settle now in a house as he has been so long on the streets. I went to see him and his home recently and the thing I noticed about Liam and all of the other homeless people. His bed place was quite clean and secure beneath the bridge. His few belongings were tucked neatly under his blanket. He had a bike locked to the railing above his bed. Liam gets up early every morning, when he's not on a bender. He washes in a public bathroom and then gets a Star bucks coffee with his bit of change he picked up from begging the day before. He then goes looking through bins and alley's for plastic bottles or cans. When he brings them to a recycling centre, he gets paid. All the other homeless people do the same and they have their own streets to collect on. Liam wouldn't dare collect on another man's allocated street! I was very impressed.

His sister Celine and Anto visit him from time to time to see how he's doing and he has a brother Derek who lives in New York who watches out for him also. The Simon community are a vital element for homeless people in New York and around the world. They make sure these homeless people are treated with dignity and respect. They give them blankets and food.

A huge problem for homeless people is that they get beaten and battered by thugs who think they can do what they want to these human beings.

Liam was battered so badly one time that every bone in his body was broken. Even his skull was fractured. Why would somebody kick a man when he's down?

I recently saw a man begging in the Dublin streets, who was so battered around his head, that blood was still flowing from his wounds. He had also lost his teeth. He looked about 50 maybe. It was around lunch time and he was looking for a few bob for a sandwich.. He spoke to me politely. He didn't ask me for money, a sandwich would do. I asked him was he ok? He said he was grand, he was having a little problem with the wife and kids and he was just out for a while. He was just going through a blip in his life. I felt really sorry for him. Why would people batter him when he's already a broken man?

I thought of Liam.

3

My Ma

Marie Kelly was born in Loughlinstown, Co Dublin with a twin sister Olive on 12th July 1941. They were the last births for Granny Kelly. Granny was 42 and had 16 other children and had four still births. Granny Kelly was a kind woman who loved lots of kids. Over the years she welcomed everybody into her home, where there was always a pot of soup on, fresh bread and some cakes. The girls did the girl chores like cleaning and cooking and the boys did the boy chores like chopping wood for the fires and stove.

It was a very simple home, but happy.

Ma was very close to all her family, but a lot of her older siblings, Julia, Alice, Vinnie, Carmel and Hubert went off to Leicestershire in England in the late 1940's and 1950's for work and opportunities. Ireland was a very poor country and offered little financial comfort to its people. They settled there ever since with families of their own, feeling the education system and medical system was better than Ireland.

Being twins, Olive and Ma had a special bond. They stayed close all through the years, even though Olive chose to live beside her mammy in Loughlinstown and Ma came to live with Da in Cabra, North side of Dublin.

Us kids were very close to Olive's kids too.

Aunty Olive had three boys, Desmond, Terrance and Mark and two girls Siobhan and Sinead and together we spent many happy summers on Bray beach.

Olive knew that Ma was having some problems with Dad, so even with her own brood of kids, during the Summer, Aunty Olive took three of us sisters at a time for a break for Ma and gave us a holiday in her house close to the beach.

We all played with our cousins in the little caves up near Shanganagh beach for hours until the tide came in, daring each other to stay till the last minute. We were never hungry and never afraid.

I loved the freedom there. We'd also be allowed to get the train by ourselves to Blackrock swimming pool. Everything was so safe then. I think people in general would watch out for children making sure that they were ok. I know that I couldn't swim at that age and we had no armbands and yet we all arrived home safe and hungry.

I was seven when my little cousin Siobhan died. She was just one and four months old. Siobhan was a gorgeous little girl with blond curls. She was quite assertive too and knew what she liked. I remember one time I was watching her in the bath, while Aunty Olive had to run downstairs for something.

Siobhan said to me "Me out! Me out, Jean!" She didn't like the bath.

I said "No, no Siobhan, you have to wait for your mammy to take you out" I was trying to hold Siobhan in the bath. She was full of fun.

Siobhan had been attending Crumlin Hospital for some tests in May 1974, after the doctor discovered a heart complaint.

Crumlin Hospital in Dublin caters for a lot of seriously ill children, and this particular time, there was an outbreak of measles at the hospital while Siobhan was in having tests. They decided it would be better to send Siobhan home to protect her, but the virus was growing inside little Siobhan already, and a few days later on a Sunday in June 1974, Siobhan went into convulsions from a high temperature while she was in Granny's house in Loughlinstown.

Aunty Olive got an awful fright and didn't know how to help her baby, she ran with her to the hospital across the busy Loughlinstown dual carriageway, but little Siobhan died on the way across in her Mother's arms.

That moment took the light from Aunty Olive's eyes. The pain of losing a child.

Aunty Olive still made time for all us Sutton girls.

Ma grew up with her brothers and sisters in a little cottage on a bit of land on the embankment of a little river running from Shankil to the Irish Sea, connecting to England.

Granny Kelly had inherited the land from her own mother.

Granddad Kelly was a poor man, so he didn't have the means to make it look fancy. The tiny cottage had a slant corrugated roof and plastered walls and as the family grew, he built another room onto the cottage.

Although they owned their own land, Granny and Granddad Kelly were still poor, and Granddad had to travel far and wide as a builder's aid for work to feed his family. He never earned much money for the hard work he did. Granny Kelly and all her daughters picked blackberries, and Granny walked the streets near and beyond to sell them.

They were a simple family, raised completely different from the harsh tenements of Dublin city. All of my ma's brothers and sisters were gentle souls; Ma saw no violence or abuse as she was growing up as there were few people living beside her and there were no pubs close by either. The nearest one was in Bray.

Although their house was small, it was scrubbed clean. They had a bathroom outside the cottage which was freezing, but welcomed! They had a fire each night and they sat for hours listening to Granddad Kelly tell his stories, after they had eaten a hot stew and homemade bread baked by the Aunties.

All in all there was great comradeship among the huge family of brother-in-laws, nieces and nephews that kept growing every year.

Ma's oldest sister, Kathleen, died four years ago, a very healthy woman just turning 90. Her second oldest sister Julia is still alive and well as I'm writing this book. Julia is 92, twenty years older than my Ma, and the youngest boy is Mick, and he's only 70.

Ma's parents didn't drink alcohol and none of her brothers were fond of it either, so they weren't affected by alcohol abuse. They did like to dance though and at all the family gatherings, they would do the twist and all sort of steps from that time.

Granny Kelly still had to raise her large family and Ma and her siblings all left school by age 10. I think my mam would have been good in school if she had the opportunity. She was good at counting and good at reading. Not many people of that time could read so well.

Granny lost two of her older sons to tragedy also.

Paddy when he was just 11 years old.

Granny used to boil water over the fire in great big pots for cooking or washing as they did in those days of the 1930s. It was a narrow sitting room and Paddy was reaching for something beside the fire, he toppled the pot over himself, he was scalded to death. Granny tried everything to help him, to free him from pain, every remedy she could think of, to prevent his skin from bubbling off him. Paddy didn't die immediately and he was in a lot of pain. Infection soon set in, and he went into a coma and died a few days later.

Granny hadn't wanted Paddy to go to the hospital as she didn't trust the doctors. That was very common in those days. Nobody went to hospital and if they did, family members were not allowed in to see them. Granny Kelly would never have a light in her eyes after that day. The pain was too great. I think she may have also suffered depression from the shock of what happened to Paddy, but in 1930, who knew what that was? She wasn't angry or bitter or resentful, but she became very sad.

A few years later came another tragedy when Granny's older son Bill was shot accidentally by his friend.

The shocked Granny Kelly further into her sadness. Granny had great faith in God and she trusted his guidance. She could only think that it was God's wishes to take her sons. She carried on through life quietly. In these days a loss of a child is still detrimental, but at least we all acknowledge the loss and recognise it for what it really means to a Mother and Father to lose a child. In those days, Granny Kelly, Granny Sutton and Maureen would never have been able to express their feelings of loss. Therefore, never grieving properly, but instead growing deeply depressed inside. This emotion would affect all of their parenting skills.

Granny Kelly was a generous woman and she welcomed everyone into her home; she shared what little food she had with others in need. She was never worried about how fancy her home was but it was clean and it had warm food.

I don't know where everyone fit when they were growing up and there was aunty Kathleen with her 13 children in an extended part of the cottage!

I remember this slightly disabled man Georgie who was taken in by Granny and Granddad, long before I came along. He was treated as part of the family. We used to call him Georgie Porgy, because he was quite fat!

Georgie loved to see us girls come from Dublin city, and delighted in us singing 'The Bay City Rollers, Bye Bye Baby' time and time again. He always gave each of us 10p.

We knew he wasn't our uncle, but we respected him because he was part of Granny's home.

Granny also took in another young woman Mary. She became another of our Aunties. When we went out to Granny's visiting, there were all these aunties and uncles and all of our cousins. There was plenty of food and cakes and the atmosphere was always full of chat and fun. The kids were all fed first, then the men and then all the women would sit around the table catching up on all the news. All of us older girls had to wash up afterwards. There was no alcohol in Granny's kitchen, it was all very simple and happy. We'd hate when we were all rounded up for the 45 bus into Dublin, to go home.

Mary was very fond of Mar, as she called Ma, and she loved all us kids too, as we were quite well mannered because of Dad's strictness. Mary is still alive and a close member of our family. Each time I see her, I ask her, 'How old are you now Mary?' She's tells me, ' Late 60's!' Now poor Mary looks like she's 95 and she has always looked like she was 95, (I hope you don't mind me saying this Mary) but whatever age she is, she loves a drop of whiskey and dances all night at all the family parties.

Granny also reared a lot of kids that she didn't give birth to, but she mothered them as if they were her own. She had enough love to go around and she loved them dearly and they loved her dearly. In those days in 1950's Ireland, children born out of wedlock were banished into Institutions as were their mothers. Granny would not allow any of her family to be taken into a home, no matter how difficult things could be. In those days there was no unmarried mother's allowance or child benefit. The mothers of those children had to go and get work and that sometimes meant leaving the country.

When Granny's in laws came to visit, they would ask, 'Where did this one come from?' Aunty Olive about 12 years old at the time had been heard to say, 'Mind your own business! You nosy cow!'

I remember when I came to see Granny with my four month old son Anthony. I had finished with Anto in America and came home without him. I was so proud to show my granny her great grandson.

'Another silly girl,' she said to me as she sat in her little chair. She was near 90 years old now. 'What did your father say?' she asked me. 'Ah, he's going mad,' I said, 'but we'll be grand.' I was trying to convince her that times had changed. It wasn't so difficult to raise a child as a single mother. In fact, times hadn't changed much in that case and Granny knew it more than I.

Us foolish young women is right. For whatever reason, we bring a child into the world and in fact we don't take into account rearing them without a father, being able to go to work and providing for them on our own as well as paying rent for accommodation. We don't think it through.

I had never thought of having an abortion. I would never have considered that.

Granny took the baby from me and held him with his big rosy cheeks and instructed one of the aunties to rub something in his gums. I was delighted. Anthony actually looks like my Granddad Kelly. His Great Grandfather Hugh Kelly.

Ma loved and lived for her children also, she was proud of her six girls.

I will always remember the smile on her face when she opened the door for us coming home from school. She was always happy to see us.

My Ma was no match for this 6 foot 5', blue eyed, stocky, butcher that charmed her. Ma was working in The Palace Restaurant, Dublin, when Christy was delivering the meat one morning. He fancied Ma at once.

Ma fancied Dad too. She was 26 now and was ready to settle down. She had lots of fun in her young years with plenty of dates. The twins Olive and Mar, with brown eyes and auburn coloured hair and freckles were very attractive. They were both married in the same year and were each other's bridesmaids.

Of course marriage was lovely for the first few years, but when children, and challenges, alcohol and recession came along, her lovely husband turned into the devil.

My lovely Ma of 5 foot 3' had started to experience mental torture that she had never experienced in her life before.

Her husband turned into an angry, violent, loud alcoholic.

Ma was very confused; she was bound by love for him and loyalty. As a Catholic, her marriage vows were strict too. She had promised to Love, Honour and Obey.

Dad wrecked her home on regular occasions. He threw countless televisions out through the front window of her house. There were holes in every wall of our house and every door, and the walls were solid brick then.

Dad hit these things to prevent him going for Ma. Then us kids would try stop him, screaming and terrified. He then grabbed us one by one and flung us against the walls. Many a time I was thrown against the wall or punched in the head, I was tough, I could take it - I was 11.

I could tell my dad off, I could protect my Ma and sisters, I was tough…

It must have been very hard for Ma.

A young woman is quick to settle to married life as she is more mature. But in 1965, when a woman married a man, she was getting the raw deal. She lost her freedom and the man became her controller, telling her where she could go and what friends to have. Dad didn't encourage Ma to have friends. He went crazy if she spent her time in a woman friend's house or invited women over to hers. He had something bad to say about any new friend she found. The truth was Dad was insecure and jealous of Ma's ease with others. She didn't need to drink to have conversations. He would say to her, 'You're so nice to everybody else and you have no time for your husband!' Dad never took responsibility for his own bad behaviour. He blamed Ma for any problems they had. Ma in turn didn't keep contact with friends. It was easier. She stopped wanting to go out with him because there was always a row in the pub. Mam didn't understand what was going on with Dad. He was needy. It seemed he was jealous of her relationship with her girls, but how could that be possible? Shouldn't he love his girls too? Dad hated everyone who took the attention away from him.

Mam had no idea how to cope with this abuse.

In those years, if the man wanted sex, the man got sex. The women had no say. Even after drunken violent episodes, the Catholic women had to give in to their husband's demands.

Many women of that time have told me, they had to lay down and think of Ireland to keep their man happy.

I don't know how a woman can have sex with a man who is selfish and disrespectful. Don't men realize it's kindness that turns a woman on after years of marriage?

Dad was a typical selfish Irish man of the times. Drinking and gambling every payday, not thinking that the woman had to nourish her children on the little remains of his wages, and try to pay the bills.

What could a woman do? How could a woman raise her kids on her own without their father?

How would a separation affect the kids?

Isn't a strict Father good for raising daughters? Would an Irish Husband do something really nasty if the woman left the home? What was the Irish man capable of? Could an Irish wife be really free?

We tried many times to get our dad locked up by the police, I begged Ma to sign him into a mad house, because we thought he was mad. She couldn't do that, because Dad would have never allowed her that control..

The scariest part was the hatchet or the knives. He used those as a threat. In a rage, he would scream, "Where's me knives, I'll kill myself!" He'd get his pack of butcher's knives from under the sink.

We were terrified, we didn't know what he would do. It was to leave a deep deep fear in me that lays still in my stomach even now. I didn't feel comfortable with sharp knives in my home until very recent years. I used to hide my knives just in case a burglar would break in at night and stab us all in our beds. No lie.

Ma's neighbours were really good though. They all witnessed their own fair share of suffering, but they watched out for each other, and each other's kids.

Mrs Tobin and Mrs Collins houses were each side of us, they had to put up with the roaring and shouting blaring into their walls, and they never interfered.

Our houses were in terraced blocks of eight and my Ma's was at the end of a block. They had three bedrooms upstairs, a sitting room and a kitchen and a bathroom downstairs, the toilet was at the back of the house. The houses were built strong. Each room partition was solid brick. The walls held in some of the noise, but my dad was such a loud shouter, that everybody could hear everything.

Mr and Mrs Duggan often came in to try to calm Dad, as did Mr Cadbury a few doors up. Even poor Mrs Herbert with her bad legs came down to try sooth him at times.

In those 1970s years, when the recession was affecting everybody, all these women passed in food, treats, and kids clothes to my Ma. As did my Ma, too, to others worse off than herself.

We loved going into Mrs Duggan's house every morning to pick up Karen for school, she had fresh buttered toast waiting for us. We didn't have a proper toaster in our house, so we'd all fight over who was running in for Karen in the mornings.

Ma did her best not to rile Dad. She didn't react to his vile verbal abuse; she couldn't be taunted into the row. If Dad was hurting us, she would try to stop him, saying "Jesus Christ stop him".

She prayed over and over a hundred Hail Mary's. She'd hurry us out the door, up to bed, out of his way. When she got us up the stairs, she came up and sat with us, trying to make a little joke, as her home was getting broken up downstairs.

The little ones, Christine and Eleanor, age seven and eight, were terrified. I had at least seven good years before Dad lost his mind, but Christine was only a baby at six years younger than me. She carries a lot of anger for the fear it caused her.

The next morning, after a house wrecking episode, Ma got up really early to clean up the mess before we'd get up and see it. She never lay in bed.

Ma forgave Dad. She never held a grudge and didn't hold resentment in her chest. God was guiding her all the way. Ma had great faith in God.

Dad couldn't cope with sickness. One time when I was 13, I caught Yellow Jaundice, an illness of the Liver. Because your Liver is not functioning properly, you feel very weak and sick all over. Dad came home in a drunken rage and wanted to kill me, violently. I was upstairs in bed when Dad charged into my room shouting abuse and grabbing for me as I tried to hide under the blankets. He had to be held back by Nick Carbury our neighbour and my poor Ma.

His reasoning was that I brought some deadly germs into his home.

I'll never forget the fear I felt that night. I was feeling shaky all over. I prayed to God to take me that night.

I knew I aggravated my Dad. He always picked on me, or went for me when he was drunk, to have a physical fight, because at 13, I could fight him back.

I remember when there was only four of us, I was about seven when Ma did leave him, and went back to Granny Kelly's for three weeks. Those three weeks were bliss in Granny Kelly's Haven.

Aunty Biddy was a great baker, and we'd have wonderful cakes, and Aunty Kathleen cooked our favourite dish, pudding gravy, we'd sop up with bread. We loved it there. It was so warm and friendly. Poor Aunty Biddy, was later to die unexpectedly in her 50's, an undetected Diabetic.

Aunty Biddy was so stylish. She was only about 5ft, and had coppery brown short styled hair and brown eyes. She must have had a million handbags, because she gave us Sutton girls one, every time we visited. Her bedroom was so full of mystery. She'd bring us in and say, "hold this" and it would be some amazing garment or fabric. I was so excited when she called us in to help sort her stuff. Her wardrobes were always filled with stuff. She was so glamorous and she smoked glamorously too! I missed her so much.

Granny Kelly had no idea what was going on for my Ma, as the women were very proud and never spoke of their problems, but Granny told her not to go back to Christy. I remember wishing we could stay, I really wanted to stay.

Dad came and took us home, and four foot Granny Kelly ran after him with a hatchet! "Put your hands on my daughter again and I'll chop you up, you blaggard!" she shouted.

Ma never told her family anything after that; she was too ashamed of the life she was living.

We didn't get to Granny's too often after that, maybe three times a year and Dad never came with us.

Mam and us six girls took the number 45 bus to Loughlinstown from Dublin city centre, with Ma paying one and six halves to Dun Laoghaire, not thinking she should pay the full fare to Loughlinstown, she was always watching the few bob. I remember the bus was stuffy and smelly and most of us would vomit on the slow bumpy trip to Loughlinstown, leaving the poor bus man to clean up the mess!

It was a trip we always looked forward to.

The cakes, the pudding gravy, the big huge family, who all arrived on Sunday for tea. It was wonderful. We then went down to Aunty Kitty's bungalow beside Granny's house, and got a gorgeous tea made for us, we were spoiled there!

I envied my cousins growing up with my favourite Aunties, and seeing Granny all the time.

Poor old Granny was getting old. She was becoming stiff with arthritis. She sat in her little chair in front of the fire and read the tea leaves for the adults, never the young ones. She had a gift of vision.

She fell over into the fire one Sunday and burned her poor hands, but she never complained, and her little hands never straightened out. She was a strong woman.

Granny loved a drop of whiskey as she got older, and used to trek on the bus into Bray to Byrne's, her local pub, for a whiskey every day. She liked her little trip. She was well known and respected in Bray and would walk around the shops greeting her friends. She visited the little graveyard in Bray where her husband Hugh lay to rest and her sons. Until one day, when she was in her mid 80's, she was attacked and robbed as she left Byrne's pub. They pushed her to the ground and the cowards got her handbag and ran off.

Granny was very shaken after that and never went into Bray again.

I know these words were said a thousand times but why aren't parents teaching their children to respect the old. Is it too difficult a job? Old people should be able to roam about in the freedom of safety.

My Ma had a great Mother and my Ma is a great Mother. These women drive me to be a better Mother also.

Their gratitude for a simple life, striving for nothing else but peace. So, although my dad was very violent at times, my mam was doing her job of being a good Mammy. We were lucky.

Ma had amazing strength. She could have easily succumbed to alcohol to block out her pain. She didn't. She prayed to God and asked him to guide her, she asked God to protect her children and guide them in his path.

We rarely heard my mother shout, she never hit us.

If we were bold, she'd give us timeout in our bedroom and lock the door.

When Olive and myself were each locked in a back bedroom, on an occasion. We were sadly looking out through the windows. Our cheeky friend June Duggan from next door called from her back garden to Ma, 'Marie, let them out to play for Jesus sake!' Ma sometimes gave in laughing.

Ma never gave us a hard time about school or homework, or said work harder. She accepted us as we were: Unconditional love from a Mother. She never tried to control us, or turn us off traveling when that time came for us. She was selfless. She was in exact contrast to our dad who judged us, criticized us, knocked our confidence, told us we were useless. Gave us hell when we wanted to travel. It was crazy.

Every Saturday, we all had our chores to do; the house had to be cleaned top to bottom. Dad went off to the pub about 1pm on Saturdays and left all us girls to it. Although I have to say on the rare occasion my Dad cleaned the house, he scrubbed it spotless. He was also a great cook and also a rarity, we savoured his flavours in the food when he did cook.

Saturdays were also bath days and we'd all share the same bath water!

Eleanor and Christine were washed first; Olive scrubbed their hairs and then took delight in rinsing with buckets of cold water. She was always playful.

Sharon and Josie were next, and then myself and Olive; We were always paired in that order. Ma was last!

Ma combed all our hairs into ringlets, after treating it with paraffin oil to keep away head lice.

This particular Saturday night when I was nine, Dad didn't come home till after 10pm. The four youngest were in bed asleep.

Ma had that worried look on her face, and she was smoking one cigarette after the other.

We heard Dad coming, she whooshed Olive and I up to bed, and told us to pretend to be asleep. I was lying in my bed with the covers over my head, and I could hear Dad come in through the front door. He was a huge man, so it was easy to feel his movements through the house.

He was starting to moan. Ma was getting his dinner. He was complaining about his burnt steak. In fairness, Ma could never cook a steak.

Then he got the smell. "What's that smell?" he shouted.

Ma explained, "It's just the stuff for the kids' hair for the lice."

"What stuff?" he shouted.

"The paraffin oil" Ma said.

And then he went crazy, "Paraffin oil in the kids hair? they'll go on fire! You stupid woman, are you stupid?" He went ballistic, wrecking the house, running up the stairs, woke all the kids, everybody was crying. I was terrified. I couldn't sleep at all that night for fear of going on fire. It would take dad ages to calm down. He would shout for hours.

Ma was also worried sick that night.

I felt so sorry for her, she was only trying to be a good mother.

When the time came for me and Olive to go to discos in town of course my dad wouldn't let us go.

Ma pretended we were going to the movies and snuck us in the window when we came home. We were silent like mice.

But occasionally, if we missed a bus or got delayed, Dad stood awake at the front door waiting to pounce. He didn't need to be drunk. Although I didn't know what nerves where then, my stomach would be in bits.

Our Ma got into a lot of trouble for letting us out, and we were grounded for weeks. In fairness to poor Olive, she was quite happy at home not upsetting Dad, but I urged her, "Come on Olive".

There was no terror on the Dublin streets that I was afraid of then. Although there were no obvious signs of drugs, or violent alcohol fuelled attacks on Dublin streets in 1980, I'm sure there was some trouble around. But it didn't scare me; my fear would only begin when I was going home.

Activities outside the home can show abused children a bit of hope. Myself and Olive and our friends joined The Mater Dei Youth Club in Cabra. It was run by a bunch of young people in their 20s, Liz Ryan, three brothers Mick, John and Des Treacy and a few other cool people that I looked up too and admired. We called them 'The leaders'. They organized club nights for different age groups and disco's once a month.

It was legitimately run, but my dad only allowed us to go after he questioned the leaders about the rules, and was happy it wasn't a den for drinking and fornication. God forbid!

The leaders spent all their nights keeping us entertained and off the streets, teaching us different board games in the club, running darts and pool competitions. They organized mountain walks teaching us lots of stuff about nature. They brought us on weekend trips to lug a La, a hostel resort in Wicklow, that not one person in Cabra will ever forget.

Lug A La was set in a valley in the Wicklow mountains. It was the most amazing beauty I had ever seen. The hostel itself was a typical country cottage, with a stream running close by. It looked tiny on the outside, but had lots of rooms on the inside. It had 8 bunk beds in the girls' room and 8 bunks in the boys' rooms with separate bathrooms. There was no central heating, just beautiful fresh cold air.

The lush green mountains and hills spread for miles and miles, covered with heathers of all colours and wild flowers everywhere. There wasn't any other houses to be seen in the vicinity, it was derelict. It was perfect. I remember arriving there one time and Lug A La was covered in beautiful daffodils everywhere, as far as my eye could see. I remember appreciating this beauty, and feeling completely happy.

The leaders brought lots of food for us and the only liquids were sodas. The leaders weren't using this weekend away for their own fun, so no alcohol came on the trips. The highlight of the trip was the nightly barbecues and the midnight feasts.

These leaders made us feel important. They played a huge part in kids' lives in Cabra.

Treating us children kindly and with respect. We were an ugly and dysfunctional bunch!

Outside influences have a huge effect on children's lives. It gives them happiness, even just for a moment, it helps them forget whatever is going on in their homes. Thanks to all you leaders of the Mater Dei, we had a bit of fun in our lives.

Living in Ireland is like living in a village. There is a great community within the people, especially during times of hardship. These people have an instinct to help the young and the suffering, giving them hope. We forgot this during the Celtic Tiger and some of us Irish stopped helping each other. It's good to see it coming back now and communities are bringing back that old helpful spirit.

Ma had got a job in Batchelor's Bean factory on Bannow road shortly after Dad had lost his job. Her hours were 5pm till 10pm. Although Dad didn't like the idea of her working outside the home, he had no choice as he was still out of work. Mam left myself aged 10 and Olive aged 11 to take care of the little ones while Dad was in the pub. When he came home, we had to lift up his dinner and clean up afterwards.

Dad was always in a bad mood. Sometimes when he was in his fury mood, Mam had to hide in the shed when she came home until he calmed down or went to bed.

They had finally got enough bricks for the extension when I was 13. Ma had applied to the Dublin Corporation for a loan of 14,000 pounds for the build and they went ahead and got a builder.

I remember seeing this skinny old man coming and going that must have been the builder. He did a bit of work and then he left his young apprentice to finish off the jobs.

The apprentice was really good looking and maybe about 18 or 20 years old. All us girls swooned around him as young as we were. It's not surprising that the extension started to crumble as soon as it was finished. Our house was bad enough with the holes my dad punched into walls, but when the joining of the extension started to come apart, even I knew that something serious was wrong with it. Pipes rose unevenly from the floor. The roof leaked with water. Damp had risen from the floors. Dad decided to take the builder to court as he wouldn't come back and fix the job.

The case dragged on for seven years before it went to court. We had to live with holes in our floors as engineers came to check things and never replaced the floors!

I was 19 then and Dad was still unemployed, but he was pretty sure they had a good case against the builder and that we would soon have a properly built extension. How my mother lived with six children and a husband in the freezing cold building site that was our kitchen for all those years, I do not know. She never lost her temper once.

When they came home from court that day, it was one of the saddest day of my life. They lost the case. The rogue builder walked away scot free, and my poor Mam and Dad were left owing money to the court. I was devastated by the unfairness of it.

There was huge corruptness in Ireland in 1986 and poor people like my parents were the victims of it. That builder was eventually caught and locked up by someone else who had more money.

Dad was deflated. He was a failure and he was crying. Sober. I was crying so hard. My friend Declan had just died recently from his motor bike crash and life was so sad.

I stopped believing in God.

The old Dad came back for a moment and he said, 'I promise I'll get this house fixed up, Jean. It's going to be ok.'
I met Anto during that time when I was 19 and Anto had a great pair of building hands and he rebuilt the whole extension free of charge for my mam! A wise move as he won my Ma's love and respect forever! And my Da's!

Then when Anto started up his construction firm a couple of years later, he gave my dad a job driving the truck! Dad loved it. He began to see a little hope for the future. Although Dad drove Anto crazy at times. It didn't matter where Dad was delivering in the country, he would always come back to Ma's house for his breakfast or lunch. He wouldn't waste his money on coffee shops or lunches out!

Ma's ongoing faith in God got her through it all.

She did her best to raise her children as normally as she could, with the knowledge she had.

Each of her six girls left their childhood home badly damaged by 'The Evil' that came into their home as children. And as adults, they had to try to find their way.

4

My School Days

When my sister Olive went to school in the September of 1970, I was 3 years 8 months. I kicked up such a fuss to go to school with her.

Mrs Le Han, the teacher let me join her in low babies, as it was called then, in St. Catherine's girls' school in Cabra west, Dublin.

St. Catherine's School was a big huge grey stone building; it was built by The Dominican Sisters in 1944.

The Dominican Sisters had acquired a vast amount of land in the early 1830s, leading from the Navan road to the back of Cabra. In 1885, they built St. Dominic's College, it would serve as a secondary school. It was built with beautiful grey stone with some beautiful architecture and design. It consisted of various buildings, including a church, and accommodations for the girls and boys. The school catered for boys till 1978; and the last boarders stayed all the way till 1999. The buildings are all surrounded by mature gardens, with plenty of fields for various sports.

Later on, it built a unit called St. Mary's which caters for intellectually disabled students. The Cabra Convent was considered one of the leading educational establishments in Ireland.

The land also housed the sisters who taught at the school, and also facilitated young ladies who became sisters themselves. The young sisters were very well educated also.

The inside of St. Catherine's school was very well maintained. It had about 30 classrooms, that catered for 42 children in each class, and it had radiators for central heating as it was quite modern for its time. We each had a proper mahogany desk, with a tilt. The school had big cloakrooms beside the well kept toilets linked to an inside shed for the children to stay at breaks if it was raining. The playgrounds were huge, with sheds also to sit in if it rained.

There was a huge hall for indoor activities, music and drama and sports.

To be fair to the Nuns who ran the schools, they took a lot of children in at 3 years of age to help the Mammys', who had about 10 kids at home and an unemployed husband.

I was delighted! I wasn't a bit afraid of Mrs La Han's long wooden cane, or when she tapped me on the head with it or my knuckles for my attention!

Mrs La Han was a huge teacher, and she reminded me a bit of Frankenstein, as she had a large head! She had a loud voice too, but I never heard any fury in it, I always thought she was a bit of a gentle giant.

I kicked up another fuss, when my sister Olive went on to high babies and I had to repeat low babies because I was too young. I was good at school. I found learning easy enough, apart from Irish. I hated Irish, our language, it was so boring.

I was good at drawing pictures too and Miss Le Han had announced an art competition. We were to draw a picture of our friend sitting beside us. Sharon Williams sat beside me. We had the same birthday and we were both 4 years of age.

I thought Sharon was so pretty. She was a petit little thing with dark brown bobbed hair with a fringe. She had brown eyes and little freckles across her nose. I drew Sharon, I thought she was easy to draw and I coloured in her hair and eyes. Everybody thought it looked like Sharon and I won the prize! I was so delighted and I received a box of sweets. It was the only thing I ever won in all my life. I can still see that picture in my mind's eye.

I did draw another picture years later for the Cabra tech. It was of 'Sting.' I think it was pretty good but I haven't seen it since. That's the good thing about computers in today's world. Everything can be scanned and saved. (Although, I'm sure my editor has wondered how I wrote this book at all with my poor computer skills!)

Sharon and I were great friends in school; we played together in the school yard all the time. One time, when we were still 4, we were playing in the school yard. Sharon asked me to hold her 3p while she fixed her shoe. Sharon always had a few pence as her mam and dad didn't have as many kids as mine. I acted quickly, and put the 2p in my pocket thinking of the sweets I could buy. I pretended to Sharon I dropped it in the grass. We looked for ages and of course we never found it. It was the only thing I ever robbed in my life and it haunted me for years. I confessed to Sharon when we were 40! she laughed so hard.

I liked the nuns. Contrary to what everyone else says about them. The Dominican nuns were very kind.

Cabra Girls needed Nuns. We were a tough bunch. They kept us on the straight and narrow. Sr. Cora and Sr. Comilla were my favourites in St Catherine's.

Sr. Cora was quite beautiful, even though you could only see her face, her hair was covered completely in a white cotton cap, and then a black cotton veil covered it. She also wore a full black cotton outfit, like a cloak, and her rosary beads hung around her neck. It was a kind face with beautiful corn flower blue eyes. She was really tall and slender and walked with grace.

Sr. Comilla was shorter, her dark hair fringe always escaped her veil as she was always very busy, running around doing something or other. She had sallow skin and bright blue eyes. Sr. Comilla was very strict, but kind. In fact, I didn't know any mean nuns there at all. There were some very old cranky nuns who still taught us at times, and we all giggled at their forgetfulness.

I still got the ruler slaps on my palm eight times every time I got sent to Sr. Cora's office, but I didn't hold it against her. It was my strong will, stubborn, cheeky behaviour that got me into trouble; Defendant of the wronged also.

I'd take up for any child the teacher picked on, saying, "She didn't do that Miss, or that's not fair Miss". I couldn't keep my mouth shut.

I didn't mind the slaps, when I'd come back from the office, all the kids gathered round me and asked, "How many did you get?" and they'd look at my poor hands and give me great sympathy.

Miss Le Han was a tough teacher but she was fair. She made us repeat our letters and numbers over and over till we got it right, whether we wanted to or not, she didn't accept tardiness. We had to go along with her or feel her wrath.

I enjoyed the challenge, even at that young age.

I remember when I made my first Holy Communion. I was about 7 years old. I remember I was the second best reader in the class at that time, I was delighted about that.

Things were still good financially at home and my dad made sure I had a new communion dress. Mine was a pretty short one, with the frilly knickers underneath, that I suppose was the fashion at the time. Everyone always asked to see my knickers; I remember feeling shy then, which must have been mortified in today's terms. I made my communion, I was lovely with my little ringlets and no teeth and I went visiting to all my aunties and I collected £9. (Which wasn't very much!)

My lovely dress got really dirty visiting all my cousins in Loughlinstown, Co. Dublin, eating jam and cream cakes and playing on the hills.

I had to wear my communion dress to school the next day as was tradition. Normally girls were delighted at the chance to show off, but my dress was scruffy.

I remember kicking up a fuss to my mam, saying 'I couldn't go to school in my communion dress, it was scruffy.'

Mam said, "Close the cardigan in front and no one will notice, you'll be grand." That was Ma, everything was grand.

Mrs Le Han used to line each girl up to have a good look at the communion dress. It came to my turn, I remember feeling really embarrassed at the state of my dress. Mrs Le Han said in her deep loud voice " Right, Miss Sutton, give me a look at your dress." She opened my cardigan, saw the dirt of it, her eyes grew wide, and then she closed it up really fast. She didn't embarrass me, I sent thank you in my eyes to her.

All the other girls' dresses seemed to be beautifully clean and perfect, even their socks. I was well clued in at seven years of age; I had washed my socks and knickers the night before myself, so at least they were clean.

We don't realize that children as young as seven and even younger are really sensitive to things going on around them and they know a lot more than we think I remember the first time I found out what the man did to the woman. I was seven years old. Breda Foley told me! She was another little girl in my class and she had found out something the night before and decided to tell us. 'Yeh, the man puts his willy inside the woman's private part,' and we all squealed, 'Ugh!' I was shocked!

I'll tell you one thing about the facts of life. There were no proper fact of life teachings. We found out, by other kids telling us. My ma didn't tell us! And the nuns just told us, 'wash up as far as possible, wash down as far as possible and then wash possible!' I kid you not!

Our Uncle Pat used to work in a sanitary factory and as ma had six pre puberty girls to cater for, she started to collect sanitary items for years. As an inquisitive ten year old, I would wonder what they were. Ma told me they were bandages, I always wondered why she needed so many bandages!

Going out to teenage disco's, Ma would say, mind yourselves, have respect for yourselves! She says the same to our teenage girls now and I say to Mam, 'You have to be more clear Mam, they don't know what you mean when you say just that!'

In today's terms it's, 'Have you got your condoms?'

I remember another occasion when I was about eight, we were working on a nature project in school. I was partnered with Barbara Wakefield. Barbara was a floaty eight year old with beautiful red hair and blue eyes. She was one of the quiet girls and we got on really well together.

We needed something for our project and Barbara said she had one at home. We decided to sneak out of school and go to her house, as she lived closest, we didn't think anybody would miss us. So, us two little girls ran across a main road to her house in Ratoath estate Cabra.

Her Ma wasn't in when we got there, so we decided to use the ladder to climb up to the back bedroom window. I held the ladder as Barbara climbed first and then I followed her up the ladder! Amazingly, no harm came to us, and we got back to school. Of course, we were found out and brought down to the office for another eight slaps!

I was a bit mischievous.

We then went on to have our senior teacher in third class, Miss Breely, (not real name, could be still alive and teaching there) and we were so excited to be moving upstairs at last.

Our excitement didn't last too long as Miss Breely didn't have much time for us Cabra girls. She was posh, and more snooty.

She was a small teacher, with red hair and freckles. She must've been very young then but she seemed older. She just did her job; she didn't seem to be very friendly and showed no real interest in anyone.

I remember telling her about one of my sisters who had just had a very bad accident and was in hospital. Sharon had fallen on some railings and a spike had gone up through her private parts and cut her badly. I suppose I was looking for some soothing words from Miss Breely, but they never came. I knew this teacher was different to Miss Le Han who was firm but kind to us little girls.

Suffer little children at the hands of adults.

Showing disdain or no interest in a child shows the child they aren't important. Miss Breely confirmed to us dysfunctional bunch that we were of no importance. We had Miss Breely for four years.

There were 42 of us in her class. It must have been quite daunting to arrive as a new teacher to us bunch of misfits. She was probably advised to appear in control, and not get too emotionally involved with a tough bunch of kids from Cabra with well-known parental dysfunctions.

There were some notoriously rough families in Cabra who were rehoused from the tenements in Dublin city, where violence and alcoholism were commonplace. Most of those kids were in my classroom.

There were a lot of tough girls. These girls were loud and pushy and cheeky to the teachers. Although a child didn't get away with too much cheek to the teachers then, or they received 10 slaps on the hand and 100 lines, 'I will not do that in class again!' Only to receive another 100 lines the next day!

Toughies could fight with anyone and win.

There were the usual few weak girls. These were generally the overweight girls, the girls with glasses, turns in their eyes or stammers, or the ones who cried when the teacher shouted at them, of course the toughies picked on the weak, because they could.

Then there were the few quiet girls, who, in fairness, nobody bothered with. The quiet girls didn't irritate anyone; they kept to themselves, sucked their thumbs if needed, did their knitting and did all their homework and were a bit floaty or airy fairy, in a creative way.

There was also another group, 'The slow girls'. The slow girls were kids with learning difficulties. Nobody knew what was wrong with these girls because there were no diagnoses in those days; those kids were just left at the bottom of the class and called slow. In our classroom the toughies left these slow girls alone.

One good friend of mine Geraldine had a different experience; she was a student in St Catherine's school 14 years before myself. Geraldine Herbert was a beautiful little blonde-haired girl with perfect tanned skin and piercing blue eyes. She was a soft, quiet girl from a big family of 13 siblings. Geraldine didn't know she had learning difficulties. She knew she was one of the 'slow' girls, or 'stupid' girls, because her teacher, Miss Gillan, (changed name, she might be still alive) told her so time and time again. "You stupid girl!" She shouted at this little 4 year old child. Miss Gillan also excluded Geraldine from lessons, saying "You're too thick for this!" She pushed her and slapped her for being slow to learn. The other children in the classroom copied this abuse from the teacher and taunted little Geraldine, bullying her, making her feel so unworthy. Hitting her and spitting at her in class with the teacher looking on.

As she grew older, the kids waited for Geraldine after school and beat her up and pulled her hair taking lumps from her scalp.

Geraldine's Confirmation was coming up in 6th class.

In those days when a child made her Confirmation, the Bishop had a question for each child before he confirmed them. The Bishop approached Geraldine, a little 11 year old girl, she was terrified. Miss Gillan stopped the Bishop, "Don't ask her anything, she's stupid, she couldn't learn her questions". The Bishop passed over Geraldine, who was left feeling worthless. She carried that feeling through life.

Geraldine left school uneducated and battered physically and emotionally.

I knew I had to hold my own in school, I had to be tough or to at least appear tough or else I'd be bashed.

I hated to see anyone getting bashed for no reason though, and I did try and break a few unnecessary fights. But I wasn't a saint and sometimes it's not always easy to do the right thing, and I'm sure I probably tortured some poor girl without really knowing the effect I'd had on her, and for that I am truly sorry.

There was another room of third class girls in St. Catherine's ran by Miss Water. (Real name, because she was so cool, and I since heard she died of cancer. Real loss). I envied those in Miss Water's Class, because she was a sporty teacher, where as our teacher was too prim and proper to prance around the mucky fields for P E (Physical Education).

Miss Water had her girls doing all sorts of Sports and activities and on occasion, we would come against them in athletics and indoor basketball.

We had great banter with Miss Water's class, we were always in our personal competitions with them. Karen Collins from my class was great fun. She was a toughie, but she had such great wit with it. She was always a bit over weight too, but it never went against her in sports, as she was good at all activities.

If Karen started the slagging match with Miss Water's class, we knew we'd win.

There was a lot of toughies in Miss Water's class too, including Martina Curley. Martina came from a big family of red heads, and had a typical Irish fiery temper with it. She was crazy too, so her and I got on really well together, we often met each other in Sr. Cora's office receiving our slaps. We giggled through our pain.

When us toughies from our class got together with Miss Water's toughies on nature walks or other outings, they was always war.

I'm pretty sure that God invented nuns just for us Cabra girls. We were hard to control. The nuns gathered in their packs to intimidate us into standing down. I'm sure they had their weapons hidden in their cloaks. I'm also sure they went to church every evening praying to God for guidance on how to stay in this path he put them in.

There was one girl who was always waiting for her chance to get me and pull my hair out. I don't even know why she targeted me. Patricia (name changed, she might still bash me) came from a notorious rough family with lots of siblings. These girls were really nasty and vicious and nobody wanted to be on the wrong end of their hate list. Although they didn't attend our school, where ever I went she was there waiting for me. Myself and Teresa Finnegan had to regularly fight Patricia and her sisters off. Patricia fought viciously and pulled lumps from my hair, one little patch has never grown back. I fought her back of course, getting as much hair from her head as I could. It was scary though.

In fairness to those toughies though, they more than likely had a reason to be vicious. They were obviously witnessing and experiencing some nasty behaviour in their homes.

Most of the Irish men were alcoholics who came home from the pub and beat up their wives. Some girls suffered different abuse in their homes, getting raped regular by their fathers or uncles and brothers.

It was early 1970's then, and us eight year old little girls were witness to a lot of violence in the home, suffering physical, verbal abuse and mental torture.

As I grew, I didn't trust men. I hadn't had a good experience of the man figure. To me, even as a young child, I always thought it was unfair.

Why was the man so important? Why had everything got to be his way? Why wasn't a woman important? Valued?

I was in danger of hating all men.

Alcohol was hugely abused by the men.

The Catholic Church wouldn't help their women. They told the wives to abide God's word and obey their Husbands.

Where was the law against men abusing their women and children? Who gave man this power? I don't know any part of the bible that says abuse your women and children. How did our devout Catholic women have to condone this behaviour in the eyes of their church?

As young as I was, I wondered where was God? Why didn't he help us?

The violence was everywhere in Cabra, in most homes with lots of children. The women weren't allowed to use contraception either. It was against the catholic religion.

Among this crazy existence, girls became good friends.

Cabra girls have a comradeship of dysfunction and abuse. It binds us together, and we have a deep understanding of each other.

For those of us who have survived, we keep going, to be better Mothers, better to ourselves. We try to live this one life that God gave us. We try to succeed in being happy, changing, growing; unaware that it's what we should be doing without struggle. We had such an ignorant start.

When we were finished school, we were told, 'Just get out there'

Just get out there and do what?

How to be a partner?

How to be a parent?

How to love?

How do we keep ourselves?

How do we do this?

Nobody told us, nobody told me.

But there is a voice or a conscience inside you, that pushes you on: Encourages you to keep going, to try again.

Some of us don't have that strength; we succumb to denial, to alcohol, to drugs, to mask the pain of failure.

It's too hard a challenge.

Then starts the circle of abuse all over again.

I can understand that attitude; I don't criticize or judge failure of others. It's really hard to be on the right road, to change yourself.

I was raised in chaos, shouting all the time, receiving anger for being sick, for being a teenager, nobody working out solutions, just hearing controlling instructions.

Receiving violence because I'd angered my parent, and I was just being a kid. I learned it was wrong to be a kid. I learned it was wrong to have a voice. I was afraid. I was afraid of my own decisions.

Then when you go into the world, into a relationship, having children, how on earth are you supposed to do it right? You have to try so hard to do it differently, to react differently. To work out problems. Of course the easy solution is to resort to alcohol or drugs or any sort of oblivion to hide the pain.

The pain is Great, its Huge, its Massive. It never goes away, because being raised in such a contorted way, causes an individual to hate themselves. To remove all this injury takes huge work. So, don't judge the weak too harshly, they can't do it. They just can't do it.

There were hundreds of times I wished myself dead from when I was 11 years old. It just goes to show you how we underestimate how strong children's emotions can be. There were thousands of times I wished my Dad was dead. I remember I really hated him then.

I thought I was really ugly at age 11. I was tall and lanky, already my full height. I was never fat, but I just hated myself. My hair was a fuzzy mess.

I wasn't getting on too well with my next sister down from me either, Josie. I blamed her for getting me grounded all the time, I felt she was always telling Dad on me. I was so angry with her; I didn't talk to her at that time for about six months. I wasn't a nice big sister. I was hateful.

I was also angry at my ma. I was so annoyed with her that she made us all stay with Dad and go through this abnormal life.

"Why don't you leave him?" I'd shout at her. I didn't know how she coped under such difficult circumstances. She also had to put up with her upcoming teenagers, now giving her grief.

How could she leave? Where would she go with six kids? In one way, Dad was also possessive with his children, he'd never let her go.

Ma was also torn, Dad was her husband; she felt sorry for him too, she knew he was in obvious need of help.

I was always very close to my ma as a little girl, I felt very secure when she was around, I was definitely a Mammy's girl.

One time when I was seven, after I got a nasty insect bite on my ankle, she took me to Temple street hospital, for a tetanus injection. When we came out from the hospital, I couldn't walk and my little Mammy carried me on her back. I remember being almost as big as my Ma.

As a teenager, I knew I was behaving badly to her. I was turning into a bad daughter.

A short time after that, on the 17th May 1974. Ma had taken us six girls into town for a bit of shopping. Olive was eight and Christine the baby, was one in the pram. We had a lovely day and we were bought ice creams before we headed for our bus on Parnell Square. We were coming from Moore Street when a big explosion happened a few hundred yards in front of us. We didn't know what it was, but everybody start screaming and running all around us. My Ma put Eleanor and Sharon, the two smallest children in the pram with Christine and us three oldest, Josie, myself and olive, had to hold on tight to the pram and just run with Ma. It was really scary.

Another big bang happened somewhere behind us. Ma was crying, saying run, run, hold on tight. I could feel the terror in my ma's voice. She was dragging us three with one arm and pushing the big pram with her other arm. We ran up past the smoke on Parnell square and we didn't stop running until we were in Cabra. We got home safe. My poor Ma got an awful fright, but while we were oblivious to what went on that day, Ma was watching on the news of the 11 people that were killed on Parnell Street by bomb explosions that day and the 14 people killed on Talbot Street from the blast behind us. Many more were maimed for life.

There were a lot of troubles in the North of Ireland during those years, but nobody claimed responsibility until 1993 when The Ulster Volunteer Force claimed they carried out the attacks.

As a teenager I started to pull away from Ma, and during those years, I wasn't nice to her. I blamed her.

I started making myself sick occasionally after eating. I didn't find it easy to get sick, so I never became completely anorexic, but it did last nearly two years.

There were a couple of times I thought about taking my own life at age 14. The only tablets in our house would be Disprin or Anadin. There were no fancy tablets for every ache and pain as in today's world.

One time after another violent episode, they would be very regular, two or three times every weekend.

I took six Anadin that night, hoping I wouldn't wake in the morning.

I hated God when I woke up the next morning. I was so angry at life.

Ma was always the good in the family, the normal. Although I never spoke to my mam about how I was feeling or my eating disorder as I didn't want to worry her any more than she was, she was the sole reason I had a choice in how I lived. I could've gone down that road of self-destruct. In my subconscious mind, I saw the good; I knew I didn't have to choose the evil.

When I was behaving really badly in my life, I could see her guidance, her wisdom, her God. I just had to find it.

I didn't know the personal sacrifice Ma was making for us then. As a Mother myself now, I understand all too well the challenges she faced.

She had six girls to raise, and she felt that fear would keep us out of trouble, and we'd be raised proper.

I started to suffer with depression, at age 11. Changes were taking place within my body and mind during puberty and I didn't know how to express those deep feelings. I had to hide how I was really feeling in order not to start a row, or invite accusations towards me. I didn't want to bring any attention on to myself.

Not being able to be yourself or express yourself freely as a young person without fear, prevents you from developing into who you should be. It gathers momentum throughout life. You lose yourself.

My friends helped as much as they could.

Myself and my sister Olive grew up with the Herbert's who lived just a few doors up from us. They were a big family and we were very close to them. Mrs Herbert had her own difficulties in raising a large family. She wasn't going to judge anyone. She just prayed for them. We played with the youngest sister Caroline and Teresa Finnegan across the road.

When we escaped Dad's violent rage, we ran to our friends' houses for comfort. We'd cry and we'd laugh at Dad's craziness.

Caroline's older sister Linda listened to our cries, and never judged, and then she'd say, "Let's get some chips and curry sauce and watch a horror movie". She loved horror movies. Linda died in 2004 aged 52 quietly in her sleep of a heart attack. I loved Linda; it must have cost her a fortune in chips and curry sauce. I can't actually watch any horror movies since then!

Linda's Ma, Mrs Herbert left her key in her hall door whenever we needed a place to go to escape the storm.

She liked Dad, as Dad was a good neighbour when he wasn't possessed by the Devil.

If I had no friends then, I wouldn't be writing this story today. My friends got me through a lot. Just being with them helped.

I didn't tell them about my bulimia or suicidal thoughts or the depth of the fear I was feeling. I knew they would help me, but I didn't want help. I just wanted to die.

I day- dreamed also, that something really amazing would happen and take me away from this life. I loved going to bed so that I could start dreaming. Two of my sister's had blue eyes and three of them had brown eyes, I had green eyes. I dreamt that Mam had got the wrong baby in hospital and that I was really someone else's. Poor Mam.

I read books also. I loved reading. I could escape into someone else's world easily through reading. It was my favourite passion.

There was a lot of violence on the streets of Carnlough road in the late 1970s.

There were lots of house fights that ended up on the street for all us young ones to see. Many young men in their late 20s in alcohol fuelled rages fought their enemies with hatchets and knives, slicing each other and leaving scars for life right on our street. The police were always on our stretch of Carnlough road trying to break up vicious fights.

Ironically, my dad kept us all on a tight rein because of this. Our friends had the same time limit, we had to be off the streets before dark and in our friend's house or home. We had another friend Lorraine Confoy, and her Ma, Mrs Confoy drove around the streets spontaneously to keep an eye on her daughter. None of us were allowed to drink or smoke, it delayed us into the ravages of alcohol till our later teens.

But Lorraine and I were the rebel's. I started to drink when I was 14 years old. I didn't drink much though as I knew I'd be killed if my dad found out. I drank only on Saturday nights and it was two or three bottles of beer: The fear of Dad always controlling my moves.

You know, my dad spoke very well, not common. So did my friends' parents. Even though his parents came from the ravages of poverty, somehow through filth and squalor, they learned table manners and grammar! I was amazed by that. There was a bit of a contradiction because we had to go to our grammar classes too, or we'd be bashed. For real. I remember it well. St Catherine's school provided after school elocution classes. All us seven year olds would line up and had to repeat, 'How Now Brown Cow,' time and time again and we still sounded like we came from Dublin!

I had my friends in school too and I loved going to school. Sadly, by age 11, I had to go across to the Secondary School, St Dominic's College, our partner school. I knew I was growing up and I didn't want to grow up. The adult world seemed very scary.

I was so defiant at that point in my life, I'm sure the teachers thought I hated school. I was horrible, angry and nasty, and I'm so sorry Miss Long, I know I gave you hell.

I was bright, but I was so disruptive in class. I was obviously very unhappy.

Sr. Adrianne was our Principal. She was a fierce Nun and she had a notorious reputation for being wicked. She had big green cat's eyes and she was big in stature. Her presence was very impressive. She spoke very low and controlled. She also wore her full 'habit'. I wasn't scared of any of the teachers but I was scared of Sr. Adrianne, but I also respected her. She only gave the strap on your hands if you were truly evil.

Many a time I was in Sr. Adrianne's office. I dared the teachers to take me down. I must've had a death wish!

Miss Long, my maths teacher had enough of me one day and finally dragged me down during a rage. She'd had lost control and I was delighted. She couldn't take any more of my cheek and disruptiveness. Miss Long was a very attractive blonde young woman. I was horrible to her. I wouldn't do any work. She threw me into the office, I deserved it. I was a Divil. Sr Adrienne never gave me the strap. She must've known I was a tortured soul. She gave me Chinese torture instead. I had to sit in Sr. Adrienne's office for nearly an hour with her just looking at me. Then she would ask me, "Why are you behaving in this disruptive way, Miss Sutton?"

I would just stare back defiantly and not answer. I didn't know, I didn't give her any information. What could I say? "My home life is mental and I don't understand it."

I never knew that I could sit down and talk to somebody about the madness in my life then. It just wasn't done.

Madness in our house was becoming very normal at that stage in my life.

The police took Dad away one Saturday night during a particularly violent attack. After he had wrecked the house, Dad was attempting to kill himself with a knife in the kitchen; he had nailed all the doors shut. Us kids were terrified. We were so relieved when the police finally came and took him away. It took them along time to talk him down. It was funny, the young police men never used force arresting Dad.

My poor ma was devastated.

We all went off to bed that night, exhausted from all the emotion, hoping to get a good night's sleep without fear.

It wasn't to happen.

Christine heard it first; She was about eight years old at the time. I saw her peep her head up from her bottom bunk bed and pull the curtain back. "It's Da!" She squealed in terror, "He's at the gate!"

We all looked through the bedroom window, and there was Dad, standing there, looking up at us in the window. He was wearing his big black overcoat. He was creaking the gate, opening and closing it, trying to scare us. It worked.

Dad was like Jack Nicolson from the movie 'The Shining', with 'The Devil' in his eyes. We were so scared that night.

We were all screaming, "Don't let him in Ma!"

Ma didn't let him back in that night and he eventually stormed off. We heard he slept on the canal that night. The police said they hadn't the power to hold him. I didn't understand that, what was the point of sending him home a couple of hours after they arrested him? He was still drunk with the whiskey.

We were worried about the repercussions of that night and we were right. Dad was on a mental rampage for two weeks solid. He hated all of us then. He came home drunk most nights starting rows. There were more holes in the walls, chairs were flung. Doors were kicked in. There was no point in calling the police.

The police couldn't make any charges on domestic violence in 1977. Regardless of what happened.

In 1782 Judge Buller in Northern Ireland ruled that assaults on wives were legal provided the husband used a stick no thicker than his thumb.

In 1840 a judge affirmed the husband's right to kidnap his wife, beat her, and imprison her in the matrimonial home.

Up until the end of the 19th century, the law supported the right of men to control their wives by force. When the Law had to intervene it was to restrain violence, not to prevent it.

Women's aid groups were only starting in 1975 in Northern Ireland and 1977 in the South.

Imagine! Less than 40 years ago!

Two official looking ladies came to our house during this time to talk to Ma about 'things'.

Ma was a proud woman. She looked after her own business and she sent them on their way. I suppose it wouldn't have made a difference what she told them. How would they have been able to help?

Dad did try sometimes. He hated being on the dole, so he took badly paid jobs here and there.

In 1977, Dad took a job as security man in the first McDonalds on O'Connell Street, Dublin. Olive and I had heard about this American burger place and we couldn't wait to hear about how the burgers were made. Dad brought home a 'Big Mac'. We were in awe. Dad explained it had two burgers inside the buns with onions and tomatoes and cheese and lettuce and sauces. I had a piece and olive had a piece and Ma and Da. The four little kids were in bed. It was delicious. I went to school the next day and told all the other kids about the 'Big Mac'.

On Carnlough road in 1975, there were at least 4 gay lads in every block of houses. As young as I was then, I knew they were a little bit different.

My Dad being old fashioned and with his growing anger and hatred for all things in life, you would imagine that this was the next thing he gave out about, but thankfully, he didn't. Dad liked the young gay men he grew up with. He sensed their difficulties in those days and had a silent respect for their courage in being different. With all of our dysfunctions on Carnlough road, It felt kind of cool to have all these gay guys living beside us.

I felt I belonged to a group. It didn't matter if we were all misfits in society.

When I left St Dominic's College after junior certificate, our third year state exam, I was sad. I loved the security of the nuns. They were wonderful people.

Although secondary school went on till 6th year, it wasn't really encouraged in our poorer families to stay on, it was better for you to leave school and get a trade.

I had met some lovely friends in that school, all sorts, some posh from nicer areas, and others like myself. Even though mad stuff was going on in our homes, we could escape in school and be a little bit normal. We laughed a lot and talked about boys that we fancied. We taught each other about periods and supported the odd girl who missed hers.

Some of the girls smoked behind the bike shed at lunchtime. I didn't smoke. There were a lot of things I was afraid to do, because my da would have bashed me.

In some cases fear is not a bad thing as I never took up smoking.

Soon after I left school, I got a hairdressing trade with Stanley James hair salon on the Cabra Road. Stan was our boss and he was a lovely chap. He was 'camp' but not gay. He had a lovely wife Mandy and four children. He was so easy to work for as he was always very pleasant, but he was a good business manager, as he didn't waste a penny on stock or materials. We had to master the trick of mixing limited bits of colour to get the shade we needed for a client. I was quite proud of my mixing ability.

I worked with a lovely bunch of girls. Anne and Marian were the senior stylists, and myself and Susan were the juniors.

Valerie was the talented florist in the flower shop attached to the salon. We had great fun in that salon and we were soon all good friends. Age didn't matter.

We witnessed Marian in her 30's then, have her first date with the handsome Desi. Marion was so adorable; it wasn't long before Desi bought Marion the ring. I thought they were really old to be getting married!

It was a beautiful love story, they were madly in love. Marion went on to have a beautiful boy and girl she adored, and got on with her life.

We lost touch over the last few years and I was devastated to hear she had died of Breast cancer.

Anne was already married and was great fun; she had a couple of kids under her belt and was a real mammy to us young girls. The hair salon was typically great fun. There was always something going on or some new gossip to hear. The clients loved coming to our happy salon and shared their own gossips. They delighted in the goings on of us 'young ones!' Anne's sister Carmel who was also a hairdresser in another salon, would come in often with a regular broken heart after finishing with one of the many boys who adored her. Carmel looked a lot like Brigid Bardot.

Anne loved her chips from The Fish Bar on the Cabra Road, and as junior, I had to go for them every Saturday.

One rainy Saturday, I ran down to the chipper for Anne. I had to cross a little road, Dowth Avenue. As I was running across the road, I got hit by a car, it knocked me down and unconscious. I opened my eyes and people were lifting me into the dry cleaners on the corner, saying somebody call an ambulance. I was mortified, "Let me up, let me up!" I said, and I got up and ran off saying 'I was fine.' The car had hit my left thigh and I had banged my head hard on the ground on impact. As soon as the shock had gone, I was in agony. I went back to the salon to work, very shaken and I had to mention what happened. My boss Stan was asking me 'Was I sure I didn't want to go in an ambulance?' I said, "No, no, I'm ok."

I didn't want any attention, and I didn't want my dad or Ma to find out, so I never told them.

In my bedroom that night, I checked my leg, and my whole left thigh was black. I was in so much pain, my head throbbed and throbbed and I thought I was going to lose my leg. I never told my Ma or I never went to the doctor, such was my fear that my dad would go mad. I just got on with it.

I was already ignoring the importance of me.

Valerie the florist was in her 30s also, but looked 20. She was into health and fitness and proper nutrition, which in 1983 was really new.

Although I didn't have a weight problem, she said it was good to live a healthy lifestyle. She soon had me under her wing, and showed me how to eat healthy and the benefits of exercise.

I decided to take up swimming, but I couldn't swim, so I went to St Vincent's pool on the Navan Road most mornings before work, and taught myself to swim. I was 17 before I start doing lengths. From then on, I always ate healthy. I had already given up red meat when I was 13, and I continued exercise throughout my life. I was never obsessive about it. It was just the way I chose to live. My healthy lifestyle helped my mind without me knowing it at the time, as food, sleep and exercise is vital to anyone who suffers with depression. I think that helped me get through a lot in those years.

I was 17 then and I still had no boyfriend. There were plenty of lads who would walk by the salon and us girls would size them up and say, 'he's lovely, he's not!' The lads didn't really come into a ladies salon. They were too embarrassed. Besides, I was still ugly then. I was still only 17. The 80's were ugly fashion years. There was no nice clothes shops in Dublin at the time. Maybe there were on Grafton street, but we hadn't heard of Grafton street yet. I was trying to find my look. My hair was shaved on various sides and coloured orange and purples.

When I did get asked out on a date, I wore my new bright yellow woollen leggings and bright yellow woollen top to match, with yellow high heels. I had no style.

The lad was one of the barbers up the road from our salon. We would have a lot of banter with those lads. I think he was a hippie, as he had long curly hair and wore long jumpers and Jeans' and said 'Man' a lot. Anyway, I was delighted.

He brought me to the Brazen Head pub and we cycled down. I didn't drive a car till I was 27! The Brazen Head is one of the oldest pubs in Dublin, it's just across The River Liffey on Bridge Street, heading towards Christ Church. It's famous for its traditional music and people bring their guitars and violins and banjos with them to sing along.

I loved being out with this grown up, but sadly, it didn't last long as he dumped me when I wouldn't have sex with him. Cheek!

Another thing I was afraid to do was have sex.

I had some bad luck with boyfriends. I didn't really have any and the odd one who asked me out was normally very ugly.

I had one really bad kiss from this ugly lad from Ballyfermot. He had a duffle coat on and black pageboy greasy hair. He rode a small moped. I really thought I might be gay after that kiss as I never wanted to do it again!

There were an awful lot of ugly teenage boys and girls in the eighties. For real.

I had a really good friendship with the most un gay, gay lad ever. John was tall, broad and all bloke with huge feet. In fact, he would have made a nice policeman. He had two children with his girlfriend and would talk about hating gay lads. When he came out, he was gas. It was great just talking to a lad with no agenda. I was really fond of John and I know he suffered himself later on through alcoholism.

It's so hard to be different.

Shortly after that I was stalked, by a man.

On Saturday nights, my girlfriends and I started to go to various nightclubs. We never had any trouble getting, as ugly as we were. They must have wanted to fill the place up. We could have been 14 years old as they never asked our age. This night, we went to Rumor's night club in O'Connell Street, Dublin. This was when they served up curry and chips in all the nightclubs then and you could smoke! I noticed this chap looking at me intently. He was another ugly fella, so I definitely didn't fancy him. Anyway, he must have been 30 something! He never said anything to me, he just watched me from the distance. Then he started to send over roses. At first, I was quite flattered to receive a red rose to my table every Saturday night.

It was a bit weird though. If we moved tables, he moved to the next table also, but he never approached me, he just looked. If we went to Rainbows for a change, a trendy bar off Georges street, he was there, just watching me. This went on for months. I never did anything about it, because I wasn't aware that I should be afraid, as I said before, there were much greater things to fear at home. I did try to ditch him though by going to different venues when he was there. One night, he followed us out, but as I was with my girlfriends and we jumped straight into a taxi. We lost him.

I did have a very good friend who was a boy; he lived a few doors up from me. I mentioned him slightly earlier on.

Declan was really tall, about 5 feet 9 inches, with brown curly hair and greeny brown eyes and freckles. He was lovely. We used to just chat at his door for ages, while he was kicking his ball around. I could talk to him about anything. He was like my brother. Declan and I made our communion together and our confirmation together and played rounders together with all the other kids on the road, John Duggan, John Quinn and Derek and Alan Dunne, and the girls being, Caroline, Teresa, Lorraine, Olive and Myself and Mandy Brown.

Declan loved motorbikes, and was really proud of his 'Scrambler' as it was called then. He took really good care of it and he was never a 'Boy Racer.'

Declan and I went to our 'Deb's' together. I borrowed Sandra Herbert's bridesmaid dress; it was blue with a high neck and long to the ground. It was the best I could get. There was no nails done or fancy hairdos or fancy limousines in those days, or fancy dresses!

Declan had hired a black tuxedo, He looked really handsome. He walked down to my house with a box of chocolates and flowers for myself. There was no fancy party either, and we went off to our Deb's at The Gresham Hotel. We had a great night. We got on so well, we decided to try dating. But there were no sparks, and it didn't really work out, so we went back to being friends then.

Declan met a girl soon after we broke up, and I didn't see too much of him then.

Then came the tragedy. One evening as Declan was driving home by The Tolka Road, between Cabra and Finglas, he was carrying a friend of his on the back of the bike, it was a wet day and Declan lost control of the bike and crashed straight into a lamp post, at full speed. He body was severely injured, and Declan was left brain dead instantly. They turned off the life support machine a few days later.

The other lad was badly injured also, with brain damage, but he recovered slowly.

I was truly broken hearted. He was my friend. He was only 19 years old. I would never see him again. I was so angry at God.

It's hard to have friends die when you're young. It's hard to understand.

Alan Dunne was one of our friends we grew up with on Carnlough road. At least the boys played with us even though we were ugly and Alan had a load of good looking brothers too! No real danger of being fancied though so we didn't fancy them. We did like them though and I was very fond of Alan. It broke our heart when he was to die a couple of years later of 'Sudden Death Syndrome' aged 22. Alan was a gorgeous lad with blond hair and blue eyes and he was a talented soccer player.

I also have to mention Brenda Farrington. Brenda worked in the flower shop when I worked in the hair salon. Stanley James owned them both and they were joined together. At break time we would all gather for tea and chat. There wasn't a bad bone among all those girls. You know, I think later on, when I have a different experience in a salon, I didn't know how life had changed so much from these fabulous co-workers. Brenda was beautiful and wholesome and had a beautiful voice. She died on a tragic motor bike accident that broke her boyfriend's heart and all of ours too. She was 22 at the time.

I guess God knew who he wanted.

I met my future husband when he came in and got his hair cut one day. The most I knew about him was that he had just come back from America after a few years working there with his brothers. He was called Anthony.

He wasn't much taller than myself, about 5 feet 7 inches. He had dark sandy coloured hair and green eyes and he was rugged looking.

I like rugged looking men.

He came in almost weekly for a haircut but never asked me out.

My work mate used to say 'He fancies you!' I did feel little sparks between us when we spoke, but he had never asked me out. I knew I had to make the first move and go down to his local pub, Matt's in Cabra.

Matt's was a buzzing pub. It was always packed to capacity with all ages of people. Great bands used to play there every weekend. All single females would dress up in their best and dance and sing along to the latest chart topping favourites of the 1980s; Michael Jackson, Celine Dion and my favourite Whitney Houston.

Downstairs it had a Disco Bar, where only the trendy and the cool people ventured.

Myself and my girlfriends preferred to go into town to really trendy bars like the Harp on D'Olier street Dublin, on our Saturday nights out. The Harp was a great bar, with great music and a great atmosphere and some good looking boys. I was 19 now and was starting to look a bit better, I had even dated a really nice lad called Charlie, but he had emigrated to Canada. Typical!

One Saturday night with no luck on meeting any boys, I was telling one of my friends Mary, about Anthony, the lad I fancied from Cabra.

Mary was a great character, red hair, blue eyes, curvy and very attractive, with a great sense of humour. She had convinced me to leave The Harp that Saturday night and find my fella in Matt's. We were giggling all the way, and fuelled with a couple of cans of Harp, off we went.

It was close to Christmas, so Matt's was packed. I was feeling really nervous when we arrived, Mary was pushing me along, 'Go on' she said, he'll be down in the disco bar. We had to push through the throng of people, walk to the back of the lounge and go down the stairs. It was all very fancy, as it was all new.

I saw Anthony at the bar and with a push from Mary, went straight over to him and gave him a big kiss on his lips. I had heard it was his birthday, he was 24.

I said "Happy Birthday".

And we were inseparable after that.

5

Having My First Child

Anthony and I were crazy about each other. He was funny and he made me laugh and my friends loved him too. I'm glad that my dad had put the fear of sex in me before now, because when you find the right person, it's corny, but it's great!

We became serious about each other very quickly and got engaged a few months after we started dating. Anthony actually went to my dad first and asked his permission to marry me. My dad loved him for that.

Both of us were very naive though. We both came from dysfunctional homes, so we didn't have the knowledge to discuss our plans, our future, our wants, what we were passionate about, having and raising children. We just thought that love and lust would be enough.

In 1988, Temple Bar area in Dublin City centre was just getting a name for itself for popular pubs and clubs and restaurants. It's situated between Dame Street, and the river Liffey and its stretches over a mile long. Over the years, it has become a great tourist attraction, as there are a maze of little boutique shops, beautiful coffee and cake shops, bars and amazing restaurants. On Saturday mornings, you will find various markets throughout the maze, with fantastic selections of homemade organic foods and artistically created gifts.

All the celebrities who come to Dublin frequent the restaurants there.

Myself and Anto had booked a table in a little quaint restaurant there one Saturday night, to celebrate our engagement. I couldn't believe when my idol Paul Young, came in with his entourage. I loved his music and was a big fan of his lyrics; I felt he spoke from his heart.

This night I was feeling really brave and I naively thought I'd go and ask him for his autograph. He had only just been seated, so I wasn't disturbing him eating or anything, but he was so rude and he unhappily gave me his autograph on a serviette. I felt really embarrassed as he nearly threw the serviette at me. I wasn't a stalker, I wasn't going to bother him for the night, I didn't think he was that famous, and there were no mobs outside the window waiting for him, just one little fan, me.

He lost a loyal fan that night.

I loved the fact that Anto had 11 brothers as I had none. I was sad to never have met his mother and father, but his brothers and their wives and all of Anto's extended family welcomed me into the Murray's. I wasn't going out too long with Anto when he began to tell me about the loss of his parents. It was obvious he was really sad. He got very emotional when he was drunk. At first, I thought his over drinking was covering his emotions.

It really affected Anto when his mam had her breakdowns . He was really embarrassed about her loss of control. He would just run out every time she started shouting. Maureen was taken into Grange Gorman mental hospital in Dublin, after the house fire and given shock treatment to her brain. The well known treatment ECT, Electroconvulsive therapy, used in mental illness in those days and some severe cases still today, administered by connecting live wires to the emotional lobes of the frontal brain and sending direct shocks to it, to jolt the brain out of depression. She died shortly after this. Anto believes this may have contributed to her massive brain bleed.

The neighbours rallied round for the boys, watching out for them. Rosana and Mrs Gorman often sent in dishes of food and Maura and Joey Hanway looked out for Anto like he was their son.

Anto had a lot of freedom after his dad had died. He was so upset about his dad that he got away with a few tantrums. It may have been easier for his mam to give in to his cries rather than give him a consequence for his bad behaviour.

After his mam had died, he had no consequence for bad behaviour at all. There was no one at home to give him a punishment for drinking so young or staying out late. Anto could basically do what he wanted. Therefore he never learned to control his drinking, leading to his alcoholism.

Later on as a Husband, he was trying to hide his addiction. As a wife, all the threats, all the tantrums and all the shouting was not going to make a difference as long as he had no consequence to his actions.

When I finally realised that I had to say, 'No! I am not living with this bad behaviour.' Only then, did he have a consequence for his bad behaviour. He was forced to make a decision because he would probably lose his children.

Anto was finally given an apprentice roofing job at age 14, from a very good friend. He learned a lot about hard work and how to earn money from the trade. Anthony had to get up at six am each morning and cycle 15 to 25 miles each day to his job.

He felt older than his years and looked older so he had no problem getting into the Dublin City pubs at 15 years of age. This brought its own dangers. He and his friends were targeted by vicious gangs from Dominic Street and Greek Street. They had fights involving hammers, hatchets and all sorts of metal weapons they could find. There were a lot of youths unemployed in the late 1970s around the streets of Dublin at that time. The youths were angry, suffering poverty and abuse themselves during the recession. They looked for fights from easy prey.

Anto also got offered heroin at age 16 years of age by a good friend of his who was injecting himself, saying, 'Try it Anto, it's great stuff.' That lad is now dead. Thankfully Anto didn't take it.

That was 1978 and drugs had arrived in Cabra.

Joe and Pascal were heading off to Texas in 1980 and took along Anthony, aged 18 then. They wanted to get him away from the Dublin scene for a while, fearing he would end up in trouble.

The three boys travelled to Texas where there was plenty of work. Anthony loved the lifestyle there and worked hard learning more and more about the roofing and carpentry trade and gaining some great skills. The boys are famously known for working on 'The Dallas County Court House' in 1982.

The brothers had no fear, and would take huge risks and climb any height. They were sought after to work all over Texas.

There was a great group of Irish lads over there with them at this point and great friends were made. Anto's cousin I mentioned earlier, Liam McMahon, was one of them. When Friday nights came, the boys partied like only the Irish can. They loved the American beer, and drank themselves 'sober'.

Anthony was getting drunk every weekend and having more and more blackouts. He would wake up in places and wonder how he got there. He also dabbled in some popular drugs in America at the time, 'Cocaine' and 'Speed'.

Joe and Pascal met two Texan girls Marcy and Darlene and got married, it quietened the two boys down nicely.

It was 1986 when Texas had its own crash, Houston and the greater part of Texas lost a massive chunk of its oil, it caused a huge depression and there was no more work.

Joe and Pascal moved on to Florida with their wives as they had a few contacts for work there. Anthony went to New York for a while and still partied wildly with his cousin Liam. The boys were good drinking buddies, both as wild as the other. They loved being out of their head! They never knew who they woke up with the next morning. Anto had decided to come home to Dublin in October 1986 at age 24, and that's when I met him.

Liam stayed in New York.

Anthony failed to mention to me the gory details of his lifestyle before we met, so I was blissfully unaware of his addiction.

My friends all had boyfriends then, and all us couples ventured into town every weekend to Benson's on Parnell Square. Anthony never came in with me as he said he was always working late, but he always arrived into Benson's fairly drunk and very late.

I suspected early on in our relationship that Anto might have a drinking problem. He was never an aggressive lad, and he held down a good job, so I wasn't overly concerned. I didn't know then that he was secretly off with the lads drinking whenever he wasn't with me.

Besides, when we were together, he paid me lots of attention, so I soon forgave him.

I was going out with Anto about 10 months when Joe and Pascal phoned him from Florida. They told him, 'Florida was having a construction boom and there was loads of work for roofers and good money to be made'. They encouraged him to go back to the States.

Although Anto had steady work in Ireland in 1987, there was no great money to be made in roofing and he asked me to go to Florida with him.

I was so excited, I was finally going to leave home at age 20.

I remember we went into town and booked our flight tickets. They cost 266 pounds each at the time and it was with Virgin Airways, Dublin to Miami.

My dad and Ma weren't too upset, they liked Anto, and they knew we were going over to his brother Pascal and his wife Darlene. I was sad to leave my sisters, I was the first to go.

The flight over was so exciting, we flew from London, Heathrow, and the Virgin plane was huge!

Richard Branson had recently launched his new airline, and it was a fancy red and white. It was my first transatlantic flight.

We arrived in Miami to the beautiful evening sun. The skies were deepest blue and it was really hot. Pascal and Darlene met us at the airport. They had a little 2 year old girl Amanda, typical American looking with blonde hair and blue eyes. She was adorable.

I was delighted to be there and was overwhelmed by the vastness of Miami. The roads went on forever with a maze of bridges and intersections. I had never seen six lane roads before and I was terrified on the heights of the bridges running across vast motorways.

Darlene and Pascal brought us straight to a typical American restaurant for cold beer and hot wings, Hooters. I loved it.

The flavours of the sauces were delicious and the beer was served ice cold in frozen glass mugs.

Darlene and Pascal had a two bedroom apartment in a place called Meadowland Circle in Naples and graciously let us stay with them. It was a beautiful apartment complex, really stylish and it had its own private swimming pool.

I was very much the guest at Darlene's home and I wasn't much help to the young Mom only 2 years older than myself.

There is a huge difference between two young women when one is a mother and one isn't. I was still young and selfish and only had time for me and Anthony. If Darlene was a bit resentful towards me in those days, she had a right to be. Anthony and I went out every weekend and Darlene was left at home taking care of her family.

I soon had myself a little hairdressing job across from the apartment, at Marilyn's hair and beauty salon. I worked with a couple of older ladies who were typically American with bouffant hair and accents to match. I loved them, and we all had great fun working together. I didn't have a green card or legal visa to work in the USA, so I gave Marilyn a false social security number.

I loved Naples. The fancy apartment blocks, the beautiful weather, the beaches, the range of food and all the different restaurants. It was all so new and exciting.

The shopping centres or 'Malls' as they were called were huge, containing all sorts of wonderful shops. My favourite was the ice cream parlours. They had the most amazing ice creams with huge servings and a thousand flavours.

One weekend Darlene and Pascal went back to Texas to visit Darlene's family. We were delighted to have the place to ourselves and planned a special night out after we both finished work that Friday evening.

I came home from work and got myself all dolled up and sat patiently waiting for Anto to come home. There were no mobile phones in 1988, so I couldn't ring up and check where Anto was, when it was getting late. So I waited and waited, and then it was dark.

Anto never came home. I didn't know what to do. I was scared by myself in the apartment also. I didn't know any of the neighbours. The only thing I thought of was, 'had he gone off drinking?' but he wouldn't do that, he knew we had booked a special night out. 'Would he?'

Finally the phone rang. It was the police. They informed me, they had picked Anthony up for drinking and driving, and that I could pick him up in the morning, they were keeping him in jail for the night.

I was in shock. What would I do? Anthony locked up! I started to cry and panic. I told the police officer that I was on my own and didn't know anybody. She suggested I phone somebody I did know that Anthony was staying locked up for the night. That would never happen in Ireland for drunkenness.

Why hadn't I listened to him talking about guys he worked with, names I could contact for help?

Luckily, Darlene's diary was on the counter, I looked frantically through it. I recognized his boss's name 'Lee'. Would I telephone him? I was really embarrassed, but I had no choice. I phoned Lee and spoke with his wife Marian; I explained who I was and what had happened. I was so upset at this stage, I couldn't stop crying. Lee and Marian came and picked me up and took me to their home. I also didn't drive then, and that was so unusual in America, because everybody learns to drive at age 16.

Their house was so beautiful; it was bigger and fancier than anything I ever saw in my life. It had its own pool on acres of land. The driveway was about 500 yards long with beautiful landscaped gardens and water fountains.

Lee and Marian were a handsome couple in their 40s. They both had dark hair and were tall and lean. I realized it was Thanks Giving, a celebration in America. All their family members were there. They had three beautiful children close to my own age, and other relatives staying also. They welcomed me into their family and home. They took care of me, and gave me a room for the night.

If you happen to be reading this book, I thank you for your kindness.

People who take the time to help another person, maybe even a kind word or a 'hello', don't realize how important and how much a difference that can make to someone's life.

I remember feeling very different from these people, lower, unworthy. I hadn't grown up in such wealth or family warmth, I felt really embarrassed.

The next morning Lee brought me to the Police Station, and we picked up Anthony and the car. If there was bail, Lee paid it. Anthony was released looking a right dishevelled state, he was to appear before a judge on Monday morning.

I was so annoyed at Anthony. I couldn't believe he would do something like this to me. Didn't he love me? I had a massive row with Anto when we went back to the apartment. This was soon to become very regular.

I was soon to discover there was another woman in Anto's life. Mrs Alcohol.

I, thankfully was never jealous or possessive of any guy in my life. I don't know why I wasn't but I was so grateful I wasn't. I didn't need the hassle.

I only had to worry about what alcohol Anto had drank.

I had later discovered that Anto had finished worked at 2pm Friday the day before. He had gone drinking with the other guys, but Anto was lashing the drink back, and was quickly 'wasted'. He got into his car to drive home to me about

7pm, when the cops stopped him and arrested him. He was driving drunk.

I didn't want to do anything with Anthony for the rest of the weekend, although he was really apologetic and begging for forgiveness. He was also really embarrassed. I was still really annoyed and I wasn't talking to him. I asked him to drop me to The Mercato Mall in Naples.

It was a few minutes' drive from where we lived. I wanted to go shopping on my own. He was to pick me up at 3pm.

It never occurred to me that Anthony may have got a ban from driving, from the arrest, but if he did, he ignored it.

When I came out of the mall at 3pm, I couldn't see him. I waited for about 20 minutes and he never came. I was still angry and behaving a bit like a martyr, I decided to walk for a bit.

I thought I would see Anto on the road. I didn't think Meadowland Circle, where we lived, was too far away. I was fairly fit anyway, and surely, after the previous day, Anthony couldn't let me down. I wanted him to worry for a bit.

I decided to walk on the Tamiami Trail road. I don't know why I started to walk without checking exactly where I was going. I presumed I was going in the right direction, I thought the Tamiami Trail road was the one we had come on earlier. I didn't know I was walking towards Miami!

I walked and walked, I couldn't see Anto's car, I kept on walking. I realized I was extremely stupid, I wasn't thinking right. I was walking for two hours now. Cars going by were looking at this mad woman walking, down this dangerous trail. I didn't look at them; I just kept walking straight ahead.

I'm sure if anyone can recall this memory, they will be amazed that I am still alive as such foolishness obviously meant I was crazy. I was wearing purple check dungaree shorts, to my mid thigh and a yellow T- shirt under them. I had dark brown curly hair just to the bottom of my neck. I was slim and young looking. I was ripe for the pickings.

Anything could have happened to me and nobody would have any idea where I had gone. Three hours passed and I was still walking, the sun was going down. I was getting tired now, and I was so hot and thirsty. I couldn't believe I hadn't reached our apartment complex yet. But there was nothing, just trees and trees and roadway. 'Could I have gone the wrong way?' I was getting really scared now.

I was saying a thousand Hail Mary's.

Eventually, a truck pulled up. I kept looking straight ahead and walking faster, my heart beating really fast. "Hey Miss? Miss?" a voice called from the truck. I looked up and saw two young good looking guys about 25 in the front seats. The one nearest me had blonde curly hair and blue eyes, he was really golden tanned. The driver had dark hair with blue eyes and was darkly tanned.

I thought, 'this is it, I'm going to be raped and murdered now, and thrown to the crocodiles.' Oh my poor Mother.

"Can we help you?" said one of the guys. "We live in the same complex as you, we recognize you, can we give you a ride home?"

They seemed genuine, but I didn't recognize them. I said "No thanks, I'm grand".

The blonde haired guy said "You've a good bit to go, it's almost dark, it's dangerous out here".

I decided to risk it. It was dusk now, and it was them or the crocodiles. I got into the truck. I said, "I'll sit on the outside seat nearest the window in case you try anything". This is all fact! As if that would make a difference if those two guys wanted to harm me.

I was really scared in the truck and was afraid to say a word to the lads. On the 20 minute journey, the guys didn't say much to me either, they could see I was scared. As they pulled up at Meadowland Circle, it was dark. They told me they had driven by me a couple of hours earlier but thought I was some crazy woman walking on the trail like that. It was only as they passed me again that they thought they recognized me from the apartment block.

I relaxed and was really grateful to them. I was safe and unharmed. I was so glad that I had met two gentlemen. Thank you to those Mothers who raised those boys. Thank you God.

Anthony was waiting for me when I got home. He had gone for a few beers and arrived at the mall at 4pm. When he couldn't find me, he went back to the bar happily, thinking I was in shopping heaven. I was so angry at this but I couldn't tell him what I did or the fear I felt.

I knew somehow the blame would fall with me and his drinking would be forgotten. I felt strangely weak.

I just told him I stayed longer at the mall, as I didn't want to be with him that day. I silently thanked my Ma for the 1000 prayers she was praying for me every day too. I needed them.

I'm telling this story so that parents embrace their children and cherish them. From the moment they are born, learn who they are, talk to them and make sure they can talk to you, anytime: Because if you don't, you're cutting their connection to safety.

Anto had to go to court and face his charge on the following Monday. The judge was kind, he liked the look of Anto as he was a likable fella, and he put up no resistance to the cops. Anto apologized for the offense. The judge told him to do a six week course on Alcoholism and sent him on his way.

Anto only did the first session on Alcoholism and never went back, saying 'I'm not an alcoholic'.

Things settled back down over the next few months and Anto was busy working with Pascal. Their boss liked the Irish lads, as they were good workers, and wanted a few more like them. Anto thought it would be better to go back home to Cabra and gather a few lads from there, as there was still huge unemployment in Ireland in 1988. It would be fun going home for Christmas to party with our friends.

Anthony gathered about 20 lads in Matt Whelan's pub who all wanted to go to the States for work. They couldn't wait to set off.

The lads planned to go in the first week of January 1989. They were going to find apartments, rent furniture, and have a few bob in their pockets before any girlfriends followed. I was going to follow a few weeks later with my pal Caroline.

Most of us were going to work in America illegal.

There was a great excitement in Cabra that Christmas. Everybody was hopeful of a new start, of permanent work, earning good money.

It was a hectic Christmas, and I subconsciously realized my period was late. I was taking the pill regularly and didn't think I could be pregnant, but maybe with the time change from the flight home, it could have been affected.

One evening before Anthony was due to fly off, I did my maths and realized I possibly was pregnant.

I did the pregnancy test in my friend Teresa's house, with Caroline and Olive looking on. I wasn't too worried if the result was positive, as myself and Anto were madly in love, and although we didn't plan a baby, I could visualize the fairy tale ending.

Little did I know. The innocence of youth. I just remember when I told Anthony I was pregnant, he was in shock, real shock! He said "How did that happen?"....

I mean, what do you think happens when you have sex at every spare minute of your life? All those little sperm fellas eventually get through the pill barrier! Duh!

No offense meant to the men of the world, but they are a little bit dumb!

I was a bit surprised at his reaction though, and a thought came to my head, had he been in lust with me? Instead of in love with me, but I quickly reassured him and myself 'All would be well'.

Anthony told me later on, that it was the worse news he had ever had. His world just collapsed! He felt he wasn't able for the responsibilities of being a Dad. He was also terrified of my Da's reaction to the news.

I told him to fly off to Florida the next day as planned, and I'd tell my Dad myself. I was worried about telling my dad, but felt Anthony was better off not there, as Dad would kill him.

All the lads flew out the next day early in January in great spirits.

My Ma knew I was pregnant just instinctively. She was worried sick. She didn't blame or judge me. She was on my side straight away, although she knew only too well, I was cutting my young free life away.

I said 'It'll be alright Ma, we love each other, it'll work out grand. Don't worry, I'll tell Da before I go to America'.

My Dad was still unemployed at this time and still in very bad form. He was drinking heavily when he could, and as we were now older and mostly out of the house with work and social lives. Dad was giving Ma a hard time. Shouting terrible abuse at her, using foul language.

It was during one of these episodes that I exploded at Dad, "Oh for God's sake, you're just giving out about nothing, here's something real to give out about, I'm Pregnant!"

I don't know what I expected, but what happened was something I'll never forget.

The Pain in my Da's face; The Howl that came out of his mouth. It sounded like a wolf losing its mate, as if it was the worst thing that would ever happen to him, to me. He cried. Then he got angry, really angry and wanted to kill me, kill Anthony, kill himself.

I had to run out of the house. I was afraid, crying, confused. I felt really guilty.

When I became a Mother myself, I could understand his pain and anguish; Because Dad was not successful in life, and he didn't have the financial means or personal security to aid us in success in our lives. He wanted us to be successful, to break the chain of poverty. He was disappointed in me. I wasn't married, my fiancé was showing signs of alcoholism. He thought I would end up a struggling single Mother. He was afraid for me.

Of course, he couldn't express those feelings with words, as he had never learned to control his anger.

The next day, I left home to go off to America. My poor Ma crying and Dad disgusted with me, "Get out you Whore, you'll never be nothing".

My poor sisters, with no one to fight the battles for them.

I left my mother and my five sisters there to suffer more mental torture and physical abuse from my father, because of me. And I escaped. I felt selfish. I abandoned my family.

My sisters were soon to follow me over, one by one.

Myself and Caroline were on a new journey, a new life in America to live with our boyfriends. Her boyfriend, John, was one of the 20 lads who had travelled over with Anthony.

I didn't suffer morning sickness during my pregnancy, but there was one little thing, I just fainted randomly. Certain smells made me faint for some reason, and I couldn't control it.

We were queuing to check in for our flight to Miami. Dublin airport was packed with people going everywhere. I was aware that if the flight attendants thought I might be sick or pregnant, that they wouldn't let me fly.

I was trying to keep calm and not smell anything to set me off. I started to feel a bit woozy, Caroline caught me, held me straight, and we got checked in. We giggled all the way on our journey like two kids, Caroline giving me rescue remedy all the way every time I felt faint. We were just kids. Going into the unknown with no money in our pockets. We were crazy. I never thought I could be putting myself or my unborn baby at any risk.

We finally arrived at Miami airport. It was so exciting. We couldn't wait to see Anto, his short name, and John waiting at the airport for us. Although it was dark, it was still really hot outside. We spotted John and then Anto. I looked at Anto and couldn't believe he wasn't shaven and his hair was like the bear's hair from the 'Hair Bear Bunch' cartoon. Did he look drunk? He definitely looked like he'd been partying for the few weeks he was there before me. I was really disappointed.

Anto told us that John just picked him up from prison a couple of hours before. Anto had been drunk 'Jay walking' the night before, when the cops arrested him and kept him in a cell for 24 hours. That's why he looked so bad. Anto thought it was very funny and I was wondering what I was letting myself in for living with the father of my unborn baby for the first time.

We set off on our two hour journey to Naples from Miami.

Anto was driving, and he decided to take the Tamiami Trail. The roads in America go on for ever, with various exits to your destination. It's a great system that Ireland only copped onto in recent years.

But the Tamiami Trail is a back road that runs from Miami to Tampa. It's 275 miles long. People often use it instead of the interstate roads. It brings you to the Vast Everglades and Indian Reservations. It's a very deserted road and we were on this road over two hours at this point. All the excited talk had stopped. We were all exhausted. It was very late. It was very dark, with no lights on the road. It was becoming very scary.

We were driving four hours now, and we were still on that road. We couldn't see a thing only blackness going on forever and ever.

I was afraid the old Corvette we were in wouldn't make the journey, and we'd be abandoned there with the crocodiles.

I was getting nose bleeds. Caroline and I were crying, 'We want to go home', we were so tired as we were traveling about 30 hours at that point.

Five hours on the road, and Anto pulled into a little rundown gas station that didn't even look open.

I was terrified some 'Chain Saw' murderer was going to jump out and kill us all. It was all those scary movies I watched with Linda Herbert. I was screaming "No Anto, don't get out of the car!"

A man came out into the headlights. He was bent over, he had a hat on and a beard, and missing teeth, he didn't look too good. He talked in a really slow voice, and he didn't smile. I couldn't believe it when the strange little man gave us directions to the right road to be on.

We had been on the wrong road. We were lucky that we didn't have an accident. The man said that nobody travelled that road anymore. We wouldn't have been found.

I wanted to kill Anto at this stage.

Finally six hours after landing in Miami, we arrived in Naples.

We fell into bed exhausted and drained.

The next morning, we woke to beautiful sunshine, it was a glorious day. Our apartment was two bedroomed, it was lovely. It had a balcony with a little patio and chairs, and it looked onto a beautiful complex with lovely green areas.

It was a great location, as both myself and Caroline didn't drive, we needed to be able to walk to the shops.

Anto had to appear in court again that day. This time he got a fine and a caution, and he had to do the alcoholism course again. He did the course, but paid no attention to it, still refusing to admit he had an alcohol problem.

Anto was a devoted boyfriend Monday to Thursday, but once the weekend came along, the drinking began.

I felt really angry, Anto was trying to convince me I was moaning about nothing. Anto didn't accept the responsibility that his drinking was affecting our relationship. I began to think it was my fault causing the rows all the time.

Myself and Caroline enjoyed a couple of weeks in the sun before we found jobs. We decided to apply for kitchen staff work from the hotel down the road. We filled in false social security numbers and got the jobs! It was great fun. Neither of us had any experience in hotel work, but we did know how to clean a kitchen! We were well taught at home. I never told them I was pregnant when I was applying for the job, and my pregnancy was still unnoticeable, (apart from the odd faint) so I had to carry the heavy trays of knives and forks and cups and plates, like everyone else.

I occasionally let a tray fall, and us girls would be in fits of giggles.

I never went to see a doctor about my pregnancy during my first 7 months. I also didn't know what to do about it. I didn't think I could legally have the baby in America, and I knew it would cost about 5,000 dollars. I assumed I would eventually go home to Ireland and have the baby, but every time I phoned home to Ma, Dad would be in the background screaming, "Tell that whore to get off the phone". Things were really bad at home. My mam was trying not to cry when I was on the phone.

My older sister Olive had left home too, and come across to Florida with her boyfriend Tony. They went to Sarasota to work for Anto's other brother Joe. I was delighted to have her over with us. That meant there were only four girls left at home, and two incomes had left the house. Ma was struggling financially, and that didn't help Dad's mood.

I eventually went to a Doctor at the end of my seven months, just to see how the baby was doing. Myself and Anto went to a local Doctor. He was amazed that I had received no pre natal care at all in during those months. I was well into my last trimester. He asked me what were my plans, 'Where was I having the baby? Had I not checked into a hospital yet?

I told him 'I was going home soon to have the baby, maybe when I was 8 months'. He told me 'you'll not be flying anywhere, your blood pressure is very low, and you need to get checked into a hospital straight away!'

That was the reason I was fainting all the time! So that was that. Decision made for me. Thank God.

My sister in law, Darlene, got me registered with Medic aid.

It's like the medical card in Ireland, which meant I could have my pre natal care for free and have the baby in Naples Community Hospital Florida.

I was really healthy during the nine months pregnancy and swam nearly every day. Apart from my big bump at the end, which made me waddle a bit.

I was due the baby on the 13th September 1989.

On Friday the 15th September at 8am, I felt a tiny twinge in my privates. I knew this was the start. I was really excited, but nervous too about the pain. I had decided I wanted the epidural, which was used in America then.

Teresa, our other pal had flew over for the arrival with Ray, her boyfriend. We were all really excited. The twinges continued all day long, but were very manageable. That night the boys were having a card game, and Teresa made us all 'Harvey Wall Bangers' cocktails.

Throughout the night the twinges were getting stronger and at 12pm, we all decided we should get a good night's sleep, as I was probably going into labour tomorrow!

I know, first baby, I didn't have a clue!

The other thing was, I didn't have any 'show', mucus, or discharge of blood, coming from my privates, and no waters were leaking. I didn't think I was in labour.

I was conscious of my Ma's advice, "don't go into hospital until your third stage of labour, they'll only be messing around with you!" That meant looking and feeling your privates to see how many centimetres you were dilated, not that I had any idea of that, because Irish mammy's leave out the words!

By 12.30am, the pains were really coming strong. Myself and Anto were reading our guide book, to see if everything was going to plan. It said you're not in your third stage of labour until there is a 'show'. No show still, but plenty of pain.

1.30am, Pain consistently. We were trying to time it, but it didn't seem to stop for breaks, again, no show.

2.30, bad bad pain, no show, deep breathing.

3.30 same.

4.30 crawling floors and chairs, pain so bad. No show.

'I must have a very low thresh hold for pain', as I thought I was still in first stages of Labour.

'Thank God I had decided to get the epidural when I got to the hospital.'

5.30am, a small show of mucus! Thank God! Pain so bad, my legs were like jelly.

Anto woke the gang, as John was driving up to the hospital.

Everybody was delighted. I was crying with pain.

Caroline said, "Get her there quick John!" I suppose I didn't look to good.

I was in the front of the car with John. Caroline, Teresa, Ray and Anto were in the back. Anto was trying to hold my hand. I wanted to kill him! I was breathing like this, like blowing out a candle, fast. I didn't feel like pushing, but the pain was unbearable. A thousand Hail Mary's.

John was speeding, through traffic lights, round corners, over ramps.

Finally, the hospital and alive! Thank God!

Through my pain, it was really funny. My five friends were running me into the hospital. It was 6am on the 16th September.

The receptionist said, "Good morning, Can you fill these forms in?" I definitely couldn't do that. I was in so much pain and breathing so fast. She said, "Ok we'll get you up first to settle you in".

Great! Epidural please.

She gave me a wheelchair, and the gang brought me up to Labour ward, where everybody was told to wait downstairs or go home, because I was going to be there a while. They'd call the Father in a few minutes.

The thing that was very important in America was marriage, and I wasn't married and I looked like a kid, like a nobody, so the first couple of nurses in the pre labour room were very aloof with me.

They told me to take all my clothes off and put the hospital gown on, by myself, I thought their behaviour was normal, until I was to have my second child, when the nurses were really helpful. I was crying in agony and could barely move to take my knickers off, and I was really scared.

I got up on the bed with the stirrups, by myself, which was scary enough, with your bits exposed to the world.

The nurse had a look, "Oh wow, you're 10 cm dilated, you're ready to deliver" she said. "You're straight to delivery"

I said, "Can you make sure I get the epidural please?"

She said almost deviously, "Too late for that, you're ready to push!"

I was moved up to the delivery suite, and then encouraged to 'push'.

I had pushed about five times now, deep bear down pushes, and nothing was happening. I remember it was six am when I had arrived into delivery and it was close to seven am now. There was a clock on the wall in front of me.

I was breathing, I was panting and pushing. Nothing. I know why they call it labour.

Anto was aloud in at this point and he was holding my hand encouraging me all the way, I wanted to kill him! He'd go down the end and have little looks and say, 'This is amazing!'

The thing I never knew was, that 'pooh' happens also during labour. Besides the pain, that is the worst thing, I was so embarrassed! My waters hadn't broken at all during this time, so a Doctor came in to have a look. I'll never forget his balding head, he was tall and wore glasses, but he didn't even glance at me.

I got the feeling that if I wasn't on medic aid and if I was a married woman, I may have been respected more by the Doctor.

Again, no pleasantries, he said, "Yes, you'll need an episiotomy, and as he said it, he cut, and I will never forget that burning pain as long as I will live. I screamed in pain, the water gushed out and so did our baby boy. It was 7am. He was fully formed, I could see he had blonde hair, and he was grey at first. They slapped his bottom and he cried. They weighed him, he was 9lb.

It was the most amazing thing, I felt immediate love for this little thing. I knew I would do anything for him.

They cleaned him off and covered him in a little blanket and a little cotton hat, and handed him to me. He was amazing. So precious.

I was very weak then, I could feel myself fading. I could hear an Irish nurse, working around me, and I asked her 'If people normally die having babies, because I think I am.'

I remember feeling completely at ease at that moment, and not afraid. It was OK. If I was dying, I was OK with that. I felt at that moment completely powerless, but that was ok. I didn't see the 'light' or 'Angels' guiding me, so I obviously wasn't dying, I just felt like I was.

The nurses whizzed around, they gave me oxygen, a drip. I was coming around. I was weak, but I was ok. My blood pressure had dropped really low, but I would be ok.

They whooshed 'Daddy' out to finish me off and Anto reassured, went off proud as punch, to phone all the families.

My lower regions felt and looked like they'd been through a slaughter house. I was so swollen below and full of stitches.

I couldn't wee, so they had to put that tube up through my vagina. I was so sore. I was to stay in one night until I was doing the wee normally again.

The nurses took our baby boy off to the baby unit and assured me he would not get kidnapped, as I thought, I reluctantly settled down for a little sleep, and Anto went off home.

He didn't come back till the next morning, and he arrived drunk as a skunk with two of his pals from Cabra, who just happened to be visiting, after doing a tour of the States.

I looked a wreck. Two gorgeous looking lads from Cabra, John Flemming and Whacker Flaherty are in my room. I was delighted to see them, but I was mortified.

Anto is saying to me as explanation in a slurred voice, "I just watered the baby's head last night with everybody, I'm just wrecked today. Look at his willy lads, he takes after his Dad!" I could've killed him!

It wasn't what I expected of my son's dad. I know he was happy and excited, but I didn't want to see him drunk and dopey. The nurses were looking at me with pity. I was embarrassed.

Caroline and John and Teresa and Ray and my sister Olive came to pick me up from the hospital. Everybody was in great form and were delighted with our new addition.

Anto insisted he could drive us home to the apartment, I was so annoyed, he was still drunk! I wouldn't let him drive and John drove us home, but Anto was in a huff, making me feel guilty.

I was tired and sore and feeling sorry for myself. I was beginning to think of raising our baby on my own. I knew for sure Anto was an alcoholic then.

He swore he loved me and I knew he loved the baby on sight, but I was beginning to think that love alone was not enough.

That woman 'The drink' was hanging around too often.

The next day, Anto sobered up and was ready to be the caring Dad and partner.

There was some funny times, we were so inexperienced, the gang of us! When I came home from the hospital, I wanted to breast feed the baby, but it wasn't working out. I felt no embarrassment as I tried to get my nipple in my baby's mouth with the gang looking on fascinated. I gave up with the baby crying hysterically for food, I sent Anto off to buy baby milk and bottles.

All us friends gathered round reading instructions on how to make the bottle, while the baby screamed for food. He had a great set of lungs!

Eventually we got it. We made the bottle. Anto fed the baby, "He must have been starving! The little fella drank the whole lot!" He said.

We were like "wow, that's great, he might sleep a bit now!" And in the next minute, the baby 'projectile' vomited across the room. We couldn't believe it. We rang the hospital straight away, thinking there was something wrong with the baby. We told the baby nurse on the helpline what had happened, and she laughed down the phone, "Read the instructions properly" she said, "you only feed a new baby 2oz not 8oz! He'll be fine, try again".

To have a little baby to be responsible for, every single moment is a huge change in a person's life. It made me grow up fast. But Anto was still behaving like a teenager.

Anto was a weekend drinker. He'd start drinking on Friday and be drunk till Sunday. I found it hard. I'd be sure that he wasn't going to get drunk, he'd convince me of it, and then he'd come home drunk or sometimes not at all. I'd beg him, I'd warn him, I tried everything to keep him from getting drunk, but I couldn't control it and I was trying to.

That's what was setting me crazy, I was watching his every move. I'd have mad arguments with him, calling him horrible names, threatening to leave him. He'd be grand for a few days and then once the weekend came around, he'd be gone again. Anto was not an aggressive drunk, he was a sleeper drunk. He'd never row back with me, but I could rile him on occasion, and one time I locked him out of our bedroom and he put his fist through the door.

The drink. She was the other woman. If there was another woman, it would be easy. I could do something about it. I could go to her and give her a slap and say, 'leave my man alone!' But I couldn't fight this woman, 'The Bitch, The Drink'.

We called our baby Anthony and he was so adorable, everybody loved him. He never slept during the day, and when I'd feed him and dress him, I'd pop him in front of the TV in his little car seat and he'd watch happily for hours.

First time parents often make the same mistake. They're so in awe of this little newborn and they pick it up at every little squeal. This little intelligent human being soon knows how to get picked up regular. As the weeks turn into months, 'The Baby' is ruling the house.

I knew I had to feed the baby every few hours, bath him, love him and put him to bed at night. Anthony was a very alert baby and he was quite happy awake.

Anto loved his baby boy and he was a great Daddy Monday till Friday, and a doting partner, but once the weekend came in, it was the other woman.

I was very low and I was crying a lot. I was having useless arguments with Anto. I had no idea I might be suffering with post natal depression.

I also had severe throbbing pain in my lower region after the baby and never thought to go to the Doctor before my six week check up. It turned out to be severe infection in my womb and the Doctor prescribed strong antibiotics. They made me feel sick and cranky.

As a Catholic, I was keen to get Anthony baptized. I walked up to our local Catholic Church with the baby in his little blue pram to book a Christening. I was talking to the priest himself and I remember he barely looked at me or the baby. I couldn't believe it when I was refused because I wasn't married. I approached two more Catholic Churches in Naples

Florida in 1989, and nobody would christen my baby because I wasn't married. I felt abandoned and ashamed.

I wasn't going to convert to another Religion from my anger, but I was witness to the huge snobbery of the Catholic Church. Should it matter where the child came from? When you just wanted to bring him into the Catholic faith?

I also felt rejected and unworthy and that my baby and I just weren't important.

I couldn't get married at that point, because I knew Anto was an alcoholic and I didn't see us having a future together.

Anthony was three months old, and I was thinking about going home. I needed to get Anthony baptized and I was going to leave Anto. I had made up my mind.

We packed up the apartment and moved up to Sarasota as Anto was going to work with his brother Joe, as the job had moved to Sarasota. We squashed everything that the four of us owned into the car and drove to Sarasota. John and Anto were in the front with things piled around them, and Caroline and myself and the baby were squashed in the back. We had so much stuff.

We were driving along the motorway at full speed when our tire blew out. Us girls were screaming in the back as Anto tried to control the car from hitting any other vehicle, the car was swerving all over the road, John was holding on tight in front. It was a miracle that we came to a stop at the side of the road and we were all ok, including the baby, who was at least strapped into his car seat as was compulsory in America.

Truly one of my most scariest moments.

I got a flight home a few weeks later with Caroline. I was leaving Anto. Anthony was just over three months old.

Anto was devastated he was losing us, but what could I do? Although Anto was completely different from my Dad, I couldn't risk raising Anthony in an alcoholic home.

Caroline and I arrived back to Dublin airport, Christmas week, 1989, more solemn than when we went off on our happy go free experience a year before.

We had grown up a lot now; each experiencing our own joys and pit falls of life; each going back to our parents' home, after living 'married' lives for a while.

I thought my dad would be delighted to see his first Grandson when I arrived into Ma's house. He was sitting on the chair, with his coat on, his arms folded looking angry. Older.

I placed Anthony on his arms and said, "Here's your Grandson Dad!" He shrugged the baby off him, "Get him off me". He walked out to the pub.

I was sick inside. The rejection was on purpose. For all that I had put him and Ma through, he wasn't going to forgive me. I was thinking, 'Oh my God, nothing has changed, I can't live here'. I was frightened for my son.

I found work straight away with my old boss Stanley, he had a new salon, in Prussia street shopping centre, and he needed staff for Christmas.

Ma was only too delighted to have her only grandson to herself, and get him into a 'proper routine'.

I paid Ma for minding Anthony and she was only too delighted, as Dad was still out of work.

I was worried about leaving Anthony in my parents' home to witness any fighting that would go on, but Ma assured me 'Granddad' loved his grandson, and when I was gone to work, he would play with him happily.

I was in my parents' home only three weeks when the inevitable happened. I had my old bedroom to myself as Olive was still in the States. I used a travel cot for Anthony as the room wasn't big enough for a cot.

One night I was in bed asleep, and the baby was asleep in his cot at the end of my bed, when I heard the shouting. Dad had come in from the pub in his horrors.

I could hear him racing up the stairs, Ma grabbing him back, "Christy don't!" she said, "Please don't".

Dad burst into my room, brandishing his knives.

My baby's eyes shot open terrified. He was four months old.

I was screaming, "Get out, get out," I was terrified. Jesus what was he doing? What was he thinking? There's a baby here for God's sake!

He was screaming, "Get out of my house you whore, you put your mother through hell, you selfish bitch! Not a thought for her or me. Get out, Get out!"

Mam was crying so sadly behind him, grabbing him.

I got him out, I shut the door. I picked up my crying baby. Oh my God, Oh my God. I prayed. I was 22 years old.

The next morning I told my Ma I was leaving, I couldn't stay there. How could I? She was devastated.

It was January 1990. I found a really nice two bedroom apartment on the top end of the New Cabra road. It was a new building. It was very American. I was delighted. It was 189.00 pounds per month and I could afford it as I was working.

Anto was back from the States, and although we were separated, he was a committed Daddy to Anthony, spending lots of time with his son, and he paid me forty pounds maintenance each week.

The people I was renting from, thought I was going to be paying them with social welfare checks, but it never entered my mind not to work. I wanted to be a 'successful career woman'. I'm not trying to make myself look so perfect here. Even though I came from a family of dysfunctionals, and I had lots of emotional issues. Something inside me was always pushing me on. I was smart. I had no learning difficulties. I found it easy to read, to learn. I knew inside me that education was the key to my success. It would guarantee me continuous work in whatever area. I took various courses throughout my life to continually educate myself.

People who live on social welfare are forced there through dysfunction. They don't know how to get out of the poverty trap through education, as the education system would have failed them in their classrooms.

Although my dad was unemployed for ten years. He hated the 'dole', his social welfare payment. He was demoralized by it. Us kids knew he hated living this way. He knew he was a smart man, but he couldn't get out of the poverty trap. His alcoholism and depression held him back.

While I was pregnant on Anthony, I had gone to Cosmetology College part time in Florida, and passed my state exams for hairdressing and beautician work, so I was qualified to manage a hair and beauty salon.

I decided to rent Stanley's hair salon from him as he wanted to cut back his working hours. I loved running my own salon and I loved my own apartment, although I was a little scared living on my own with my baby. I wasn't sleeping well. I had dreams of someone coming to get me overnight with a hatchet and knives.

I was always terrified to sleep soundly.

My sister Eleanor moved in with me gladly as she had enough of home life. At 17, Eleanor was the second youngest in the family. She was really pretty, with blonde hair and brown eyes. She had sallow skin and she was tall. She was really quiet and never interfered with the mad goings on of my father. I worried about Eleanor being more affected than she let on. She also moved over to Florida a couple of years later.

I was able to give Ma a few bob per week for minding Anthony and she was truly grateful. She was also truly grateful to me for letting her mind her grandson, as she loved him so much.

The Cabra road wasn't far from Carnlough road and I cycled up to 'Nanny's' with Anthony on a seat at the back and dropped him into my Ma.

I still wasn't talking to my dad, and sometimes he shouted through the front door after me, when I picked up my son. Anthony had good clear language from very young, he asked me, "Why is Granddad shouting, Mammy?"

I told him, "Grandad's not feeling too well, it's ok, don't worry". I never slated my dad in front of my son. I knew Grandad loved him, and Anthony loved him too, so, I didn't want to destroy that relationship. I worried about my son every moment I wasn't with him. I was afraid of Da's behaviour while I wasn't there.

Although I didn't think I had panic attacks this early in my life I remember going through some nervous feelings and shallow breaths. I was worried about life and death. I went to see our Priest in Precious Blood Parish, Cabra.

Father Brendan Madden was only a couple of years older than me at this time and he was only just ordained. I had some tough questions for him.

I was questioning God. How does it all work? What happens when we die? Where do we go? I was breathing fast and shallow. I was panicking. I was upset. I was scared.

I must have made Fr. Brendan question his own beliefs then also. How could he comfort this young troubled woman? Providing the right answers.

He explained the best he could and told me God is there guiding me, it'll be ok. I wasn't so sure.

Father Brendan is one of a few very good Catholic priests, who work on the same level as ordinary people, forgetting the trappings of wealth that the Catholic Church stood for in the old days. These priests try to instil a simple guidance on how to live without resentment and hate. To appreciate life as we live it.

These priests are solely responsible for Irish people returning to the Catholic faith after enduring the selfish abuse inflicted on them as children from paedophile Catholic Priests.

I kept praying to God for guidance. I was going to the Al Anon Group for families living with alcoholism and I was working on my own behaviour. I was more understanding of Alcoholic behaviour. When the Alcoholic's partner tries to control the Alcoholic, it takes up all their own mental space. I had been obsessed by Anto's drinking and what he was up to. It made me angry when he was unreliable and let me down.

When I let go of trying to control Anto, things ran more smoothly for me. I had to change the way I reacted to situations, therefore changing my bad behaviour. I realized that Anto and I could get back together as we still loved each other.

Although, like any affair, in order for the marriage to have another chance, the man would inevitably have to give up the other woman, or in Anto's case, The Drink. Anto realized that he couldn't continue his binge drinking. It was leaving him very ill and it frightened him that he couldn't remember the night before. One morning he had woke up in his car with his hair chopped off him and his eyebrows gone, not knowing what happened to him. He decided to try to give up the drink, or take a break from it. He had stopped drinking alcohol for the first time when Anthony was nearly two, in 1991.

I liked this change in Anto and I could see a future together after all. We decided to give our relationship another chance.

We moved into Anthony's family home on St Attracta road.

Anto didn't stay off the drink too long. He began a pattern of binge drinking. He would drink himself silly till he couldn't drink another drop and this normally lasted about three weeks. He'd stay sober for about a week or two until he felt well again and then he'd go on the binge again.

Alcoholism is a disease that gets progressively worse, so Anto continued on in this pattern over the next four years with his symptoms getting worse. It was difficult to cope with my partner passed out on the floor more often than not but when Anto sobered up, he became the doting partner again.

One night he had a massive car crash in Store Street Dublin, right across from Garda Headquarters. His van was crushed as he had a head on collision into parked cars. He miraculously walked away from the crash unharmed, and thankfully nobody else was injured.

He handed himself in to the guards the next day, which in fairness, the guards appreciated. They were lenient on him, he was given a hefty fine of 5,000 pounds and more endorsements on his license. Anto had to pay the highest cost of vehicle insurance for years because of the endorsements on his license.

I was doing very well in the Al Anon program and coped very well with Anto's on, off, drinking through the next few years.

We decided to get married when Anthony was nearly six years of age. Anto blames my friend Lorraine Confoy suggesting to me that a wedding was needed in the gang. He said he was quite happy not being married!

It was 1994 and we had invited 115 of our friends and family to our wedding in Precious Blood Church. Father Brendan Madden married us on the 18th of August. We had planned to say our own vows, but I was really emotional and could barely say I do!

Anto was feeling paranoid after smoking a joint earlier and he thought I was having second thoughts! Thank fully I didn't cop this as I may have walked back down the aisle alone.

We then went on to the CoolQuay Lodge in Ashbourne. The CoolQuay lodge was a restaurant and a function room. It was a stylish venue and I never even thought to look at hotels. We would never have had that much money.

The day went great and we didn't want to leave our wedding party at the end of the night. Anto didn't get drunk which was great and his oldest brother Johnny had started his speech after dinner to represent Anto. Johnny burst into song, 'If I was a rich man', it got everybody singing all night long and it was a typical Irish wedding.

My Dad got drunk, but even he behaved himself on the day.

I had booked into a wedding Bed and Breakfast further up in Ashbourne for 115 pounds, for two rooms, one for myself and Anto and one for my sister Christine to take care of Anthony. We never thought to have a car, and the coach driver Con Keenan had to drive us to our B and B in his 30ft coach, and had a job trying to turn on the narrow country roads.

When we arrived at the B and B, they had let our room out, and sent us on to a cold pokey little place further into the County of Ashbourne. I was furious just for a moment. The day had been too good.

The 'Celtic Tiger' was only just beginning in 1994. Everything was still affordable. Weddings were cheap, houses were under 100,000 pounds.

Style was slowly starting to creep in though. Women were looking at designer kitchens and fancy curtains for their homes.

All my girlfriends searched the shops for the perfect dress for the wedding. They were gorgeous.

My dress was a fairytale type dress, It was made with ivory Chantilly silk, it sat off the shoulder's and had a puffy skirt, and it cost 350 pounds from Alexander's in Dorset street. I wore a tiara and a veil, and I felt like a princess. As a hairdresser, I was able to do all my bridesmaids hairs myself, but my flowers were made by Val the Florist and they were beautiful. They were the latest design in white lilies.

Although Anto had regular work in his business, he was only on a wage from the company and we counted out our 1,100 pounds savings for the cost of our wedding. We had no bills or mortgages.

Things were really simple then.

6

Sarah

When my second child was born on 9th August 1995, out popped this cuddly 9lb baby girl. She had a head of black hair, and a red birthmark on her forehead covering her eyelids. She looked a bit bashed up, but she was the most beautiful baby. I was euphoric.

I was delighted to dress her in little pink baby grows, and little pink hats and little pink cardigans. She was adorable. We called her Sarah after Anto's aunty Sadie.

I had her in the Rotunda hospital in Dublin. I was only a public patient so I was in a room with 3 other women, and we all had baby girls. We were all in great spirits in that ward and got along really well. The care from the nurses and midwives was wonderful, and the hospital was spotless.

I had a straight forward birth, but the doctor discovered that Sarah had a heart murmur, an opening in her heart, and moved her to special care for three days. I was worried sick, but they soon reassured me, that Sarah's heart murmur should close within the next two years, and didn't need surgery. They encouraged me to breast feed Sarah as it would build up her immunity.

Sarah was a really good baby, and so full of smiles from early on. She giggled at eight weeks! I was really enjoying my time at home with Sarah, and decided to stay off a few months more from my job as a stylist, at a well known hairdressing chain in Ireland called Peter Mark.

We had no great financial outgoings then, and I could afford to stay at home for a while longer.

Anto loved his baby girl, Sarah.

He was a hands on Dad and had no problem changing nappy's. He loved giving Sarah a bath. She was really cuddly, so easy to grip in the water.

Sarah went through colic when I finished breast feeding her at seven weeks old. The only thing that would quiet her was to bring her for a long walk in her pram at all hours in the night and Anto would happily take her.

He was still going through his binge drinking every few weeks, and it was a tough time. My emotions were all over the place.

We went on holiday to Orlando, Florida, when Sarah was about 12 months old. My sister Sharon came with her baby Ryan, and her husband Myles, who since died in 2012 of Lung cancer aged just 50.

Both Anto and Myles were drinkers, so they found it hard to get out of bed as early as our small children did every morning. Sharon and I headed down to the pool of the Holiday Inn as early as 8am in the mornings.

Anthony was nearly seven years old and he was a good swimmer, he was jumping in as I was settling Sarah in her pram. Ryan was only 1 year old then and was happy to splash at the water. I brought our niece Carolyn Murray along on holidays, she was 13 years old and she was great with the little ones. She perched herself on a sun bed looking forward to a tan.

Anthony called to me, "Mam! look at me doing a back flip" I was four feet from him, and as I turned to stop him, he landed on his head at the side of the pool before falling into the deep end, unconscious. I screamed and jumped in straight away and retrieved him from the pool, I thought he was dead! The pool filled with blood! Sharon ran to the lobby to call an ambulance and I running behind her carrying Anthony. I was in complete shock myself. I was shaking like a leaf, and praying to God.

Anto arrived to the lobby in shock after hearing the commotion. Anthony was still unconscious, and the top of his head was split open and bleeding fast. I was holding the wound, and I am not good with blood! There didn't appear to be first aid in the hotel but the receptionist brought me a towel with ice to press on Anthony's head, but Anto revived him gently and the ambulance arrived then.

Anthony was brought to the hospital and thankfully we had taken out a holiday insurance policy, because he was given an MRI scan to the brain to see was there any further damage to the brain or skull. He received 10 staples to his head after they shaved his hair off, and kept him in for the night for observation.

That had a huge effect on me. I blamed Anto for not being there, and I blamed myself for letting it happen, Anto consoled himself with more drink the next day.

I thought I was managing things well, as I appeared calm on the outside, but as I bathed Sarah the next evening, she slipped in the bath and busted her lip with her front two teeth. Blood everywhere again! My nerves were in bits. We were also trying to take care of Carolyn who had gotten sun stroke, while I was busy at the hospital. She was burnt to bits!

I don't know how I didn't turn to the drink myself. It was a difficult time in my life. I knew I had to be the sensible parent though, I had to show the kids a consistent normality at least from one of us.

My sister Sharon's nerves was also in bits from that holiday, but she is great fun and she had me laughing through my tears.

Anto and Myles had many hangovers in the mornings, so Sharon and I would be waiting for them to wake up and drive us to parks, not being able to drive myself in America.

This one morning I said to Sharon, 'Come on, enough of this waiting, I'll drive!' We strapped the kids in the car van and off I went. It was also my first time to drive an automatic and after a few difficult starts, we were off. It was hilarious. Once on the motorway, I didn't know how to get off at an exit as all the other cars were speeding and I couldn't get in. Sharon was getting worried as it seemed we were leaving Orlando but a couple of hours later, we arrived at our destination!

When we returned home to Ireland, we heard news of Val, one of my Husband's brother's. He lived in England and was struggling to take care of his three children after his wife Kathleen had died the year previously of cervical cancer. She was 37 years old. Val was an alcoholic and things were falling apart for him. His three children were taken into care in London.

Mark was 15, Catherine was 13 and Clara was just 5 years old. Anthony and his brothers decided the children would be better off with family in Ireland. Billy and Peter Anto's older brothers went and brought the children back to Ireland.

I offered to take care of Catherine, and when the brothers phoned me on the day of their return to confirm that I was taking on Catherine, I said yes as I looked at my husband who was passed out on the floor, drunk.

I wasn't thinking of myself. I was thinking of that poor child without her beloved Mother and I wanted to give her a good home. I was still going to my AL Anon sessions and working on my behaviour and personal growth. I'm not saying it was perfect, but it was good considering I was now married to an active alcoholic.

Anto at 34 years old was quite ill himself at this point. He could binge drink for 5 days in a row, and then become so ill. He would be in bed for days with black stuff coming from both ends of him.

It was 1995, and Anto was running a successful construction company. I will add that he wouldn't have been able to do that without his good team of friends he had employed then, and are still with him today, Paul O Connor (Littler), Derek Ward (Wardy), John Thormy (Frog), Patrick Doyle (Whacker) Matt who was a great foreman who died a few years ago from Cancer and my dad also, who drove the truck and watched Anto's stock like a Hawk. Dad died from Cancer shortly after Matt. There was also, Brian Dunne who was a great roofer and Anthony Costello (Gozzi) who died suddenly of a heart attack aged 42.

My younger sister Christine worked in Anto's office and she kept everything organized. I helped in the office as well as everything else.

It was a community affair. Anto's brothers and his best friends Paul and Steven helped at every opportunity, watching his back.

Catherine arrived to us, this beautiful blonde haired, green eyed 13 year old girl. Catherine was devastated to be separated from her little sister Clara. Peter and his wife Betty happily took on Clara having no children of their own.

We started Catherine in St Dominic's College, secondary school, where I had gone. She started first year and went all the way through sixth year. Catherine was really bright and creative and did really well in school, but she had so much trauma in her short life, I had a difficult time trying to bond with her. She was a great girl and gave me no trouble in the seven years she lived with me. She was great to Anthony and Sarah, she was so kind, but I was worried about her just functioning, never showing her emotions. I could see the turmoil she went through since losing her mother and that had a huge effect on me. I could see the devastating effects to a child in a dysfunctional family when she loses her Mother.

After suffering appendicitis, Anto thought we should go away for a week by ourselves and work on our relationship. He was off the drink again for a few weeks at this point. I guess with everything going on in my life then, I wasn't giving my husband much attention. I thought a break would be good.

My sister Elle and her husband Hugo moved into my house for that week to take care of the kids. They had no kids of their own, so it was less disruptive.

I had booked a holiday in Majorca, and off we went to Dublin airport.

I had never left the kids before for any length of time, and I was starting to feel very nervous while we were waiting for our plane. As we were flying further and further away from Dublin, I was having huge doubts. I didn't want to be away from the kids, 'Why did I want to leave my baby?' 'Was I crazy?' I conveyed the feelings to my husband. He didn't understand me saying this now; he was looking forward to us having some quality time together.

So, I put on a brave face, and we arrived in Majorca. But there was a knot in my stomach and I couldn't relax.

I got on with it the best way I could, and just kept focusing on 'being home soon'.

One day after we had come back from a walk, Anthony had fallen asleep in our room. I picked up his 'Focus' magazine to have a read. Saddam Hussein was all over the magazine, and his nuclear weapons, and the destruction it would cause if they went off.

I couldn't believe it! 'Oh My God! What if it happens now? I'll never see my children again, they'll die without their mammy, or I'll die, and they'll be left without me'.

I was in an awful state, I didn't even wake Anto. I had to go to the TV room to see the news. (there were no TVs in the bedrooms then) I remember vividly how I was feeling on the way to the TV room. I needed to find out any details of Saddam Hussein's war. When and where he was going to strike. I was racing down to the TV room, when I bumped into the two lovely Scottish women I had met earlier in the week.

They could see I was very upset as I told them what I feared, that Saddam Hussein was going to destroy us all. I could see tears in their eyes. They were worried for me, they tried to console me, to reassure me, but I had to see the TV with my own eyes. The TV didn't have fancy Sky channels in Majorca! I didn't find out any information about Saddam's war. I just had to pray and pray to ask God to mind my children.

Anto found me then, and I just wanted to go home to Ireland.

Finally the day to go home came, and I couldn't wait. I was so worried that I would never get home to the kids.

The weather was really stormy that day, and the gales were fierce. I was afraid the flight would be cancelled, but it wasn't.

As we waited to board the plane, I looked around at all the passengers, children, adults, grandparents. I thought, 'Oh My God! These people are all going to die'.

Finally we got on the plane, buckled in, and the engines started. As we were speeding down the runway, the Captain made an announcement; "It's going to be a rocky flight as it's quite turbulent outside".

That was it; I started screaming hysterically, "Oh God, we're going to crash, we're going to crash!"

My husband near died of shock, I was inconsolable, crying hysterically, I buried my head in his lap, and cried and cried, I couldn't breathe. My Husband reassured the cabin crew, he would look after me. The other people on the plane were terrified of my reaction. Anto said most of them had their rosemary beads in their hands, praying. I didn't stop crying till I landed in Dublin.

I was home safe. My children were ok. Saddam Hussein had not bombed all of Europe.

I was back to normal.

I had no idea I was suffering with Post Natal depression then. I had no idea I had a panic attack on that flight. I didn't realize I was acting irrationally during that period since Sarah was born. Those Scottish women in Majorca would have seen that I was unbalanced, but they didn't know me well enough to interfere.

I didn't go to the doctor about it when I returned home, because I went back to 'normal'. I was still terrified of flying after that incident, but because I loved going over to America to see Anto's family. I knew I had to fly. I would never fly without my children again though. I had to accept the possibility that the plane would crash. I would accept I was completely powerless to God, but if anything where to happen, please God don't let my children suffer.

In the years that followed, I had to say to myself a thousand times, 'I'm on a bus, I'm on a bus, I'm on a bus', and I could never look out the window.

I went back to work a few months after that trip in 1996, for the same hairdressing chain. I only wanted part time work, so I was transferred to a branch in Tallaght.

I had previously worked in Peter Mark in Blanchardstown village with a wonderful bunch of girls and guys.

Tallaght branch had a lovely fancy Salon and it was really busy. I was looking forward to working there.

That was of course, till I met the manageress of the salon. (Doris is not her real name, she had a fancy name, but she didn't look like her fancy name, she looked like a Doris, no offense to any other Doris's out there).

Doris was mean to all the staff in the salon, so I wasn't too put out when she was mean to me. In fact, I used to defend her to the other girls in the staff room when they bitched about her.

Doris was mid 40s then, and not very attractive and not very stylish either. She didn't have a nice personality either, but I felt sorry for her and said 'Ah leave her alone girls'.

I was about 29 then, and I think I kind of looked ok, I was fairly stylish, and I didn't carry any weight.

I knew Doris didn't like me, it didn't matter what I did, that was the way it was. I got on with it.

One day I came in wearing a 'bandana' over my short hair. I thought I looked ok, but I noticed Doris watching me all morning with her cigarette in her mouth, (you could smoke in salons then).

Eventually she said to me, "What's that on your head?" and I looked at her and for one moment I thought she was going to admire it.

I said, "Oh, I need to get my haircut at lunch time, I'm just hiding it for now".

"Well" She said, "I'm sorry, but my staff are too busy to do your hair today, (there were only three clients in the salon at that time) you'll have to take your break now, and ask the other salon upstairs if they'll do it for you".

I was quite taken aback; there was no mistaking her nastiness here.

Like a fool, I went up to the other salon, when I got there I made small talk but didn't have the guts to ask someone to cut my hair as I knew I would make Doris look bad and I was so embarrassed. I then went upstairs to a barber shop. There wasn't one client in the barber shop and there was two staff just standing there at their reception area. I asked, 'Could they cut my hair?' as I wore it really short, it would be like doing a boy's haircut. They replied 'No, we only cut men's hair'.

I was choking back the tears at this stage. I was sick with nerves in my tummy. I went back down to my salon, and feebly told 'Doris' nobody could cut my hair, and she said "oh just wash it there then, that'll have to do".

I was a good hairdresser, and I loved the customers, I was good with them; but my confidence had taken a huge dive after Doris's bullying towards me in the few months I worked with her. I finished work that evening and walked out of that salon and never went back. I felt so small, so unworthy.

Human Resources from Peter Mark offices rang me and wanted to know why I left, and if I would work in a different salon. I never told them about 'Doris' or reported her bullying behaviour towards me or others at the salon.. I think I was afraid of her word against mine. I didn't feel important enough.

I figured someone that nasty and mean spirited was obviously living a horrible life anyway. I didn't want to make it worse for her.

During that time, Sarah was about 18 months old, I went for a routine smear test. The results came back and showed I had CIN 3, which meant the full thickness of the lining covering the cervix had abnormal cells, and I was requested to go for a colposcopy in the Mater Hospital to have a closer look and take a biopsy.

I got quite a fright about this and was really worried of the outcome, at 29, I knew about the dangers of cervical cancer.

Like everything else, I kept all this fear to myself. Anto was going through his own struggles with alcohol and I didn't want to make a big thing of my procedures.

A lovely, kind female doctor took my biopsy and reassured me all would be fine and not to worry.

The results came back as grade 3 abnormal cells, and the Doctor needed to perform a LLETZ procedure. This is a large Loop Excision of the Transformation Zone; it means cutting out the area of the cervix where the abnormal cells develop.

The transformation zone is the area just inside the cervical canal.

I was sent off home with a good result and I was to return in three weeks time for a checkup. I was still bleeding, but the Doctor said that was normal and not to worry.

I bled for eight more months, not heavily, but it was always there. I was convinced I had cervical cancer, but I never went back to the Doctor. I know that sounds crazy, but I was just ignoring it, hoping it would go away.

Eventually though, in an awful state at this point, I arrived without an appointment to the Mater Hospital, really upset, on my own. I hadn't told Anto, or anybody, I never wanted to make a big fuss I found the Doctor who had treated me and I was crying and crying telling her that I was sure I had cervical cancer.

She examined me straight away, and found that I had an infection in the wound that was causing the bleeding, not cancer. The doctor prescribed strong antibiotics to clear the infection.

I was relieved, but I had spent all that time worrying and burying the fear in my stomach. It's amazing about the body; I was also suffering severe constipation all my life, even though I ate healthy and drank loads of water. I couldn't understand it then, but now I know it was me burying all my fears and worries in my tummy and keeping them there. I have no constipation problems since I really start working on me.

It was coming up to Sarah's third birthday, 9th August 1998. My husband was very ill. His benders affected his health hugely. He wasn't eating. He lost complete control of his bodily functions.

I couldn't look at him doing this to himself any longer, so I made a decision.

I phoned his brother Fergus to come and take him away one Saturday morning. I couldn't live this way any longer. It broke my heart, but I felt his illness was now very obvious to the kids, and I had to protect them from this.

Fergus came up to the bedroom where Anto was laying on the bed. He said "Come on Anto, let's get you out for some air".

I wanted to make it clearer though, Fergus walked out to the landing, I was very upset, crying, I said, "Anto, I'm sorry, but I can't live this way any longer, and I don't want you back, do you understand?" I was hoping he would take me in his arms and hug me and tell me it was all going to be alright, like he always would, but he didn't.

Anto looked at me, and I gasped with shock, because it wasn't Anto staring back at me. It was the Devil. He spoke, he said words I didn't recognize, they came in a different voice. I knew then that my Husband had been possessed by this evil. The Devil had been able to get into Anthony, because he was weak, he was vulnerable.

Through an orifice, with alcohol.

Anto left. I was broken hearted. But I was confident I was doing the right thing, taking control of my situation. I wasn't doing it from some nasty resentment. This had to happen. I couldn't control Anto or his drinking, but I could control the bad behaviour from coming into my home.

I was learning.

He returned home that night from another drinking session, he tried to open the front door. I had it locked. It was the first time I had locked my husband out of his home. I told him to go away, he wasn't coming in. He was angry, he climbed up the drainpipe on the front of the house to get in, but I had all the windows locked.

He said, "This is my house, my family home, you can't put me out". I told him, "you can have your house back, but not tonight". He was angry, he smashed a downstairs window. I threatened to call the police. He left: Deflated.

My dad couldn't believe that I had put my husband out of his home, insisting I go find him. My Ma was also worried about Anto, she didn't think this was right. Anto needed help not banishment.

I never listened to my Dad before, so I wasn't going to start now. It was hard to come to this decision, I didn't rush into it. Of course my life that I knew was going to change, my kids weren't going to have their daddy putting them to bed each night. But I had no choice. I couldn't live with active alcoholism any more.

Anto came back three weeks later, the day before Sarah's birthday. He asked to see me. He was sober. He had gone on a massive bender during the last three weeks, he stayed in a caravan in Cavan that we had bought there.

His body had been through huge neglect through his years of alcoholism. During his blackout periods, he had woken up to find himself battered and robbed. He had withdrawn from family and friends who cared for him. He had experienced the worst moments of his life, where he was cold and alone and afraid, dirty from soiling himself. He lost a good wife who stood by him through his lies and his unreliability.

Anto's personality had changed over the years. Suffering alcoholism had left him very insecure. He became paranoid and jealous in the marriage. He couldn't trust anymore. He had lost his children. The Devil had controlled his body. Anto had let him in. This was his rock bottom.

I could see he was sober about two days, by the look of him. He was clean and shaved. He was nervous. My heart ached for him.

He told me he was an Alcoholic and he was attending Alcoholics Anonymous. He decided he would never drink again, but he could only take it one day at a time. I was happy for him. He wanted to come back home, would I take him back?

I didn't want to take Anto back. It had been a tough 12 years.

I was badly affected myself by Alcohol. I was constantly working on my own bitterness and resentfulness. How did I know this time he meant every word? I couldn't be watching and waiting for the next relapse.

I had to weigh up the pros and cons. Did I believe in him?

Anto was a good father who loved his children and did the best for them. He had put a lovely home around his wife and children. He provided well for us.

I wasn't perfect myself with the baggage I carried. I had made my marriage vows in God's Presence. In Sickness and in Health. Should I give him another chance?

I could've decided that day to walk away and take my new path of single life. Somehow I knew Anto would never drink again. He was afraid. I believed in him.

I let Anto back into our home that day. He was relieved and grateful. The kids were delighted to see their daddy home that evening.

Now we were on a new road.

Living with a sober alcoholic has its own challenges. Although Anto was running a successful business, there was a void in his life left from alcohol. He also decided to give up smoking cigarettes and hash as he wanted to be healthy again. Anto smoked John Player blue, and he could get through three packets a day. He had smoked hash casually over the years and looked forward to rolling a joint each evening, as it really relaxed him. Anto had an additive personality, so like the alcohol, he was now becoming dependent on hash. He made the tough decision to go cold turkey, as he didn't want his kids seeing him rolling joints as they were becoming more aware.

Anto had developed a heavy chesty cough that took two years to go away. It also took those two years for his body to recover from the effects of his addictions. He didn't escape injury from the early start his body consumed alcohol, he was now left with a debilitating kidney disease, that needs constant medication and monitoring. He may eventually need dialysis and a kidney transplant when he's older.

He became moody and sullen when he hadn't got the vices that got him through his days. He also stopped doing little things for me. This was very gradual, I didn't notice it at first because I didn't ask him to do much as a Husband or Father while he was recovering. I didn't want to put pressure on him. If I moaned about the things he wasn't doing for me, he said 'I'm doing enough. I'm off the drink".

He had to find a hobby for himself.

I focused on being busy myself. I had taken up Camogie with Beatrice's ladies team at Finbarr's GAA Club. I loved the sport. Beatrice was a great trainer. Although she was only a young girl, she was big into fitness and health. She trained us girls hard.

I loved the training sessions; the camogie matches that left me covered in muck and bruises. It was great fun. Us ladies went to the clubhouse after each match for a couple of bottles of Budweiser before our dinner on Sunday's.

Catherine Kirby, Ursula Lambe, Stephanie Mooney and myself were the older ladies in the group while a lot of the team were teenage girls. We all became great friends.

I really enjoyed that part of my life. I was sorry I never took up the sport when I was much younger. I wasn't very skilled at scoring or hitting the ball far, but I was a good defender, I was strong and if I got the slither, I could balance it on my hurl stick and run like the wind. The girls used to call me 'Forest Gump', because I could run.

Anto was beginning to grow jealous of my ability to continue on my own activities outside the home. While he couldn't drink anymore, he didn't know how to fill his time, besides working. He had never had a weight problem, as he always did physical hard work, so he never had a sport. He didn't think I should want to drink since he didn't. I didn't drink much; I would generally have about 3 bottles of beer socially. I liked my health, I liked being slim, I'm a bit of a control freak myself, so I never liked the feeling of being drunk, but I do like to drink. I thought that was selfish of him.

He wasn't always supportive. I had to overlook this side of Anto. I did feel guilty that I was having some fun with the girls, but I was always worried about Anto in the background.

I was still fulfilling my obligations as a mother and a wife. I kept my house spotless, I cooked good food and looked after the kids homework and activities. I put myself under a lot of pressure to do all these things, so I could never be told off for preferring sport to my family life.

I encouraged Anto to take up sports, join a gym.

I loved the outdoor lifestyle, and encouraged my kids to be into sports also. My son Anthony joined the hurling team for Finbarr's when he was seven. Anto and myself enjoyed watching him on the sidelines and following his match's every Saturday.

I'd have a picnic for Sarah and a flask of hot tea for me, and we'd be soaked. I loved the rain and muck, and my kids loved it too.

Anthony's true passion was Motor Cross Scrambler bikes and he left the hurling team at age 12 to race. I was devastated to discover that, especially after my friend Declan's death from his Scrambler bike. I didn't discourage him though, but I was always afraid to watch him race.

Catherine joined the Camogie team too, she was a great sports person, and it gave her an outlet from her problems. She had team support. The girls encouraged her and supported her, when she felt she couldn't confide in me about her becoming a lesbian and other problems.

Catherine spent those vulnerable years holding in all her emotions and fears, dealing with things by herself. Being part of a team is a huge help to people feeling alone.

When Catherine left my home when she was 20, she went on her own road of self destruct and discovery. Taking her down the route of alcohol and depression.

Today aged 30, she is a beautiful, talented hard worker. She continues to deal with the pitfalls of life, but now she does it sober. We are now very close and we talk to each other about anything. I'm so proud of her.

Sarah was a late walker and talker, and she was very immature for her age. Once she turned four in August 1999, she was able start school. I knew Sarah was very babyish for her age, but she was a big child and I was wrongly thinking size was more important than social skills. I wanted her small and cute in her communion dress at age seven. True.

Sarah received a lovely teacher for junior infants, Miss Cummins, in St Mary Help of Christians on the Navan Road. Miss Cummins was a stern looking woman who wore glasses and had a severe page boy haircut, but she was a very good teacher. She approached me in the school yard as I dropped Sarah to school one day in October and suggested I have Sarah assessed for learning difficulties as she was struggling to cope in the classroom.

Miss Cummins pointed out to me, that school is a huge pressure for children with learning difficulties, as they are unable to take commands, listen to instructions and they cannot focus in class, making it difficult for them to sit for five hours.

I was so sorry I started Sarah at such a young age. I was worried sick. I wanted to take her out of school for another year. Miss Cummins advised me against it, she said Sarah was happy enough in school and suggested Sarah repeat junior infants again next September, so I went with her decision.

She told me that she thought that Sarah was going to be very talented in art, saying Sarah's detail in drawing animals and horses, was really good, that she can express the animals character in his eyes.

That made me feel better, she was saying that Sarah was talented, not dumb.

I was very emotional during those couple of years; I felt I had a lot on my plate.

Sarah was assessed privately first of all by a speech and language therapist. I had to pay privately because the Health Service had a long queue. I was all very new to this, and when the therapist told me Sarah was very immature for her age and had poor comprehension. I didn't know what that meant for Sarah in the classroom. I just knew that Sarah was babyish for her age. I followed the therapist's instructions and brought Sarah to her privately for speech and language sessions weekly for 18 months, and Sarah progressed well.

Sarah was seven years old when she was assessed privately with the ACLD in Suffolk Street Dublin, Dyslexia association of Ireland. They diagnosed Sarah with a severe learning difficulty, Dyslexia.

Sarah had to go to a dyslexia workshop weekly all the way through primary school.

Sarah was a good little girl and she responded well to the teachers, she worked really hard and she came on really well in school. The teachers were delighted in her artistic talent.

After hearing a talk on dyslexia and eye tracking problems with Martin F Murphy, The Author of the book, Dyslexia. Martin was also behind the making of the first brain scan machine. He fascinated me with his knowledge of the brain. I brought Sarah to see him also privately, he sat in Dun Laoghaire.

Martin explained that Sarah had a severe eye tracking problem also, which affects the muscles of her eyes. He gave her exercises to do regularly and lots of valuable information, which made me relax a little. Sarah could be educated just like her peers. She just had to work a little harder.

The exercises helped a lot, but as Sarah got older, she was experiencing bad headaches and she would lose her vision while reading. She had a huge difficulty focusing. She was then referred to Marita Mcgeady who was able to do the special eye test required using the Irlen Method. Sarah was prescribed the Irlen lenses to help shield her eyes from glare and light. These glasses worked well for Sarah, although all Sarah's eye symptoms haven't disappeared, they are much better.

Sarah's educational costs were up to a few thousand by now. There were no free assessments offered and there was no information available about learning difficulties when Sarah started school in 1999.

A parent might not know there was anything wrong with their child until they are eight or nine years. I was lucky Miss Cummins told me early, so I was able to seek the proper help for Sarah.

I loved living on St Attracta road as a young married woman. I loved my house and I felt really at home there as there was a growing community spirit on the road. I was very close to Aunty Josie across the road from me and after a rocky start, Josie and I got on really well. Josie was very protective of Anto and didn't appreciate it in the beginning if I gave out about his drinking or bad habits. I won her over when she realized I was a good hard working Mother.

One Thursday evening when Anto was away, Aunty Josie came running over to me, telling me Uncle Billy, her brother of 82, had collapsed. I ran over and realised he wasn't breathing. Without thinking, myself and Catherine's brother, Mark, performed mouth to mouth resuscitation. Mark took out uncle Billy's teeth and I blew into his mouth while Mark pumped his chest.

The ambulance men came and took over from us and Uncle Billy was revived. Mark was only a young lad about 19 at the time, I thought it was a really brave thing for him to do.

Living in Anthony's family home was really good, but I began to feel overwhelmed. Uncle Thomas was Aunty Josie's brother from Canada. He was divorced from his wife because of his alcoholism and came back to Ireland with terminal throat cancer to Aunty Josie's house. I met Uncle Thomas before, in the earlier days when we lived in Florida. He often took Anto on drinking sessions. He was a nice man though and I felt sorry for his suffering. He couldn't speak now as he lost his voice box through the cancer and he had a tracheotomy feeding tube in his throat. I did find that difficult but I was happy to see him and do little things for him. One day, as I arrived home from work, he was waving at me in alarm from his hall door. I went straight over and into the house, where Anto's brother Val was having some sort of a seizure. He was unconscious and foaming from the mouth. I called the ambulance and Val was whipped off in emergency. Poor old Thomas got an awful shock. Josie had been in the shops at the time. Val had suffered a massive brain bleed and underwent a ten hour operation to repair it. His skull was open from ear to ear. The Doctor wasn't sure of his recovery ability and told Anto it would be unlikely that he would wake up for a few days.

Anto was always caring towards his brothers and he sat with Val looking at all the different types of tubes coming out of him. Next he heard, 'Have you got my teeth?' 'Anto, have you got my teeth and my wedding ring?' Anto laughed out loud and called the Doctor who came flying in. Val was awake and talking normally. The Doctor said it was a miracle. Anto reckons that from all the alcohol in Val's system and that each day his body received alcohol, his body had woken up looking for its fix!

Five days later, Val was released and sat having a pint in Matt Whelan's pub. Val did eventually die a couple of years after that from a massive heart attack that left him in a coma for a year before dying. Val was a lovely chap. He was also a great worker. He helped Anto out in work with labouring and he was great fun also. I enjoyed the few conversations we had when he was sober. Val had loved his children but alcoholism had him in a firm grip and he couldn't let go. He gave his children to his family because he knew they would be educated and nourished.

The Gorman's were my neighbours next door. Mrs Gorman was a lovely woman from Donegal. She lived with her husband Peter and daughter Caroline. I remember when I moved into Anto's house initially, Caroline said to me, 'Jean, you're a bit loud,' and I was like, 'Me? loud?' I had no idea! Of course I was loud. I was shouting my head off at any stressful situation. I didn't know there was a different way to deal with stress. I thought everybody shouted. Anto wasn't a shouter and neither was his family. I thought he was only pretending! Eventually he was going to shout. Only when really riled would he raise his voice!

I became very fond of Caroline. She had never married and had no children of her own, she often had a few sweets for the kids. I loved her gardens front and back as she had them blossoming with flowers. Mrs Gorman and her husband Peter were getting on in years and just before Peter died, he fell down the stairs and split his head open. I ran in to help. I never saw so much blood in my life on the lino floor. I cleaned it up while the ambulance men took care of Peter. After wards, the shock of the congealed blood stayed in my mind. That's the way it was on Attracta road. The neighbours rallied round in times of trouble. Peter died shortly after that and then Mrs Gorman followed a couple of years later.

I loved all of Anto's family, but with all of our own problems, I felt their pressures an extra strain.

Anto and I were struggling. He was jealous of my sports hobby and I felt I should try a bit harder on the relationship as we were very close to splitting up. I made a decision to move from Cabra to Ratoath, to try and start again.

I was going to miss Attracta road hugely. I had made some great friends there.

On Saturdays when I cleaned my house, I could hear Joey Hanway blasting his opera music from his garage across from me and I loved singing along to Mario Lanzo. Joey advised me on my small garden and when to plant things. He gave me a load of garden tools to start me off.

It was going to be strange not being around all my friends and I would miss Aunty Josie too. We had grown close over the years.

When we moved to Ratoath, Catherine was turning 20. She didn't settle into Ratoath at all. She loved Dublin and she left and moved in with Anto's other brother Fergus. I was sad to see Catherine leave the nest!

I was getting fed up with hairdressing. It was hard work, the hours were unsocial and I wasn't making great money from it. I decided to go for a change. I had been helping out in my husband's office over the years, and had gained experience doing payroll.

I applied for a cashier job in Ulster Bank in Dublin in 1991. I had to go to the main offices on the quays in Dublin for the interview. It was a huge impressive building, full of wealth.

A lovely young woman interviewed me. I had no college degrees at that point, but my CV impressed her with the amount of courses I had done, and qualifications I had received over the years. I was 34 years old. I looked well, she knew I was smart, and felt I could do the job. I was delighted, she gave me a chance and I got the job.

My working hours were 10am till 2pm, Monday till Friday, I couldn't wait to start.

A lovely older woman showed me the job I was to do, she had worked there for years, she was attractive with dark brown eyes and brown hair. I was really excited. I couldn't believe I had got a good job.

I settled in really well on the first day and I was proud of my cash balances. I was sitting on my stool quite smugly, thinking there was nothing to this banking work at all. There was an overall 17,000 Euro's, (the new currency had just come in) gone missing from the cash balances. I could see all the staff running around trying to find it. Adding figures as they went. I was oblivious to their stares at me, knowing it was me who had caused the deficit somehow. I had actually made the mistake of counting the cash bags inaccurately. I had no idea until they went through my coins. They were cool about it since it was my first day and it made me more cautious.

One of my most memorable moments while I was working there, was when Gerry Ryan, (2FM Radio Celebrity) came in to lodge his salary cheque. He would often come in quite regular, but I had never served him before up until this day.

After I said, 'Good morning Gerry', he handed me his cheque to lodge.

After my first incident of counting change wrong, I wasn't taking any chances. I was looking at the numbers on the cheque and I was counting the zero's with my finger, to make sure I typed in the right figure. I was obviously holding the cheque too long, whilst still looking at it, (I wasn't mesmerized, I had seen bigger cheques).

"Excuse me, Miss, I can guarantee its real! Will you put it in my account before they cancel it and say I'm not worth that much?" Gerry joked. "I'm sorry Gerry" I said, giggling. "I know it's real!" I was all starstruck.

I loved working in the bank and took to it like a 'duck to water'. I loved doing the foreign exchange and working out the conversion figures. If the other girls were on lunch break and I wasn't busy, I would answer the phones and follow people's requests; Posting out statements, reminding accounts to call people back that were looking for something particular.

I loved it especially when it was busy, but there seemed to be a problem with a couple of the young girls who worked on the accounts table.

They weren't too long out of college and they had to work hard to get their jobs. I liked the job and I was happy to do all the extra bits and pieces and I'm old school, I wasn't used to sitting around doing nothing. I had to keep busy. These girls would just do what they had to do, and finish dead on the button.

I was irritating them, I caught them slagging me off a couple of times when I came back from my lunch. They ignored me quite regularly and one time asked me, 'How I actually got the job there with no college education?'

I told them 'I was obviously educated enough, or else I wouldn't have got the job!' They didn't believe me; they were convinced I must've known someone to get the job!

My manager was the same age as me, and she was very attractive, tall and slim with brown hair and dark eyes. She was a really nice person, I think I made her a bit uncomfortable. She said to me one time that 'she couldn't afford nice clothes because all her money went on her horse'. I was amazed at her negativity about herself. I thought she looked really stylish, but we never really bonded.

I was beginning to think that these girls thought I was after their job, but I wasn't looking for brownie points. I didn't want to climb higher in the bank. Part time suited me grand with two children at home.

Although there was a team leader in the branch and I voiced my concerns to her, the bullying behaviour hadn't changed with the younger girls.

After a few months of feeling alienated, I was feeling really low. The Team leader and Manager had a meeting with myself and the couple of girls involved.

I was really upset, crying, I told them I wasn't chasing their jobs. I suppose they thought I was mad, but they did apologize, apart from one girl who wasn't in that day.

I got on with my job; I was surprised that the management or team leader hadn't sorted out the problem before. I didn't think to go to Human Resources with the bullying issue.

Soon after that incident I discovered I had missed a period. I did a test and it confirmed I was pregnant. I figured I was about six weeks.

Sarah was seven years old then, Anthony was 13, Catherine was 19 and doing a college course in travel and tourism.

Anto and I were surprised but delighted.

It wasn't to be though. A few days later, I was heading to my car after finishing work. It was particularly stressful that day in work and I was a bit late coming out. I saw the guys lifting my car to tow it. I raced to the car, begging them to let it go, apologizing for being late back. They released my car, Thank God! They're not all bad.

My boobs stopped being painful the next morning, I knew I was going to miscarriage. I was ok about it, I knew it was barely a cluster of cells but I wasn't prepared for the emotional rollercoaster that happened to me really quickly after the miscarriage.

I didn't take any time off work, I just got on with it as usual. What I went through then was crazy, I was an emotional wreck, crying spontaneously during working hours. Behaving erratically, crying as I was serving customers, snot running down my nose. I had no idea it was post natal depression. I was only pregnant for seven weeks at most.

Maybe the staff were very inexperienced, although two of them were older than myself, but did nobody see that at the very least I had some form of depression? And at least suggest I go home for a couple of days! It was a very busy bank and I guess they must have needed the staff, no matter how ill the staff member was. Mental illness wasn't obvious to me so I suppose it wasn't obvious to them either.

Why didn't I just go to the Doctor? I didn't, and I continued to feel low in the job.

I eventually said to my manager that maybe I should leave the job, as there were a lot of barricades against me, with the extra distance I now had to travel from Ratoath and now crèche fees.

She agreed I should. I gave up my job. I should have been sent off sick and got treated for depression.

I wrote a letter of complaint to Human Resources a few weeks after I'd left, explaining the bullying I had experienced in that branch.

They sent me a reply, 'Good luck in your future'.

I felt rejected. Employers didn't want troubled people.

I got back to normal a few weeks later and I just got on with things. Life in our new home didn't go as easy as I planned. After the initial holiday period of a new house. I kind of wanted to go back to Cabra. I felt a lot of guilt living in a big house. We were arguing a lot. Anto hadn't really wanted to move from his house in the first place and then he blamed me.

In September 1993, I started a full time college course taking Business Studies in St Peter's College in Dunboyne.

I liked the bank work and I wanted to educate myself in that area. There were nine modules in the course, including, law, finance, media studies, health and safety, first aid, computers, business management. I graduated with all distinctions and student of the year!

I was really proud of myself. I liked the finance section and thought I'd follow it on and maybe do a degree in it.

During that year, I became pregnant on Yasmin. We were really happy about it and our relationship flourished. I relaxed a little.

Until.

A good friend of mine fell out with me when I was going into my fourth month of pregnancy in 2004. I found it hard to come to terms with, I really didn't know what went wrong. There was no closure. I cried and cried for the next 5 months. I didn't know that depression could hit you when you're pregnant, but it hit me. I had to really look at myself then. What was wrong with me? How come things can't just be easy for five minutes? Do I attract trouble?

Why is there always a big drama with us women?

When I was growing up, there was always plenty of drama and talk about affairs. Us girls saw plenty of fights in the Disco's with women fighting over their man. I learned the rule young. You never fancied friend's, sister's or any woman's boyfriends or husbands, and thankfully for my own mental health, I was never attracted to anybody else's man.

I had a good moral etiquette. Besides, I knew affairs caused trouble, big trouble and I was always afraid of trouble.

But the rejection was huge.

I was already depressed before my little Yasmin came into this world.

I doubted myself. If others didn't like me, I wasn't worthy of being liked.

In my mind I was thinking. Did I come across as cocky? Was I not aware of people's needs?

I deserved punishment; self-hatred was routed deep in my brain.

7

Forgiveness

In 1993 Dad got his first full-time permanent job since the mid 1970's. He was now 51. That recession had lasted 17 years and Dad had been unemployed for most of that time.

When Anto started his company in 1991 He called it Custom Crew Construction Ltd. Dad was to drive the construction truck, picking up materials and delivering them to sites.

While Anthony had been in America, he worked on beautifully customized homes, which was how he named his company.

The 70s and 80s were finally gone in Ireland, and people were starting to renovate their homes. Everywhere was extending or renovating. Business started to boom, there was work everywhere.

For the first time ever, the ordinary trade's people of Ireland were starting to earn really good money. Gardens were getting landscaped in council areas, people had new cars, houses were fashioning state of the art kitchens. The women were becoming really stylish, hair and makeup done regularly.

People were going on exotic holidays.

Children were being sent to private fee-paying schools.

People were buying new houses home and abroad; and property prices started to rise fast.

It was called The 'Celtic Tiger.'

My dad was happy in work. He was finally earning a proper wage and paying into a pension. He loved the lads and he began to feel like he belonged. The Devil didn't appear too often.

During these years, we brought Ma and Da away to Florida a few times and there are a few incidents with my dad that were funny, sad and scary.

The first time was when Olive and Tony were getting married and Anto had organised the stag party in Sarasota.

There were about 40 lads including the two Dad's.

The guys did the usual pub crawl and were soon getting happily drunk, even Dad at this point. There were two buses picking the guys up each time and bringing them to the next venue. One bus carried the guys who were smoking pot which included Anto and the other bus had no pot and my dad onboard. All was going to plan and they arrived at the last venue. A Strip Club. My dad had never been to one of those in his life, so he wasn't sure what to expect. They sat around the bar and ordered their beer and when a naked girl walked onto the bar to pass out their beer with her bum and bits hanging out! Dad went ballistic! He wanted to kill Anto for bringing him to a brothel and he would to kill his soon to be son in law for going to a brothel. Of course he was thrown off the premises!

When we were flying home from that trip, we had proceeded to check in. Mam and Dad's luggage was somehow over weight and the baggage guy was trying to charge my dad 300 dollars! It's just as well that was before security had become really strict because Dad went ballistic again. If Dad thought he was right about something, he would never give in. He was shouting, demanding to see a manager, refusing to fly with Aeroflot. It was gas. We were all really embarrassed.

Eventually, they gave up and let Dad on the plane.

This time my sister Sharon came with her two kids, and we brought a couple of cousins too. My son Anthony was about 13 and Sarah was seven.

My dad was terrified of flying, so naturally he had a couple of whisky's in the airport before we boarded the plane. Once the plane was up in the air, he couldn't breathe. He was panicking. My ma and Anto comforted him and he settled down. Sharon and I were staying clear in case he roared at us!

We rented a big house near Sarasota, where Joe and Marcy live.

It was quite ambitious for us lot to stay under the one roof, but I thought we might manage it.

It was ambitious. Where I had begun to learn how not to annoy my da, Sharon hadn't. She also drove him crazy. Sharon and my Dad were niggling at each other. He moaned that she was never ready and she moaned at him for annoying her. Ma and myself were managing to keep the peace though and all was going well. Anto took Dad on the huge bridge in Clearwater and Dad was terrified! He hated heights. He was having fun though and enjoyed the beautiful weather and the boat trips we took to go fishing. He loved the cold draft beer in the sports bars.

Accidents were never too far from my door and young Anthony dove head first into the pool and broke his front teeth. I was grateful he hadn't broke his neck but I was really upset over this and overreacted completely, crying for hours. We found a dentist who temporarily fixed him up till we got home and Anthony was fine. I was stressed now though and it changed the mood in the house.

A couple of evenings later we were going out on a big family meal. Anto's brother Pascal was down from Texas with his four children and Darlene. We had booked our huge group into a bar as Joe and Marcy would be there too.

Dad was picking on Sharon for not being organized, Sharon snapped at Dad, and he got in a mood and wouldn't come with us.

We all went anyway as we were already dressed. We met up with the family and had a great night. I was sad for Dad that he missed it. The banter and the chat was great. That was the thing with Dad, when he got moody, he couldn't just snap out of it.

When we came home a few hours later, it was dark. The lights were out in the house and the music was blaring. The front door was open. Dad wasn't there. An empty bottle of whiskey stood on the coffee table. We walked in slowly and turned on the lights, no sign of Dad.

We put the kids to bed and then Dad came out of one of the bedrooms and made us jump with fright!

Whisky changed my dad completely. He lost all control and any self-respect.

He was roaring and shouting and going ballistic. I was 31 years old, and he still wanted to get at me and strangle me.

I went crazy back at him this time and told him, "No way, not here, not in front of my kids!"

The kids were awake at this point and terrified. Anto's 13 year old nephew Darren was looking at the scene in fright.

I called the police in Florida that night. They arrived within minutes to arrest my dad. I only thought afterwards that we might be on TV! You know that program that goes in after the police?

My poor Mother, she said "Please don't let him get locked up, Jean, please!"

The police agreed to let him go to a hotel that night to cool off. There were no weapons involved, so, they didn't see him as a big threat.

Ma went off with Dad to the hotel that night, their heads bowed down. I never felt so ashamed of myself.

What had I done?

A strange thing happened to me that night. It took two people to have a fight, and I was in there ready, just like my dad, but he got all the blame.

I was an adult now, and I was reacting just as I always reacted, in there, giving it as much as my dad, behaving just as badly. Who was I to judge him? I was no better.

I was so embarrassed. I had to accept my responsibility for my part in the row. For putting my mother through that. My ma had to stay in a hotel that night, ashamed. Dad of course felt guilty and ashamed. He'd done it again. He lost control of himself in the whisky. He was angry at himself.

He hated himself. He didn't know how to stop though.

I'll never forget that hurt look in my mother's eyes that night, I had let her down, and my dad. I could've reacted differently and ignored my dad.

Did I ever say I'm sorry for that night? I don't know. I'm so sorry Ma and Dad.

Things were naturally strained for the rest of the holiday, with Ma and Dad afraid to say too much.

They bought me a beautiful glass dolphin to thank me for the holiday. It was the last holiday they came on.

Dad settled back to work at home and the holiday was soon forgotten.

He loved being at work, with the other lads. He'd meet them for a pint on Fridays after work; He was much happier in himself. He wasn't better or 'cured' and he still had terrible rows at home. He'd still throw you out if you annoyed him; He'd work a half day on Saturdays and rush home to shower and change to go off down the pub.

I remember when I had Yasmin, I was 37 then, and Yasmin was a few months old. I'd go down to Ma's every Saturday and do everybody's hair colour and cut. I used to carry Yasmin into Ma's house in her little carry tot car seat. She always used to cry hysterically in Ma's house.

I was convinced she could sense my unease there. (Later on, I would find out, that at three months, loud sounds were painful to Yasmin's ears). Even when Dad was being nice to her and she would cry and cry, he would say impatiently "What's she crying for?"

This particular Saturday, we were all there in Ma's house, with all our kids, safe in the knowledge that Dad would be in the pub for ages.

All us sisters were in great form, and we all took turns in buying the cakes. We'd have a bit of a laugh on those Saturdays.

I was just finished doing all the hairs and Dad arrived back early, (obviously lost all his money in the bookies). I was rushing to finish, I knew he was in bad form, ready for a row.

Each sister was packing up and rushing out the door with their kids, Dad shouting after them. Eventually the roaring escalated, Dad shouting crazily at us, 'Get out and stay out!', (using foul language I can't write).

There was a crowd of 5 year olds gathering outside Ma's house, watching confused, as us adults were thrown out!

It was my turn to exit, Yasmin was screaming hysterically, Dad roared "Get Out! Get Out!". I escaped into my car. Oh my God, when would this ever end? It was crazy.

Dad had a lot of respect for Anto and he liked him. Anto would talk to him, and treat him like one of the lads.

Although my relationship with my dad wasn't fantastic, as I blamed him for all the damage he had caused.

That hate and resentment wasn't good for me or my children. I was aware of how I reacted to Dad in his times of anger. As I was getting older, I realized I had been behaving just as badly as he had in during our fights, I could be just as nasty and just as vicious. I had to change. After that holiday, I started to change, to detach from the rows, to avoid going to the house if Dad had been drinking, to consciously talk more respectfully to my Ma and Dad.

Regardless of maybe getting thrown out if I arrived, I would always visit my parents with the Grand kids. My parents loved to see their Grand kids.

Dad had a good ten happy years in the job, when he developed Cancer of the Oesophagus. In the latter couple of years of Dad's life, I could be genuinely nice to him, making him a sandwich if he was up my way, in Ratoath.

He was really good to me, he'd move anything in the garden for me, or do little jobs if he had the time, or pick up the kids from school if I was stuck. I really appreciated that.

I felt I was getting the Dad back from when I was little.

For the two years my dad fought oesophageal cancer, he suffered terribly. He couldn't swallow anymore as the tumour blocked his throat. He opted to have the tumour removed. The success rate of this operation was very small and was extremely painful. We were glad to see he survived the operation and the Doctor had removed the tumour and replaced the oesophagus with another piece of tissue. For the next six months, Dad was very ill in hospital. He couldn't eat, he had no energy, the cancer was spreading. He received chemo and the side effects from that was very severe. He also received radiotherapy and he felt excruciating burning inside his skin. Eventually he got out from the hospital. He had lost a lot of weight. The cancer had spread to his prostate at this point and there was no more chemo offered. There was nothing more they could do.

After he healed from all the procedures he had received, he began to have a relative quality of life. He was able to eat again which was a great comfort to him. He was also on the morphine pump which kept him from pain. I worked a lot more on my relationship with my dad, showing compassion. It wasn't really hard, as anybody going through the 'fight with cancer' knows, the suffering is tough.

Although Josie, my sister, took on a lot of the care with my dad, because she lived closer, we all did our share of going to hospitals and visiting him, and supporting him and my Ma.

When Dad's bowels started to give way, he went into St Francis Hospice Raheny. It was a beautiful place, and Dad was cared for with kindness.

I made my chicken soup for him, and he ate it every night till his final sleep.

Dad was an awful character at times though. There was a Brother in the Hospice who went to each of the patients to bless them each night and give them communion.

When the Brother was approaching Dad on his first night there, Dad was reclining in his bed, "Don't let that fucker near me!" He'd say to us with fear on his face. Dad had grown to hate the Catholic Church and everything it represented. He said they were a load of hypocrites. Brother Patrick came over to Dad, "God bless you son, will you have communion?"

Dad replied, "Good evening Father, I will."

We were laughing at his own hypocrisy.

Yasmin was only turned two at that time and Christine's Isabella was just 12 months. We were able to spend a lot of our days at the hospice as we were off work. Yasmin had only started walking at 19 months and Isabella was already walking at 12 months, so the two toddlers toddled around the corridors happily each day. The other patients were happy to see the little girls, it put a smile on their faces. The hospice tolerated the babies as it was very family orientated. It had beautiful gardens we could go and walk in and push Dad in his wheel chair for some fresh air. It was a beautiful autumn, and the sun always seemed to be shining down on us all. It also had a great family room with TV, where families could be close by their loved ones, and still be comfortable. There was a fantastic toy room for the children also, so they were happy when we had to go to see Dad often.

Dad enjoyed the attention he was receiving from us all, but occasionally, when he'd see the toddlers arriving, he'd say, 'Could you not get them minded for God's sake?' He was a bit moody at times, but Christine and I would giggle and say, 'They wanted to see you Granddad!'

It was hard for Dad to acknowledge that he would never see his 14 grandchildren growing, or be there for their special occasions. Dad loved my son Anthony, his oldest grandchild who was 18 at the time. Dad was very proud of him. It's funny, he never raised his voice at him ever and Anthony had a good bond with his granddad. When Dad was seven weeks in the hospice, his time was close. His movements and voice had become very slow. I think the saddest part for me was when a piece of his tooth was breaking away.

Dad was always careful about his appearance. He hated the dentist and after a visit a few years earlier, when they told him he had Pyorrhoea gum disease and would need all his teeth out, he refused to go back and managed his teeth himself. He did a good job as he hadn't lost any till now.

He was trying to remove the piece of tooth from his mouth and he had very little control of his hands at that point. I brushed it away with tissue, but it was the finality of that tooth. Another piece of him broken. I could see the sadness in his eyes. He knew he was dying.

He had been in the final sleep three days now. All us sisters were going to stay the night as he would be gone before dawn the nurses said. I went home to sort the kids out and get my toothbrush.

On my return, an hour later, I arrived to see Dad in the garden, having a smoke. He looked like death, but he was still alive. We called him Lazarus.

He obviously had unfinished business to do.

We had some funny times in the hospice and funny talks. Families become very close to other families there also, often seeking them out for comfort or reassurance.

Dad had always wanted his body to be donated to the college of surgeons for science. It was funny that in all his drinking years his liver was never damaged, not even touched by cancer till the very end. Doctors were inquisitive about that.

I thought that was a fair enough request, but Christine had a big problem with it. She told Dad she didn't fancy knowing that Dad's body was dismembered in a science lab and the thought gave her nightmares. I think Dad thought it would prolong the inevitable burial that he feared so much.

Ma wanted to cremate him because that's what she's getting done!

It was like a discussion for a hair treatment not a funeral!

Dad didn't want the hassle of the mourners coming to the house. We were laughing with Christine adding, 'It won't bother you, you'll be the dead one!'

This was the talk around his bed while we were all supping our tea and coffee. It was just as well Dad was on morphine to dull the effect as well as the pain. He didn't like being the butt of a joke!

I had grown a lot in the past couple of years, and I had already forgiven Dad, even without an apology.

This one day, a couple of weeks before he died; He said to me, "I fecked up!" "I made a mess of my life; I didn't do a good job as a Father."

I really felt for him. He'd had a hard life himself and he succumbed to alcohol because it seemed easier. I knew he hated himself for his failures. I now understood as I was making my own mistakes in parenting. Life wasn't easy.

I was able to say to my da, "You didn't feck up, you didn't have the knowledge, you did the best you could with the knowledge you had".

I have to convey how important forgiveness is to Spiritual growth. It frees you.

I was growing, I was looking at my own ways I was raising my Children. The mistakes I was making. I couldn't judge another.

What happened when I was a kid was terrible, but that was then. I couldn't live my life being resentful. It would hold me back. I wanted to grow, to be spiritual, to be happy, to make my children happy. To teach them. To show them the way. Dad had little instructions for all us girls after he died. He told me to look after Ma and never see her short. He knew I'd honour his wish as long as I could.

Dad died 6 weeks after the Lazarus resurrection. It was the 16th of December 2006 at 11am on Saturday morning. It was a beautiful sunny fresh morning and there was a calm in the air. Dad had been in the final sleep for a couple of days now and his eyes were just flickering at our voices. He looked really well groomed as the hospice nurses had bathed him and even cut his nails. One of the nurses was swabbing Dad's dried lips with whiskey on cotton wool. He was breathing easily.

For some reason I decided to go home and have a shower. I thought Dad would be still there when I got back. Dad had died minutes after I left.

I couldn't believe I wasn't there. My sister Christine said it was just as well I missed Dad passing, as he woke in panic fighting for breath, struggling to let go. He was always scared of dying.

I had often heard of how corpses go back to their youth on dying, but I had never really believed it, until I saw my Dad.

His hair had seemed almost black again against the paleness of his skin. The wrinkles and bags left his face and he looked so peaceful. His hands laying weakly on his non existing tummy. I thought he looked really good looking.

He didn't get his wish for the science lab after all; As he died on a Saturday, the college didn't open and they had to preserve him on the day he died!

I felt sad for my Dad dying at age 64, especially when he was getting a second chance, he was trying to live his life better.

I miss having a Dad to do the little things that Dad's do for their daughters. There's too much politics between a husband and wife; 'I did that last time', 'I always do it', 'Can I never have a bit of rest?' But there's something about Fathers and daughters. I see it with my husband and our girls. He would do anything for them. He might moan a bit about the cost of them, but he'd still do it for them.

My Dad was like that with me in those last few years of his life. He was relatively healthy and he was working, so he was happy to do things around my garden. He loved his garden before the devil got hold of him. He's notoriously remembered for his 5ft sunflowers that he grew in our front garden one year. They were his pride and joy. He also grew all sorts of vegetables when we were little. We had to help mix in the manure, which was cow's pooh, that he brought home from the abattoir. He told us it was very good for our chilblains.

Everything was homeopathic in those days! I think Dad would have made a good farmer, given the opportunity. He loved all animals and nature. He loved all birds and knew all their names. He told us that when he moved to Cabra first as a young teenager, he got himself some chickens, as he always wanted to keep chickens.

When the neighbours eventually complained about the noise of the rooster in the early dawn, he moved all his chickens to his back bedroom. No wonder his mam bashed him!

My Dad loved the years of rock and roll, and Elvis was his king. He had quite a good singing voice and he had a cousin Rose Tynan who was a popular Irish singer in Cabaret shows around Ireland. He loved singing Elvis songs. I was 10 years of age, sitting in our sitting room reading a book, when the news came on the radio. Dad was there too and he was devastated that his idol Elvis, 46 years of age, was dead.

Dad was really upset.

He also loved Tina Turner and he played her songs at every occasion.

One of my most memorable moments I like to remember is when I got tickets for Ma and Da and Anto and myself to go see Tina Turner in July 2000. She was playing in the RDS Dublin.

At nearly 60, and with the energy she performed with, Ma and Da were really looking forward to seeing her.

It was a beautiful Summer evening as we set off. Anto decided to wear his new Adidas tracksuit I had bought for him, as he thought it would be more comfortable. Ma had her standard high heels on and her handbag she couldn't part with. Dad had his suit on, carrying his overcoat in case it rained. I was in my jeans and runners. Anto had parked close to Ballsbridge, and we went into one of the pubs in the area to have a drink before the concert. Everywhere was packed and there was a great buzz in the air.

We left the pub in plenty of time to walk across to the RDS venue. There were people everywhere. Anto was laughing and chatting to my Dad as he walked along behind Ma and myself.

Next of all two beefy looking men grabbed him, put him up against the wall and frisked him. Just like that!

We were all in shock!

When they found nothing they wanted, they asked Anto for his ID. They apologized and released him, only, after my Ma went over to them threateningly with her handbag, and said "Hey! leave him alone! that's my son in law, we're only on our way to see Tina Turner!"

The men were plain clothes detectives and they thought that Anto with his swagger and tracksuit was a classic ticket tout and probably a drug dealer as well! We all got a good giggle from that. My dad was laughing heartedly.

Gardai! Not everybody in a tracksuit is a drug dealer or a crook!

My Ma and Dad loved the concert. We were right at the front. Tina was truly an amazing performer. We danced to every song, Dad holding his overcoat and Ma in her heals and handbag!

When Lionel Ritchie came on as a surprise act, I couldn't believe it. He was my Idol and I loved his songs. I felt he was singing them to me. It was a beautiful balmy summer night. It was perfect.

I like to remember that night with my Dad, just being normal, and happy. He'd had a hard life. He had a lot of scars. It was hard for him to relax and be kind to himself. To feel worthy as any other human being.

On that night he was Ma's young Christy.

8

Yasmin

Yasmin age 6, 2010.

Yasmin screamed at high pitch, "Aghh! "My toe! It hurts!" She moved her position. "Aghhh, my leg!" She screamed in agony, I checked to see if somehow she had managed to dislocate some body part within inches of me sitting beside her, because it sounded like she had; Her face contorted in agony, her body writhing in pain.

But I knew she hadn't physically hurt herself. It was her brain, fighting against learning to write this simple sentence 'Mr Nog sat and got fat'.

It was a struggle for Yasmin to write, to sound out words, to read, "I can't do it!" she screamed, "I'm so itchy."

"You can do it!" I said firmly and kindly, "Don't bite yourself! That's unacceptable! Take a deep breath," I said.

"I can't!" she screamed.

"Let's breathe together," I said, "In through your nose, slowly out through your mouth, again, now let's try it again." I feel like giving up myself, I don't want to see my little girl suffer. I'm crying inside, and having a hot cappuccino on the outside. Thank God for coffee!

But I'm ok, I can do this, I can help my little girl to learn. Her challenge is bigger than mine. She's the one who has to try to learn to read, learn to write, learn to count, with her brain which is all in a fluster. It won't let a letter go in and stay in. It doesn't remember how to write a letter. "What is SN Mammy? I can't remember!" she cried.

"SN SN SN," I said over and over, gently, firmly," Snow starts with SN". She gets the SN! "Well done! Great work!

Great writing!" I praise her. She smiles. We get to the next difficult sound, 'Sh'.

The pain starts again, the screaming, the wriggling, the scratching. "I can't do it!" she cries. "Why is my brain like this, Mammy?" she cries.

I try to help Yasmin understand what's going on for her without giving her too much information on her disability.

I say, "Yasmin, you have a little allergy to learning, it causes you to itch and squirm and fidget. It makes it a little hard for your brain to let in information and words. But don't worry, I can rub some cream on you to take away the itch and I can give you some vitamins to help your brain, it'll be ok," I say kindly.

"It won't be ok, I can't do it Mammy!" Yasmin cries in frustration.

I try to think of something she was really impressed by and I tell her, "Remember Winter the Dolphin? The little baby Dolphin in Florida who got stuff in nets and lost her tail? She learned to swim! You can learn to read and write! It's not easy, but you can do it!" I tell her.

The Clearwater Marine aquarium in Florida saved the baby dolphin and taught her to swim again without a tail. Because Winter was using different muscles to swim he was damaging his spine. An artificial tail was created by Hanger Prosthetics and Orthotics in Clearwater with Dr. Mike Walsh leading the team to get his tail area to swim properly. We went to see Winter that summer, and Yasmin was really amazed by Winter.

Yasmin tries again.

What an amazing little girl! She tries so hard. She wants to give up, but she tries again.

Can you imagine something that you find really difficult to do but you have to do it every day? That's what it's like for Yasmin. She finds it really difficult to learn to read, to write, to concentrate.

She inspires me.

I look at her and God is speaking to me through her. 'This is how you do it, don't give up, try again. Come out smiling!' Like my little angel, who smiles a lot.

She's funny, she loves farty jokes and silly things. She loves our dogs, and plays happily for hours with them. She loves horses and talks incessantly to Sarah about horses, because Sarah loves horses too. She loves to sing, of course she can't put a song together yet, but she would give any good traveling child a run for their money on Grafton Street.

She loves 'One Direction'. She says, "Mam, you know when I grow up and if I marry Niall Horan. I will be called Yasmin Amy Murray Horan".

She has no fear. The immaturity part of her frees her up to ask personal questions of people.

"Who are you?"

"Why are you here?"

"Why are you wearing that?"

"You're fat!"

Many a time, I've politely pulled her away from people. Some people look at her with disdain. Yasmin is a tall girl and people expect more of her. They don't understand that when she behaving like a three old that in her social development she is a three old, even at age seven.

Traveling on airplanes are particularly challenging, as it requires Yasmin to sit in one place for a lot of hours. Yasmin gets very itchy and uncomfortable. Many times, people in the seat in front, give me glaring looks and make rude comments about Yasmin. Yasmin pretends not to hear them. She has a disability and she's very sensitive but she's not stupid. She knows when people are annoyed at her.

Yasmin needs constant entertainment to keep her busy on an airplane. She is so excited to be on the flight, but she fidgets and squirms a lot in her seat and can't concentrate on any one thing for long.

Yasmin isn't rude or bold to anybody, as it's not in her nature to be bold. Her disability isn't as obvious as other known disabilities, so most people aren't aware. I was so affected by people's comments or stares at Yasmin that one time I alerted the air stewards on boarding that Yasmin has a little difficulty in sitting down.

As soon as the flight took off the steward was down checking on Yasmin to see if she's was going to have a fit! I was trying to protect my child from rude passengers and the steward was thinking of protecting the passengers from Yasmin!

I feel people have no patience for children traveling. Regardless if they have no disabilities, it's difficult for children to travel in confined spaces.

And no, children shouldn't be left at home till they're older!

Although the traveling exhausts Yasmin and myself, she loves going on holidays with her family and cousins.

People should consider next time they think a child is bold, that maybe there's something else going on, and to show a little kindness.

It's hard for the parents too. When I see people looking at my beautiful child with distain on their faces. It breaks my heart. Why can't they see she is a beautiful child?

There are lovely kind people too though, like my recent experience in The Kildare Outlet on Saturday 26th October 2013.

I feel I should mention this because the woman was beautiful in Spirit, and I was grateful for her kindness towards my child.

Myself and my sister Christine were taking Yasmin and Isabella communion dress shopping, as both their communion's are coming in May 2014. Little Catholic girl's First Holy Communion is a big occasion in Ireland. The dress is very important to each child. Yasmin and Isabella are very close cousins, as they see each other every day. They're like the terrible twins sometimes, as they can squabble like sisters. Yasmin has blonde hair, grey blue eyes and fair skinned and Isabella has brown hair, brown eyes and dark skin. Yasmin is a year older than Bella at nine, but Bella is three years older than Yasmin at eight. They're similar in height at about four feet.

We spent nearly two hours in Cathy's Communion Dress shop in Johnstown, Co Kildare.

The owner had hundreds of different styles of dresses and tiara's and veils. Both Yasmin and Isabella were delighted to try on lots of dresses. There were mirrors everywhere, so the girls could admire themselves at every angle.

It was a perfect day out for us Mammy's and our little girls. Yasmin's big sister Sarah came along too to share this special occasion. The girls picked their favourite dress and then they were given a Hello Kitty goody bag from the owner, packed with sweets and little toys.

Yasmin and Isabella were so happy, comparing what they had.

We decided we'd stop at the Kildare outlet and maybe Sarah could have a little treat in the SuperDry clothes shop.

It had started to rain heavily and we were darting into each shop. To be fair, it was the first bad day of Autumn.

I brought Yasmin and Isabella into a luxury dish shop. I thought I might get myself a few new dinner plates. It was nearly decked out for Christmas with lots of Santa and Rudolf cups and plates. Yasmin spotted a reindeer family made of twigs just inside the door. The first thing she did was pick Rudolf up and the other reindeers fell to the floor.

Yasmin looking for someone else to blame and said, "Isabella, you're not supposed to touch the stuff in the shop!" Thankfully, nothing had broken but I was scrambling to pick things up.

The lovely woman who worked in the shop came over to us. I think she may have been late 60's, it was hard to tell as she looked very stylish.

"It's perfectly ok for these little ones to touch the reindeers," she said, "it's a small shop, and things are going to fall down. Come over to me girls and I'll give you both a little gift for yourselves ."

That's all it takes in life.

A small piece of kindness to make somebody happy.

I would have gladly bought everything in the shop as there was a great selection and it was beautifully displayed. My budget for luxury buying is limited now, so I had to leave the goods behind!

Although it rained hard that day, it was perfect day out.

Yasmin will try anything, athletics, swimming, horse riding, ballet. She wants to do everything her friends do.

One of my most favourite moments, was when she was 6. She was a member of The Monica Loughman's Ballet in Ratoath. Monica was previous Prima Ballerina for the Russian Ballet, and she was radiantly beautiful.

Monica was putting on her first show in the Draiocht Theatre Blanchardstown. All the little girls had a part, and Yasmin was beautiful in her TuTu. I provided my hairdressing services and styled all the girls hairs into their buns. It was a beautiful show.

Yasmin had danced her part, but she was so happy, she wanted to do more. As the helpers were dressing the next group of girls to perform, Yasmin jumped in the queue and got dressed for the next scene that she wasn't supposed to be in!

She went onto the stage, and did her own little routine! It was so funny and yet amazing. She loved being in the spotlight. She tries so hard in all these activities, even if she's not the best, she keeps going. I'm so glad she isn't aware of shyness yet.

Yasmin was born on 2nd September 2004 weighing 7lbs and arriving three weeks early. She whimpered into the world, this tiny little thing with white blond hair and red birth mark on her forehead. It was love at first sight for my husband and myself. I was a private patient at Rotunda Hospital this time. We had health insurance and I availed of the luxury. The hospital stay wasn't as nice this time as I was placed in a tiny room by myself and only my husband and children were allowed to visit because of new rules. I was to be there for three days.

Some say that it was the fault of the foreign nationals that used to visit with 20 members of their family and often left their toddlers there to be minded by their mothers having just delivered a new born baby.

Strict health and safety rules came into place and visitors were restricted.

I felt very lonely in the little room and because this was my third child, the nurses didn't feel the need to help me with the baby as I was an experienced mother. I signed myself out on the second day.

On the way home we stopped by Ma's house in Cabra. Yasmin was tiny in her car seat and she didn't look comfortable, it was as if she was sitting up. I decided not to go into Ma's house. I was feeling really panicky and wanted to get the baby straight home. My poor Ma and Dad, they must have felt rejection from me numerous times as their child. I feel really sad about that, but it was irrational behaviour from me and also a sign that I was already in depression.

On a return to the Rotunda Hospital to have my tubes tied in February 2005. I was left for 4 hours after the operation unattended without a drink of water or a cup of tea. I had to go looking for a nurse for a cup of tea, which she answered, 'That's not my area, I'll send kitchen staff to you,' She appeared to be chatting to another nurse. A couple of more hours after that, the Doctor said I could go home when a nurse detached my drip, I was waiting another two hours without seeing a nurse and I had to go looking again, at this point, I was nearly taking the needle out myself. I found a nurse who disgruntledly removed my drip and sent me home.

A lot had changed in that Hospital since I had Sarah in 1995 and Yasmin in 2004, for the worse. Health insurance was no benefit for me there. I felt the hospital had gone downhill hugely. The bathrooms were not clean, and the nurses hadn't got the time to help you.

Every time I picked Yasmin up, there was a little silver angel feather where ever she lay; I knew immediately that Angels were minding her. I knew she was a special gift from God, but I didn't know the reason yet.

She was sleeping in her own bedroom at six weeks and I'd wake to hear her giggling in the night, I'd run in to see her eyes wide open staring and smiling from her cot. I didn't see anything, but I knew it was the angels. I stopped seeing the angels feathers when Yasmin was about 19 months, when I think they knew I was well enough to take care of Yasmin myself.

When Yasmin was seven weeks old, I knew I had post natal depression. I had watched Ireland am that morning and it was discussing post natal depression and the seven symptoms.

I had the seven symptoms, couldn't sleep, couldn't eat, couldn't wash my self, couldn't peel potatoes, was crying all the time, couldn't get organized. I had huge angry out bursts at my husband when he came in from work. The kids were really scared and upset, and my husband didn't know what was going on.

On one occasion, when I was feeling really frustrated, I had Yasmin in one arm and I threw her baby bath off the table and let out a frustrated scream. My little seven week old baby had fear in her eyes!

I knew I needed help. I remember feeling totally worthless and a really bad Mother, and more than once, I wanted to leave. I loved my kids so much, I didn't want them to go through the madness I grew up in, and I thought my husband would be a much better father to the kids than I was.

I used to cry 'Let me leave, I want to leave!' As my husband stood in front of the door, blocking my way.

I just couldn't understand why I was like this. Why I had angry outbursts. I couldn't control them and I really hated myself. I really thought I was no use to anybody. I wished I was dead.

Eventually, I went to my doctor, and was diagnosed with post natal depression and was prescribed with anti-depressants. I had never been on medication before and to my amazement after a few days the clouds started to clear in my head and I could think clearly. I felt huge relief, I found help. I also didn't suffer any of the side effects people fear. I was more worried about the dry mouth I had seen from Jack Nickolson's portrayal of a mentally ill patient on 'One flew over the cuckoo's nest'. But thankfully, that didn't happen.

The doctor also advised to me to book private counselling, as well as being in Alcoholics Anonymous, my self-help group. I didn't go to private counselling at that time. I thought I was doing ok on the medication.

When Yasmin was about 15 months old, I was carrying a basket of washing from the clothes line into the house. It was a wet day and as I came in through the sunroom, I slipped on my tiled floor. I fell flat on my back, knocking Yasmin with my feet as I fell. I checked Yasmin and she was fine, and I seemed to escape any injury.

The next morning as I tried to get out of bed, I was in a lot of pain. I felt really strange and I looked in the mirror and couldn't believe I was crooked. My right hip was sticking out sideways from the top of my body, I got a bit of a shock. I knew my back had come out of place.

I don't know why I didn't go to a hospital but I looked for Chiropractor and thought that would be best as he deals with back pain. As it was Saturday, I left Anto with the kids and I drove to a Chiropractor in Dublin myself. I don't know how!

Yasmin couldn't get in a car without getting car sick at this stage, and I thought it wiser to leave her at home with Dad. I was also reluctant to leave her with anybody else. I had an automatic car, so I didn't need to manoeuvre my legs much.

The Chiropractor X Rayed my body, and we both could easily see on the screen that my back had come out on the lower end of my spine. He explained he needed to do some manoeuvres on my back to ease it back into place. I was very reluctant as I was in a lot of pain. I had to lay down face forward on a strange looking contraption. He proceeded to pull levers which manoeuvred the wood beneath me, its aim was to gently ease my bones back where they should be.

Although it was fast, the pain still killed me. I got up from the bed feeling stiff with my hip still jutting out sideways. He told me it would take a few days to go back in. I paid him the 150 euro, which included the X Ray cost and struggled to my car.

I called him the body popper and I would never go back.

I eventually had to go to my doctor, and she wisely told me that the back actually slots back in itself. A person can help it along by standing straight and gently reaching for the sky, one arm at a time, and also, ordinary walking, not a power walk!

While in bed, I was to support my back with a cushion placed below my bum if I was sleeping on my back, and between my knees if sleeping on my side. This worked and I do this all the time and I'm free from pain in my back!

I'm just trying to fill you in on the constant craziness in my life.

The doctor also sent me off for X Rays just to check it out. I was to phone for the results a couple of weeks later.

The receptionist in the doctor's surgery was a little strange. She was mostly unhelpful and rude to the patients, for daring to bother her while she was busy. A lot of us patients were really scared of her! I phoned the surgery and the receptionist answered the phone; I meekly explained I just needed to talk to the Doc about my results and she answered, "She's really busy at the moment!" she said tartly, 'I'll just have a look for you, yeah, it's just wear and tear, it's your age, it's not going to get any better, just worse. I have it myself!"

I'm sure she thought she was being helpful, but I was shocked. I thanked her and hung up amused at the very least!

She didn't last too long at that job!

I worked on my back with walking and swimming when I could and I was lucky, the problem didn't last too long.

It wasn't till Yasmin was three, that I eventually booked the private counselling sessions, after I had become an emotional wreck.

I had been taking the medication for nearly two years since I was first prescribed, and I didn't want to stay on it forever. It was also really expensive at 80 euros a month. I was feeling really well and thought I was ready to come off it. I was grand for a while....

But a lot of things were happening at this time in 2007.

My son Anthony had left home. I started to see I was losing Anthony when he was about 16. I was hard on Anthony. He wasn't too interested in school and I thought that was such a waste as he had a great Maths brain. I pushed him to study. I remember I shouted at him a lot. Anthony never spoke to me about his worries or fears; he was always a quiet lad.

I remember when he was seven and he had gone off with his friends for an hour and a half, to the Cabra road without my permission. I was worried sick as I didn't know where he was. When he arrived home I was livid with anger. I smacked him so hard on his bottom, with his clothes on, at least seven times. I was shouting at him for causing me so much worry. I actually lost Anthony then, he never trusted me after that.

He did really well in his Leaving Certificate state exams when he was 18, getting 325 points but I could sense Anthony felt it wasn't good enough for me. I was happy at the result, but he needed 345 points for the course he wanted, so he decided not to take a different college course and he took the roofing trade working for his Dad's company. He had wanted to do that at Junior Certificate level, but I wanted him to continue his education. I don't regret that decision; at least he was 18 after Leaving cert and he was a bit more mature making his decisions. Sometimes a mother is not popular even when she's doing the right stuff, but I also feel Anthony would have done just as well at the roofing trade at age 16.

I never met Anthony's emotional needs when he was a child. I remember one time his friends were bashing him on the street and I told him to take the hurl stick and hit them with it. I couldn't understand why he couldn't stand up for himself. I was always on alert for self-defence; I didn't understand that Anthony didn't want to be that way. He didn't want to fight. He didn't need to fight.

I loved Anthony and I thought I was doing an ok job as a parent . I performed the duties of a mother. I cleaned, I cooked, I took him to his activities and I loved him so much but I don't think I showed it in the right way. There's no point in telling someone you love them, then you treat them with disrespect. That's not love.

I did try to do fun things with him and when President Clinton came to visit in December 1995, I was so excited. I liked Clinton, he was a rogue. If my husband was in American

Office, he probably would have done the same with Monica! I didn't hold it against him.

Anthony was just six years old and I took him on the back of my bike and I cycled into town where Clinton was speaking at the Central Bank of Ireland, Dame Street. I pushed my way to the throngs of people trying to find a place for my son to see. There was a vacant postbox as close to the front as I could get. I popped Anthony on top with me beside him. Everybody was in great form and they helped this little lad see a great President. Anthony asked me, 'Who is it, Mam?'

I said, "It's The President of The United States of America. He's a good man!" I had heard the Herald newspaper had a photo of myself and my son on that postbox that day, but I couldn't find it.

Where I fell down was my controlling way of parenting. I shouted a lot to get him to do his stuff. I used violence when I thought he was bold and I scared him. The result of that was I lost my child. For good. The damage I did as a parent in those early years of Anthony's life turned him off me as a parent forever. I can never get it back again no matter how hard I try.

I messed up in those early years of child rearing. My strictness helped sometimes. I feel I taught him to always be a worker, even if college wasn't for him at that time, he should always leave the door open to education.

Anthony has a great work ethic; he's an early riser and goes to work at 6.30 am to pick up other lads. He's really skilled at his job and I'm really proud of him. He's good with his hands.

Anthony never answered me back as a child, he was softly spoken. He was a good kid and gave me no trouble, but it was hard for me to know how he was feeling. I think when Sarah came along, and there was so much going on in my life during those years, that I let the bond slip with my son. I hadn't taken the time to listen to Anthony, or Sarah.

Anthony's love was Motor Cross track racing and his Yamaha 450 scrambler. He loved fixing up his bike and racing in Gorman's town every weekend. And Skerries. His good pals Thomas and John arrived at our house early on Sunday mornings getting the bikes ready to go racing. I was really proud of Anthony's strength and skill. He was a handsome lad, at six feet tall, fit and lean with fair hair and blue eyes.

Anthony left home when he was just over 18. I was devastated. I knew Anthony left home because I was a bad mother to him. I hated myself.

The recession had also hit in 2007. Myself and my husband had invested all our money into property, and the property market hit the floor. Although our properties were rented out, the rental income decreased and the mortgage repayments increased, we had to find money to subsidize the repayments.

Our two daughters educational needs were high cost and necessary. We didn't apply for any social welfare help, we knew we weren't entitled to it because we were still working and earning an income. We heard horror stories of how people were belittled by the people who worked in the social welfare offices, making them feel like they were beggars. It wasn't these people's fault that the construction industry fell, leaving quantity surveyors and architects unemployed.

It demoralized these previous PAYE workers.

One day my husband's aunty Phoebe and her husband Dave came to see us from London. They had a gift of some money for Yasmin's needs. I was mortified and of course I didn't want to take it, but that was a huge help that month. Thanks Aunty Phoebe.

There were lots of little things like that the family did to help. For the kids' birthdays my sister-in-law Carmel and Aunty Josie and our friends gave money for their birthdays. It got them the things they needed.

I started to shop around for my groceries in Lidl and Aldi comparing prices. I became an expert in prices everywhere, even in fashion and utilities! I had a teenager who loved fashion and makeup, I had to find the brands she wanted, at the best price.

I normally bought a cappuccino every day in a coffee shop, now I made my own coffee, I bought a little coffee pot in TK Maxx for 12 euro, and I use Roberts's coffee, now I make myself an espresso at home, its great! Still conscious of feeding my family nutritiously I bought fruit and vegetables sometimes on Moore Street in Dublin and I mastered making delicious chicken or beef stews that could last two or three days. My Ma would also make a pot of beef stew every Tuesday for me and I'm not too bad at baking muffins, I must take after my aunty Biddy!

I didn't buy luxury moisturizers anymore for myself anymore, even Nivea Q10 was a luxury. I shopped for cheaper ladies essentials and bought the proper simple face washes for Sarah's teenage spots. I searched the last date in the meat section, so I could still buy steak and chicken and fish for my family at a cheaper price. Our other bills like mortgage and fuel bills were high so they had to be paid. Grocery costs was the only place I could save. I stopped wasting money on food. My bins got lighter! I felt no shame if I had to put a few things back at checkout.

A mother does what she has to do.

I still couldn't help the worry I felt inside when my husband had to try balance the huge outgoings every month.

I don't know how my husband didn't succumb to alcohol during that time or collapse with stress or depression himself. Every time another loss came in, I reminded him that we always had suffered losses even in during the boom time. There was one company in the height of the boom that just refused to pay my husband's company 100,000 pounds, as was the currency in the year 2000. That put a deep hole in his company even then and he had survived. I told him not to think of what's gone, just move forward.

Companies were going bankrupt every day, Zoe development, and Pierce Contractors and many more that my husband's company contracted for, all went out of business. NAMA, National Asset Management Agency, was set up to repossess all the property that had failed on its loans. They would re-sell them and try regain some of the money back for the state. NAMA annihilated many large companies, putting them out of business.

My husband's company had losses of hundreds of thousands of Euros, and the losses were still coming. People my husband knew were taking their own lives violently. Good friends of his were annihilated by the tax man and the banks.

I couldn't understand the logic of our government. Shouldn't they be doing everything in their power to keep companies employing people instead of shutting them down because they were late on their taxes or bank loans?

Didn't we take the hit from the government bailing out the banks? What about the ordinary people? Struggling to pay their mortgages and keeping their homes they worked hard for.

Our other political parties were happy to blame Fianna Fail for the collapse of our country, not taking into consideration the rest of the world was under economic collapse also; nor the master redevelopment of our country during the boom years. Building competitive roads, redesigning Dublin city with new modern buildings and bridges to attract tourists worldwide. We have beautiful hotels and restaurants throughout Ireland because of Fianna Fail.

Fianna Fail would never have let the banks shut down great construction companies and let the industry fall purposefully. Forcing thousands of talented workers on the dole queue, or again, to emigrate to Australia and the wild west of Canada in search of better futures for their children, like my beloved sister Elle and husband Hugo and children Sean and Grace

There was doom and gloom everywhere. It was really sad to see people lose everything they worked hard for. We had our worries, but I really felt the pain of all our friends suffering.

I tried playing the Euro lotto for a while, convinced when I'd win, I'd help everyone I knew. I never won and thankfully because I'm not a gambler, I didn't continue on that losing road.

I remember that Ireland changed during the Celtic Tiger . There was a huge divide. The ordinary working person had never experienced The Tiger. They had no opportunity to earn extra income. It did seem that riches followed riches. The wealthy were able to invest money into successful ventures leaving ordinary workers resentful. When all of it failed, it was the ordinary person left carrying the debt and that is why the Irish are resentful.

Ok, so there was a fair amount of work and risk attached to becoming wealthy. It took hard work, consistency and drive. Their motivation was to earn money, but they got greedy, forgetting others.

For the smaller businesses like my husband's, there was a lot of risk involved. The stress and long hours often play havoc with these men's health and their marriages. The wives had to carry the weight of rearing the children on their own with many lonely nights, or the husbands with preoccupied minds of how to pay the bills.

I don't know how my husband's company survived after the losses he received. He had to deal with the devil himself a couple of times to keep his company afloat.

After putting millions of euros through the bank in the previous 20 years and continuing to pay his way, the bank wasn't very helpful for other things.

The Tax man was the annihilator himself!

Finding small amounts owing from years previously had now grown ten times the debt! It was crazy.

Similar issues were happening to many businesses because of incompetent staff in the tax office, forcing them into solvency because they couldn't afford to pay the debt.

There was actually no benefit in investing in property for our old age. The government had his back covered every way. As we all have experienced the new high costs of property tax, not taking into account the stamp duty tax and huge planning permission costs. It seems the government is telling you where to put your money, when it suits them, but actually, even if you have invested in a good pension fund, you can't take it out in a lump sum when you retire at 65. A person with an average 70,000 euro pension saved can take 10,000 out on retirement, and the rest gets paid monthly at a measly sum of 130.00 euros a month, for the rest of your life! Unless of course you're in government and then you can receive your pension in lump sum on retirement!! Very fair.

My husband kept at it. He had a good team of men working for him and he had a good head for business. He chased any kind of work all over the country.

So Merkel may be delighted with Enda's dedication in paying back the deficit . but unfortunately, he took the money from the poor.

Would our politicians swap places with the working class Ireland? Would they say that they worked their way up to the top? They deserve to be there maybe?

Maybe we should remind them that we voted for them on good principle that they wouldn't leave us behind....

Life was very stressful; it was hard not to be an emotional mess.

It affected my sex drive also, I had little or no libido. I knew the importance of continuing our intimacy. I was very conscious that my hubby needed the physical connection, whereas most of the time, I'd be happy to just go to sleep.

I felt guilty if I didn't perform. That was another weight on my shoulders. I personally blame the young people's magazines when I was young, telling us young women that our men need to have regular sex every night, in all sorts of positions or your man will get bored. I was brainwashed by this!

I grew up in the 70s where men still had a lot of rights. Us girls were conditioned to look after our men.

You know, I don't buy this anymore. A woman has times when she feels in the mood. If her man isn't around, she quietly looks after herself.

If a man is in the mood, and his woman is tired, ill or just not in the mood. Instead of a sulk, can't he just sort himself out? Who's to say his orgasm is more important than a woman's orgasm? Or more needed? Who's to say that it's better for a man if he enters an orifice? Doesn't he climax just as well from sorting himself out?

Or is it really that a man is just so used to women looking after their needs that they are conditioned to thinking it's their right?

Of course, sorting himself out would require effort from the man …I'm just saying…

Either way, myself and my husband focused on keeping our sex life going throughout the years and that probably wasn't a bad thing.

I booked private counselling with an English woman, Linda Keen. She was in her mid-50s and had lots of life experiences as well as lots of qualifications. I was in bits when I arrived to Linda. I didn't know which problem to talk about at first. There were so many!

It took two years to work through my stuff with my Husband. I would still be going there if Linda hadn't moved back to England!

It was really expensive but valuable to us. Linda was really good and made us delve deep into our lives to try work a lot of things out. We had taken each other for granted in our marriage and forgotten what was important to each of us. We stopped giving each other attention.

We were suspicious of each other and resented each other.

Linda also helped me work on my relationship with our son Anthony. I had to respect the fact that he wanted to live away from home, and be grateful for all that he was. He was independent, self-sufficient. He was a worker.

I had to try focus on the positive. Instead of phoning Anthony just to ask him to do a chore for me, I had to just phone him to see how he was getting on. It was a start down the right road. It really improved our relationship.

I had got out of the habit of taking care of myself since I had Yasmin. I needed to make time for myself. While Yasmin was in Montessori I went swimming twice a week and went walking regularly. I made a better effort on eating well.

And I went back on medication for the second time.

Some people believe that you don't need medication, that you can get well on your own, but that wasn't true for me, believe me I tried. I obviously have no serotonin in my brain and I needed that chemical. Likewise, you can't just take medication and not do the work to find out why you suffer with depression, why you hate yourself, why you have such low self-esteem.

So, all of this combined really helped me, and I really started to get to know me then, I was 41. It wasn't an easy road, and I was only starting.

Some Psychiatrists have a theory about depression; If a child is malnourished in his childhood, the brain does not develop properly, so leading into various forms of Depression, or maybe passing on an imperfect gene to the next generation.

Bi-Polar and Schizophrenia are some well known conditions that Psychiatrists are working on, as there seems to be direct connections with children with Learning difficulties and their parents who have depression. There seems to be such an epidemic of children with learning difficulties in Ireland today, 2013.

Both mine and my husband's grandparents' were born in the 1900s in Ireland when poverty and hunger was commonplace. Vital nutrients were missing in our ancestor's brain growth, therefore, causing faults in the brain development that is passed on through the generations.

Besides everything going on in my life, I loved being at home with Yasmin. She was adorable. When it was time to have solids, I made all my own soups and I gave her every variety of food. She was really good at eating finger foods at eight months and I proudly sat her on the potty from nine months so she was toilet trained by two years old.

She started to get car sickness when she was about 11 months and it continued all the way till she was a good year in Occupation therapy at about six and a half years old.

It was quite violent and everything in her tummy would come up. It happened on every journey, no matter how short a distance and often twice a day. I went through a lot of car seats and spent many times stopping on the side of the road cleaning her off.

One time, I was picking up Sarah from her horse at Broadmeadow Equestrian Stables on the Swords road. It was a wintry dark evening about 6.30. Yasmin started to scream in the back, "sick, sick!" She would get very scared getting sick. Sarah's stomach would turn when Yasmin got sick so she didn't like help Yasmin in the car. I asked Sarah to pass a bag quickly to Yasmin and Sarah without looking passed a bag back to her in the back seat. Yasmin would make a lot of noise while throwing up and Sarah was complaining. Yasmin was finished and couldn't hold the bag so I asked Sarah to take it from her to prevent it spilling all over the car. Sarah reluctantly took the bag of sick without looking. Sarah was complaining about holding the bag of sick. She shouted, "For God's sake its leaking!" and I said "Oh just throw it quickly out through the window then!" I was still driving and I just wanted to get home. Yasmin also needed to have all the windows open in the car while driving, even in freezing temperatures. Actually, Sarah did too when she was little. I can tell you, it was very uncomfortable driving with my girls!

Sarah threw the bag out of the front window. The sick flew in the window in the back all over Yasmin and the car!

We were all screaming then, it was chaos!

You might wonder why I didn't stop the car, but more often than not, I stopped the car. Sometimes, I just couldn't. I couldn't do anything. It was one of the most difficult parts of Yasmin's difficulty.

I couldn't tackle the clean-up job on the car till the next day. I was weary.

I was always praying to God for help and guidance, every morning, to keep us all safe and well and every night to thank him for doing so.

I woke in the mornings feeling guilty, for everything, for anything. I couldn't do anything right. I was hard on myself over everything. I felt guilty I wasn't a good enough Mother, I felt guilty I wasn't a good enough wife, I felt guilty I wasn't a good earner. I blamed myself a lot. I was anxious all the time. I prayed to Mother Mary every night also, to help me do it better.

Yasmin was also extremely clingy to me and I found it hard to go anywhere without her being attached to my leg. She wouldn't even stay with her daddy then. Anto felt slightly put out but because she would get so hysterical he was happy I took the job.

She cried hysterically and had huge tantrums, she couldn't be consoled, it was quite scary. She was extremely nervous of new people or places, and she cried for no apparent reason.

Yasmin hated having baths, she screamed when she getting washed at all even her hands and face. She was terrified of showers and she hated getting her teeth washed. She begged me not to wash her hair. I didn't understand this at all because Sarah had loved her baths and would play for hours in them.

I just got on with it as gently and firmly as I could. She had to be washed!

She did suffer badly with eczema and I only used Silcock's base but it didn't seem to make a difference. I did think she had some allergies at that point that was causing her distress and proceeded to have all the blood tests. The first time Yasmin noticed she was having an injection, she screamed and pulled her arm away leaving quite a tear in her skin. The nurse got a terrible fright.

Yasmin has a beautiful thick main of hair, and I often left it two weeks without washing, because of the stress involved.

Yasmin had contracted her first and only case of head lice when she was three and a half years old. As I treated her head and washed and combed out the nits, she screamed hysterically and cried, "Please Mammy stop, please Mammy stop!". I knew she wasn't being bold, she was in genuine pain. She sobbed herself to sleep while I was still combing her hair. I was really scared for Yasmin and confused, I knew something wasn't right.

I was giving Yasmin a bath one evening, and she was screaming hysterically, in obvious pain. This screaming was the worst I had ever heard. It was like she had been scaled to bits. She was screaming in pain. She was holding her privates area. I was checking and couldn't see any rash or redness but I couldn't console her. I was terrified!

I didn't know how to help Yasmin.

Yasmin was very impulsive and easily excited, she was extremely hyper. She never sat and watched television.

She had lots of falls and I couldn't take my eyes off her. If I did, something would surely happen. I felt she was still a baby, that she hadn't matured much at age three. Her speech was still very babyish.

I did at least get Yasmin to start Montessori school in Ratoath when she was three. It took three weeks to settle her in.

Yasmin's Montessori teacher Andrea Magennus was really kind and she had a lot of patients for Yasmin. The classroom was like a home environment so Yasmin felt very comfortable there.

Yasmin had an age three developmental check-up in Dunshaughlin Health Centre. The nurse suggested that Yasmin have a speech and language assessment, because of her poor speech and proceeded to put Yasmin on the waiting list.

I wasn't overly concerned with Yasmin's speech problem then and thought her difficulties were similar to Sarah's and that she inevitably would be fine.

Although I didn't have any assessments for Yasmin at that time, I knew Yasmin had a delayed mental development. In layman's terms it means if your 3 year old still behaves like a baby, then its most likely that they are still a baby in their brains. I knew I didn't need to rush that appointment.

I knew Yasmin was more babyish than other kids, but I was more concerned about her behaviour in those early years. She was hyper active, never sitting still even to sit and watch TV for a while. Then, the strangest thing was, she would complain about being really tired, but she still couldn't sit still.

At 4 years of age, Yasmin said to me, 'Why are my bones so tired mammy?' I didn't understand it myself.

She was traumatized easily. She was terrified of things, sounds. She had no sense of danger. She would approach strangers in shopping centres. She would wander away from me in the grocery store and not answer my calls. One time when I was in River Island in Blanchardstown mall, Yasmin disappeared from my sight for 20 minutes. I was hysterical, insisting they close the shop till we found her.

Yasmin was sitting under a hanger of clothes unaware that the fuss was for her.

Another time when she was four years of age we went away on a weekend to Cavan to a show jumping event with lots of Sarah's friends from Broadmeadows.

Yasmin was all excited as Ma and I checked into the hotel while Anto and the rest of our party checked into the stables.

Ma and I decided to have a class of wine in the lobby and some milk and cookies for Yasmin.

Yasmin got up to wander around when she was finished. I never took my eyes off Yasmin because at the very least, I thought she was accident prone. As Yasmin approached a cabinet I got up from my chair to take her away. I also called out the instruction, she was only a few feet from me.

When the huge piece of furniture collapsed onto my little girl, I was traumatised. Ma and I lifted the cabinet off Yasmin and I figured it was about 20 stone in weight. Yasmin's arms were across her chest which prevented her heart from being crushed but her right knee was purple instantly and it was limp. She was screaming in agony. I somehow functioned as a Mother and called an ambulance. Yasmin didn't stop screaming in pain till the nurses administered morphine at the hospital. She had broken her leg really badly. Thankfully she recovered well as children do but I was devastated to see my baby suffer like that.

I couldn't believe it, I was always right beside her and still, she would hurt herself. She had broken arms, wrists, elbows and deep cuts from various falls.

I felt such a failure as her mammy. I was on edge all the time. I needed help.

I called the ADHD helpline around that time, and spoke to a lovely man who was great help. I voiced my concerns to him about Yasmin, how she would scream and hit me when I was washing her, I was sure she had ADHD from what I knew about it. He told me wisely to take control of Yasmin's bad behaviour at that point; He said if Yasmin is behaving badly, give her a warning and then a consequence. Tell her bad behaviour is unacceptable and give her time out and not to allow her to hit.

Now, as parents, we may all say, 'That's what I do and it doesn't work!' I didn't say that because I didn't know what to do, I was too emotionally attached. So I took his advice and tried his method. I had nothing to lose.

I decided to wait for my first assessment for Yasmin and follow the advice from there on. All young children with learning difficulties show similar ADHD symptoms because of their frustrations. I needed to have Yasmin properly assessed.

I was really comforted from the help line. I felt there was hope and I calmed down. I started putting to practice the advice the man gave me. When Yasmin started her tantrums and hitting, I would tell her it was unacceptable, give her a warning and if she continued, I would give her time out on the bottom stair.

I was to be firm but kind, but to carry out the time out.

This really worked for Yasmin, maybe because she was a girl, or maybe because she was only four and a half, I don't know. I knew she was scared when she was out of control. Now when I corrected her behaviour constructively, I saw in her eyes the relief that I now, was in control in a loving way. She used to say, "Not the step, Mammy, not the step!"

She would have to say sorry for the bad behaviour, and then I would forgive her and hug her: Poor little pet.

During this time, my husband didn't really think Yasmin had any difficulties. He thought that my depression had affected everybody in the house including Yasmin and he was just hoping it would all work out in the end.

I did try to perform and cope as best I could with my depression. It was a good thing that Sarah's horse sport took up a lot of our time. Preparing Sarah for training and traveling to various events added a bit of fun to the kids' lives. Yasmin loved the horses too and loved going to watch Sarah and her friend Anna compete at high level in show jumping events. They were Yasmin's hero's. She was so excited going to the RDS qualifiers to see Anna and Sarah succeed and also other girls from Broadmeadow.

I'd pack a picnic and Anto would get the trailer ready, Sarah would get her horse ready with Yasmin looking on, eager to help with any little thing. It was mostly 5.30am starts every weekend, so it kept me focused, and my mind occupied.

It was one of my most proudest moments, when Sarah did qualify for the RDS when she was 14. Although it was the Equitation Class, based on how you perform as a rider and how you control your horse, we were really proud of her.

Anna and her dad Brian had qualified too for higher classes, so we all packed up and off we went. Yasmin dreams of one day going in the truck with Anna!

Yasmin and I loved the buzz of the early 5.30am start in the stables and I'd get a coffee. We'd eagerly await the girl's jumping class.

The crowds and shopping stalls were too much stimulation for Yasmin, she was much happier hanging in the stables.

During my hectic life of mobile hairdressing, I also travelled to a Day centre once a week for Alzheimer patients to style their hairs. It was located at Heskin court, close to Blackrock, South Dublin.

I styled all the ladies and gent's hairs, cut and sets, perms, colours and blow dry. I loved being with the old people, doing their hairs and talking to them. Some of them with early Alzheimer's were really funny and they'd laugh at their own oddities, knowing that soon enough, they would be like the others with no knowledge of where they were or who they were.

The carer's that took care of them in that centre and others were doing an amazing job. I saw them treat these people with the fondness of an infant.

They didn't all have Alzheimer's and I met some lovely women, who will stay in my heart. Sarah, who was 72 suffered kidney failure and had to travel to the Mater Hospital three times a week for dialysis. She walked with a walking frame as she was recovering from a broken pelvis, 'She was in bits!' She often said. One day she told me how she had received her broken shoulder. She told me her friend took her to a big Department store in Dublin to buy a dress for an upcoming wedding. Sarah was in her wheelchair, but it was easy to manoeuvre around the big store and they had caught the lift up to the first floor. When they had bought the dress for Sarah there was a big queue for the lift. Her friend, impatient to leave, decided to risk the escalator with Sarah in the wheelchair!

The inevitable happened. Sarah toppled head first down the steps of the escalator in her wheelchair! People all around her were in shock, screaming for help. Sarah was miraculously fine and there were no new injuries to her load!

The department store called an ambulance for precaution, to get Sarah checked out. Sarah was mortified as she was strapped to the ambulance stretcher and taken away to the hospital.

On arrival at the hospital, the ambulance men proceeded to remove Sarah from the ambulance and deliver her into the casualty department. As the two paramedics lifted the stretcher from the ambulance, one of their hands slipped and the stretcher fell heavily to the ground with Sarah strapped in it! Unable to save herself, she landed on her shoulder and shattered it, leaving her in unmerciful pain. Afterwards, she was left strapped up for months disabling her already bad mobility.

Sarah was laughing so hard telling me the story. She was great. She had six sons, and Mark was her youngest at 37. Mark came over often and helped Sarah a lot. As a gay man, he had a great personality and a caring disposition.

While Sarah sat for hours in the salon getting her hair done, Mark would bring down sandwiches for Sarah and myself. We got on really well.

There was another lovely woman Maureen. She was a quite gentle lady, not 60 yet. Maureen loved coming to get her hair done. She told me of the depression she suffered, and sometimes when it got very dark for her. I told her of my struggles. She encouraged me to keep going.

Maureen had one son whom she adored. The high light of her life was his upcoming wedding to a girl she loved too. We talked about what she would wear and how I would do her hair. She was so excited and also worried like any Mother of the groom, how the day would go with the in Law's and relatives.

The day went off without a hitch and Maureen was so happy.

I was very stressed when I arrived at Heskin. I knew my time was limited between school pick up and I was always rushing. I would only make about 50 euro at the day centre because I hadn't the heart to charge them much money. To save time, I would go through the Port tunnel and it cost 10 euro in the morning and 10 euro on the way back. Petrol was so expensive, so I wasn't actually making any money.

I was going through an emotional tough time at that point, so I had to give up doing the Day Centre. I know those women missed me coming there, like I missed them. I was so sad to hear that Maureen died shortly after that.

That summer 2009, we booked a holiday to Santa Monica in Los Angeles. We brought my sister Josie's daughter Rebecca along with Sarah and Yasmin. It was our first time on the west coast and we were all in good form, even Anto, who was getting quite grumbly at the cost of everything in life!

Santa Monica is very family orientated. It has the well-known Santa Monica Pier where the Santa Monica officials decided Route 66 should end to attract tourism. The famous Chicago to Los Angeles Route 66 officially ended on the corner of 7th street and Broadway in downtown Los Angeles. Forest Gump made his first stop on the Santa Monica Harbour before running across to the east of the Country. Patrons have built a restaurant in his honour on the pier called Bubba Gump and it sells all kind of good memorabilia and dishes up great fish.

The Pier has all sorts of family amusements, with a big wheel and also little game stands. They also have a not too scary roller coaster that I actually got on!

The Pacific Ocean's waves are huge and they entice kids and adults alike to enter the water on body boards and surf boards.

It reminded me of Bray beach, maybe it was just a bit warmer and it was sandy, not stony.

Los Angeles doesn't have the humid heat of Florida, so when five pm arrives, so does a chill. I always loved swimming in the Ocean. Dalkey beach is my most favourite. It has beautiful clean deep fresh water. I haven't been there since I was 20.

Santa Monica beach was very similar though and I stood in the ocean looking onto the beach with the sun on my back. It was beautiful. The kids all loved the simple beach holiday.

After a few days in Santa Monica, our next stop was Las Vegas. It was a four and a half hour drive and our route took us through the Mojave Desert. It was dry orange sand all the way in the steep grade heading up to Cajon Pass.

Cajon pass is a mountain pass between the San Bernardino Mountains and San Gabriel Mountains. It went on for hundreds of miles.

The sights were breathtaking. I could imagine the old Wild West movies being made there, as the land was dry and thirsty. There was a mile long freight train that chugged all the way to Vegas.

As we approached the end of our journey, we could see Vegas in the distance, I couldn't believe we were in Las Vegas. It was so exciting. We were booked into The Grand MGM Hotel. It was really cheap to stay there, but we were very impressed. The lobby was huge, with spectacular chandeliers and life size gold ornaments. There was a city of restaurants and shops in our hotel!

Anto went straight to the casino to check it out and us girls went straight to the pool, which was a fancy maze of different interconnecting sections of water paradise for the kids.

The deep blue sky and the heat was brilliant and the three days in Las Vegas was really relaxing. I also found the shopping there so much cheaper for our kids favourite designer brands.

On the way back to Los Angeles, we were all giggling in the car. We were all in good form after being awed by the sights of Vegas. Anto had won 1100 dollars on a game of craps, which involve dice. Thankfully Anto is not a gambler, so he took his money and ran, but he could not believe the people beside him betting hundreds of thousands of dollars.

Three hours in on our journey back to Los Angeles, Yasmin needed to go the toilet. As it was near dusk, I didn't fancy stopping in the desert, for fear of snakes and spiders. I had a bucket in the car and told Yasmin to go on it while we were still driving. When Yasmin finished, the teenagers were having a fit in the back of the car, screaming, 'Throw it out! ugh!'

Yasmin was laughing and laughing and I said to Anto, 'Just pull over anywhere. I'll dump this out!'

Anto was also laughing so hard too at the teenagers who were kicking up a fuss. The strong descending sun was blinding his eyes and he somehow lost control of the car. It skidded on its side. We were all screaming then in terror, until he managed to finally get it to a standstill, after crashing into a road sign called, 'Death Valley!'

Amazingly the bucket of pooh didn't spill over!

Death Valley is in the town Beatty, Nevada, in the eastern part of the Mojave Desert and is known for devastatingly beautiful sunsets, which I indeed did witness.

We all got out of the car to survey the damage and laughed at the state of it. It was drivable though. Thank God we had taken out the extra insurance.

Death Valley, as the names suggests, is very creepy. It's famous for being one of the hottest places on earth and the driest. Even as the sun descended fast behind the mountains it was still really hot. The others were eager to look around but I was keen to get into the car to safety and away from poisonous snakes. There were times when our holidays went really good and I was really grateful for that.

Anthony is a great Daddy in the house, the fun element, where I am the serious one. I get all the stuff done, homework, activities, nutrition and when Daddy comes home he just makes everyone laugh.

I always felt that I had to be the proper parent, or the serious one in raising the kids, especially where education was involved.

Anthony didn't see what all the fuss was about with education, as he had none and he was a good business man. I felt I was on my own sometimes, I felt I didn't get the support I needed from him. It caused me to resent him, causing other problems in our marriage.

I did resent the fact that he could laugh all the time in the family and I was so tense! Sometimes he laughed Yasmin out of bad behaviour and that wasn't a good idea at all.

I've since discovered my husband has being doing exactly that all through our marriage, laughing off his bad behaviour.

When I want to talk serious, he listens for a minute until he hears something he doesn't like. He then shrugs it off, not wanting to or not able to deal with anything serious, because then he would have to take responsibility for his behaviour and inevitably, address the bad behaviour, or maybe grow up? So, he actually finds laughing easier than dealing with problems.

Eventually though, Anto did get on board a little with the new tactics because he could see the good results coming through.

Yasmin was aged five now and had finished two years in montessori. She had just started Rathbeggan National School and my little happy child turned into an anxious child in those first two weeks. Yasmin had started to wet her pants and her bed, something she never did before.

Yasmin's first assessment with Louise Mc Donaugh came for the 12th September 2009. Louise was head of the Speech and Language department in Dunboyne. It was a free service provided by the HSE, Health Service Executive, for children on a waiting list referred to by their doctor or health visitor. Yasmin was waiting two years for this appointment.

Yasmin's montessori teacher Andrea had previously performed an early assessment on Yasmin. She had showed significant difficulties. She suggested Yasmin not start school till the following year. I did agree with her. I knew it made sense, but the recession was well under way in 2009 and sometimes school seems the more affordable option.

Louise Mc Donaugh was a young woman about 30. She was very precise and direct and came across a bit abrupt, but she knew her job well and she was keen to help Yasmin.

She found that Yasmin had no comprehension of tasks or commands. That was huge. That meant that Yasmin basically had no idea of what was going on around her, so although she was five, she really was like a two year old.

I was relieved to find this out. I knew we had to go on at a slower pace for Yasmin. Some might not want such a result for their child, but when a child gets a proper diagnosis, they can start getting proper help.

I never once aloud myself to think that Yasmin wouldn't come on. She was a beautiful loving child. She had mastered eating, sleeping, toilet training. She was hugely interested in the stars, the planets, the ocean. She loved sea shells and stones and she tasted everything in her mouth!

She loved our dogs and they loved her back. She loved her big brother Anthony and her big sister Sarah and was a regular at Broad meadows horse yard where Sarah kept her horse Marley.

She showed no fear walking between the horse's legs. The horses watched Yasmin walking with her Mother and they with their Colts, I could feel their understanding of Mother and Child.

I then took the unprecedented step of taking Yasmin out of school and putting her back into the montessori/preschool environment. That was to give Yasmin time to learn at her own pace. If she had no comprehension of tasks or commands, that meant she couldn't process the information in the classroom.

Yasmin settled back easily into the montessori.

She immediately calmed down and soon stopped wetting her pants, she was happier in herself.

Most parents don't realize that school is very formal and children are expected to perform as young as four years of age. It puts even clever children under a lot of pressure, to sit still for long hours, to take in information, to follow instructions.

We were now on the right road to Yasmin's education.

Louise Mc Donaugh was to be 'Core' help for Yasmin. She was continuously helping Yasmin with her speech and language comprehension difficulties for two years and guiding me to various assessments.

Yasmin was then moved to James Delaganey in Dunshaughlin for further help with comprehension and I found him professional kind and patient.

In October 2009 Louise also referred Yasmin to Jan Meyer, a child Psychiatrist for the HSE. He assessed Yasmin for her anxiety and nervousness.

Jan was in his mid-40s and had children of his own. He was really kind and patient with Yasmin. She liked him straight away. He asked me about my history as it's really important in order to help the child. Jan needed to see how we lived at home warts and all. I wasn't afraid to give Jan all my gory details, because at this point in my life I knew everybody has their own personal struggles and you need to face them in order to change and grow. He also asked about the other kids in the family.

I mentioned my other daughter Sarah who was going through some strange behaviour at the time. She was 14 and was excessively washing her hands. I put it down to the changes of secondary school. She was also increasingly worried about germs. She had got so bad she wouldn't even touch clothes that fell onto the floor!

Jan had Sarah seen to straight away by Martina O Shea psychologist nurse for children and adolescents for mental health in Navan, also HSE.

Both Anto and I and Sarah had to attend Martina's sessions. Martina was a wonderful lady and was there to help Sarah. She was direct and firm to Anto and I.

Sarah hated going to these sessions initially, because she didn't want to talk about anything. Actually, she didn't know how to express herself as she always felt she had no voice in the family. When she did start opening up and talking, there was a lot of things she said about me that I didn't like to hear. But I told her it was ok, she could say anything she wanted to. Martina pointed things out to me that was not proper parenting. I respected her and I was glad she was on Sarah's side. We went there for nearly two years and it really changed things in our house.

I think all parents have a difficultly adapting to their children becoming teenagers. We forget that we need to listen to them. Sarah needed to have a voice in the family.

I felt very lucky to be receiving this help from the HSE. The therapists were really helpful to my children.

Jan saw Yasmin for about a year. He determined that Yasmin didn't appear to have mental issues, but there was something there that needed to be addressed. I appreciated the help Jan gave us.

He referred Yasmin on to Emir Crowley, an Occupational Therapist who could do a special assessment on fine motor skills. At this point I had to start paying privately as the waiting list for OT assessments were two years long on the HSE. In fact Yasmin was called just over three years later on that list.

Up until now, we were covered by the HSE. Now we had to make a decision. In order to help our five year old child, we would have to pay hundreds and thousands of euros throughout the coming years for private help.

We had to make a lot of personal sacrifices, but we were both still working and we were able to cover Yasmin's costs, just about!

Yasmin was one of the lucky ones. She received help.

It made me angry and annoyed that other children had to wait three years to get Occupation assessments and other necessary assessments. In those two to three years, those little children had to suffer. Suffer in school, not being able to cope with processing information, suffer in social areas of their life, affecting their self-esteem hugely. Their parents struggling to cope at home, not able to help their beloved children.

I was so mad! I rang up the Joe Duffy radio show, angry. I was angry about the recession. I was angry about the children's educational needs being cut again. They didn't put me on air, obviously thinking I was a mad woman, I was.

In the days following the Fianna Gail electoral, the new government start cutting poor people's allowances. What was wrong with these men in power? Didn't they realize, that with poverty comes dysfunction? Families had no resources to help to educate their children. Had they no idea that these poor people had no way of paying for their children's necessary assessments as it was?

Our government doesn't have a clue.

In the future, every Mother in this country will be looking for a government who will provide the educational needs for their children.

It saddened me. I felt guilty that we could provide for Yasmin needs, barely. Education is especially important for children with learning difficulties or disabilities. They need it more, not less than the average child. Our children with disabilities can be educated and they can make a vital contribution to this world. They should have every chance. Our government knows this, but chooses to put the children last.

Like any mother, I will sacrifice everything to have Yasmin's educational and emotional needs met.

We got an appointment with Emir Crowley Occupational Therapist in 2009. Emir was a young married woman with children of her own.

She's a petit little thing, and passionate about her job. She diagnosed Yasmin with Dyspraxia and severe sensory difficulties; This explains Yasmin's hatred of washing as water felt like pain on her skin! Hair brushing feels like stabbing her scalp.

Yasmin was also referred by Emir to Dr Sinead Hearty in Drogheda Hospital to confirm Dyspraxia. This did scare me, because Dyspraxia is a Neurological disorder, it affects the three processes of Ideation, Organisation and Execution. It effects Yasmin's processing information, effecting her learning ability and carrying out tasks and normal body movements.

This diagnosis was important to the educational department. They allocated resource hours to Yasmin in school, to help her learn, she ended up getting two and half hours each week. This meant that Yasmin was taken out of class for a half hour each day and given some physical exercises and phonics and maths help.

A child can only get these resources when they have had their assessments and diagnosis! So children on two and three year waiting lists have no diagnosis and therefore receive no help in those important early years.

Teachers are trying to help by meeting the needs of children with learning difficulties with no assistance, leaving them stressed and overworked; Mrs Clinton, Yasmin's resource teacher, does lots of work with Yasmin and gives her lots of praise and encouragement, she has loads of patience. She also works many unpaid hours trying to help other children with no diagnosis, who are struggling in school.

Yasmin started to see Emir regularly for OT. Emir works on Yasmin's muscles, balance, coordination and finger muscles. She has used various methods for Yasmin's sensory difficulties also. Within a year, there was an immediate improvement in car sickness alone.

There were still a lot of difficulties though and Yasmin was in school at this point. Getting out of the house in the morning to school was a huge struggle. As washing was so difficult, hair brushing caused hysteria and certain knickers wouldn't work. Yasmin couldn't wear vests, socks were a nightmare!

I felt and looked like I was going through a crazy obstacle course each morning. I had come off the medication again when Yasmin turned 6 because I felt well and thought I could do without it.

I was really stressed at this point and when Yasmin went through the school doors, my own tears would come.

I don't know how I coped then. Looking back, I didn't tell anyone how hard I was finding everything, not even my husband, or my family. I didn't want anyone feeling sorry for me.

I was very possessive with Yasmin. Although I let her go on a few play dates, I was terrified she would fall and hurt herself, or eat loads of junk food, which made her hyper. I tried to tell the Mammys, 'You can't really take your eyes off Yasmin...' praying that they wouldn't.

I don't think they knew then, that Yasmin was just that bit different to their five and six year olds, or the responsibility they had to watch over Yasmin.

Of course I didn't want Yasmin to be affected by my behaviour, but I didn't know what else to do. If I didn't give the parents the instructions on how to watch over Yasmin, she was at risk to be injured.

It was a catch 22.

Yasmin was my motivation to keep going. I had to educate her. I didn't accept it was too hard a challenge. I wanted Yasmin to learn to read and write and do maths. I wanted her to have every exercise and activity that would strengthen her muscle development.

I remember when I was a kid at home and after a big violent storm from my Dad. The next morning, my Mam and Dad got up early. They never stayed in bed. Mam cleaned up the mess and got on about her house wifely duties. Neither of them addressing the night before, nor acknowledging wounds.

I retain the same sort of stamina. My body can keep going till my mind starts to break it down.

I found 2011 chaotic. I felt I was running all over the place, but there were good things happening around me, positive things.

Queen Elizabeth II of England was coming to Ireland for a visit on 17th May 2011. It was the first visit by a British monarch since 1911 when Elizabeth's grandfather King George V visited Ireland when it was still part of the United Kingdom.

I like the Queen and I thought it was very honourable of her to bow her head in apology at the hand of any wrong doing that she was involved in during her reign. She was a good age at 85 years old and carried a beautiful style. I admired her courage and growth.

That was great leadership she performed that day, to admit wrongdoing and move forward. Let go of resentments and regrets.

Nelson Mandela had the same qualities all his life, move forward, don't look back. Focus on the positive.

President Obama followed to Ireland seven days later on the 24th May. I like Obama. I think America is so lucky once again to have a great leader with a good woman Michelle by his side. It was really good of him to run around Ireland that day. I followed his path on televisions as I went from house to house doing hairs. I felt connected to him and I felt his hyper activity of running from place to place, trying to get his job done, just like me!

I thought that pace is going to catch up on him one day.

Each time we went to Louise McDonagh, she suggested a new assessment for Yasmin. She told me Yasmin would need an Educational Report from a Psychologist; a Dyslexia assessment.

Like the other assessments, she said if I could afford private, it was a shorter time to wait as the HSE list were long.

Again, we had to pay hundreds of euros for an assessment for Yasmin. While only one child from every school can apply for a free Educational assessment, or one child in every 300 children, it was up to the school principal to decide who was the worst case.

Can you imagine a principal of a school trying to choose that one child from increasing high levels of children now with learning difficulties?

Are you having a laugh Enda Kenny? Our Taoiseach.

Yasmin saw Lisa Flanagan Education Psychologist at the ACLD Dyslexia Association of Ireland, in Suffolk Street, Dublin in 2011.

Yasmin was diagnosed with dyslexia and the maths difficulty; Dyscalculia also. On Lisa's instructions, because Yasmin scored really low, I proceeded to get private tuition for dyslexia outside school, which is another cost every week, but necessary, and showing huge benefits.

Louise was not surprised when I showed her the report from the ACLD, but she was happy with Yasmin's slow progress. She also suggested I get Yasmin assessed for ADHD, as she was still showing signs of hyperactivity, impulsivity and fidgety behaviour.

I brought Yasmin to Professor Michael Fitzpatrick in 2012 privately in Castle knock.

My husband was really frustrated now at the high costs of assessments.

Professor Fitzpatrick did think it looked like ADHD as Yasmin was particularly hyper on that appointment. He said Yasmin should get another two and half hours resource in school, but I would have to make an appointment with CAMH's, Children and Adolescents Mental Health at HSE in Trim also, and they would do a thorough assessment.

Actually, children diagnosed with ADHD, who receive prescribed medication, are only then allocated five hours resource and that is to monitor the child.

Resource is like gold dust in Ireland.

Yasmin was assessed by Fiona Coyle in CAMH in Trim in May 2013. She was a lovely woman, who was thorough in her interviewing of me and Yasmin.

On every assessment for Yasmin, I and the school teacher had to fill out lots of questionnaires about Yasmin, describing Yasmin's behaviour and habits. On top of everything else the primary school teacher had to do, this was no easy chore.

On Fiona's diagnosis, Yasmin hadn't got ADHD! I was actually delighted with that news, it was just Yasmin's disability and what it entails that causes her behaviours.

So, Yasmin's disability is Dyspraxia, with that, she has a Severe language Receptive Disorder, she has Severe Sensory Difficulties she has learning difficulties dyslexia and dyscalculia.

I was happy. We knew the areas we needed to focus on with Yasmin. There was a lot, but now I had the knowledge to help my daughter.

Also in 2011, I looked into the early primary movements that some babies miss out on. I went to see a therapist with another private fee, but a valuable assessment.

The lady conveyed to me the importance of proper nutrition for children like Yasmin, with learning difficulties.

Although I didn't take on her program for Yasmin, as Yasmin was doing quite a lot at this stage, I did follow her nutrition plan. Omegas 6 and 9 are very important for brain function and development. Proteins and non-processed food are also very important and bad fats are not good. (saturated fats) Even though you might be giving your child the good omegas 3,6,9, eating the bad fats will take the good effects of the omegas away.

The lady agreed exercise is hugely important for Yasmin and encouraged trampoline, swimming, and horse riding, which is hugely important for keeping the fluids flowing in Yasmin's brain, and also for muscular movements.

I cannot convey how important all these people were in Yasmin's life and what a wonderful job they do to help our children, both private practices and HSE Services.

The therapists work so hard and the results are amazing. As a parent, you have to participate hugely. The parent has to work with all these psychologists to help their child.

The parent has to be consistent. The parent has to do most of the work.

Information and help and guidelines for parents with children with difficulties is not easy to find, nor readily available. It's solely up to the parent to research her suspicions!

First time parents are the worst hit. They have no idea if their child has a difficulty. As a first parent, you only see perfection. Your love clouds your vision. It deafens your ears.

Yasmin was my third child. My oldest, Anthony was 16, when she arrived. My second child Sarah was 9 when Yasmin arrived.

Sarah had already been diagnosed with Dyslexia.

I had experience with some 'big scary names' like, Psychiatrist, Psychologist, already. I witnessed Sarah thrive through the scary world of the big names.

I learned by my mistakes I had made with my older children, how not to do things. I always say, that if God had sent Yasmin to me first, she would be a different child today, in a negative way, because I had no clue how to parent a childlike Yasmin.

When Yasmin came along, I also, saw perfection.

But when the 'big scary name people' told me things, I listened without prejudice. I knew they were giving me this information to help me help my child.

I would advise any parents experiencing difficulties with a child to ask other parents, don't be embarrassed. More and more children have learning difficulties than ever before.

Google help lines, get as much information as possible.

Other mammy's will be only too happy to give advice and tips. Because funnily enough, the government doesn't hand out any leaflets with that information on it!

How to find free assessments?

The HSE is your best bet, as they are really professional, but start as early as you can; On your child's three year old health check from your community health centre, don't let it be rushed. Have any questions or concerns about your child that you need addressed. Get her name put on the speech and language list, even for a small issue, because if it's something else, they'll send you to the right section.

Don't panic! Most children with learning difficulties have a delayed mental development. If she's five by the time it's her first assessment, that is ok. Once you're on the list though, you can ring for cancellation appointments and be seen to earlier, if you are really worried.

The school can have a one in 300 children, freely assessed for dyslexia. Maybe in your school it will be your child. Pursue the school. Don't be embarrassed, it's your child's right to be properly educated.

Tax credits in relation to children with disabilities? It's called an incapacitated child tax allowance. If your child has a disability that requires constant payouts for their educational needs, you are entitled to it. It's easy, go to the revenue site and you can apply online.

Don't be put off by other disabilities on the site. It's your right as a tax payer to get the proper allowances for your family.

Disability benefits if eligible? It's called Domiciliary Care Allowance. This is a social welfare payment. It's applied through the social welfare office and your working status is not affected. If you have a child with a disability that needs your constant attention, you are entitled to apply for this allowance.

Don't be embarrassed! It's your right as a parent to provide all the activity and educational needs for your child to help him or her progress through life: If you're refused then appeal.

Our government is entitled to meet our children's educational and emotional needs, when we can't afford them.

Can I also urge people to look at their children's diet. Missing nutrients in children's food today may seem ok while they're tackling primary school. But when secondary school comes along, and they need to focus, their brain will not have the stamina.

Yasmin is an amazing child, despite her many challenges. Although we are doing everything for Yasmin, there's no quick fix. She's not 'better'. I'm like Yasmin's SNA, special needs assistance, as I do everything for her at home to help her cope with when she's not in my care. I remind her about drinking water, her manners, while she's not with me, and hygiene rules. It's a huge task for her to function in school all day and when she comes home, she might be a little sad or easily angered.

Yasmin's sensory disorder makes day to day routines painful for Yasmin, brushing her hair, washing her teeth, blowing her nose. All these things hurt Yasmin, yet she wants to be pretty, so she knows it has to be done. She cries in pain throughout the ordeal.

Yasmin's dyspraxia makes it really hard for her to sit for any length of time and to focus and process information in the classroom, yet she loves school and tries really hard to learn. It causes an immaturity in Yasmin that other children get bored with her playing after a while. She gets aggravated easily causing her to react a little angry at things, banging the table or the doll, blaming it for the game going wrong, so that even her cousins get a little bit scared and go home early from play dates.

I will stress though, that whenever Yasmin is badly behaved, I give her a warning first, then if it continues I give her the consequence. I have to carry it through. It doesn't have to be a huge punishment but it is very important that Yasmin knows that she cannot be allowed to get away with bad behaviour for any reason.

This action alone is contributing to Yasmin being acceptable in all social occasions.

My heart breaks for her at these times. I feel her rejection. Not only am I trying to keep myself focused on the positives and my mind away from my depression, I feel sad for Yasmin and her challenges. She's impulsive and quite hyper, resulting in many falls and injuries.

We had hired a camper van in June 2013 to attend a weekend show jumping event in Mullingar, that Sarah was jumping in.

We had just arrived on site and Anto was plugging us in for electricity. Yasmin was on the top bunk bed, delightedly playing with her monster high dolls. I was at the little kitchen sink right beside the beds area. Next thing she came crashing down backwards, I couldn't catch her from the angle I was standing. She landed backwards on her head and neck. She was screaming in pain. I was terrified she had broken her neck and screamed for Anto. Yasmin was hysterical and we tried to calm her. We checked her over and she was able to move, but she had a nasty bump on her head. We had to go to Mulligar Hospital to have her checked out. We were relieved some hours later, when all her observations were fine. Yasmin has always fallen a lot and when she does, she falls awkwardly and can't save herself in any way, often resulting in severe injuries. Recently she fell off her bike, just standing there talking, but she fell right down on her elbow, and a lump of skin came off right to the bone. I became a nurse then as I dressed it and cleaned it for the two weeks it took to heal.

Yasmin's muscular difficulty makes it hard to write, for her to catch balls, skip rope, and do handstands and cartwheels, but she wants to do it, so she keeps trying. She can do handstands in the swimming pool!

Yasmin is teaching me strength and courage every day.

Working at home with Yasmin is imperative and very challenging.

Parents just like me, all over the country and the world, are doing this work with our children every day, often without help.

It is up to our governments to provide for the educational needs of all our children, with and without disabilities.

Our children with disabilities can be educated! It is the parents' right and responsibility to make sure their child gets educated.

With the circle of dysfunction, certain children will never get that help. That is why it is imperative for our governments to step in and meet the needs of all those children from poor families, who will never be able to meet the costs of special education. Poverty shouldn't stand in the way.

Our governments have known this for a long time: that poverty leads to dysfunction leads to learning difficulties, leads to suicide and crime in their teenage years.

Why is our government allowing this?

Forget the free medical card for children under five years. Assessments for children's learning difficulties should be provided for all children from age five as early intervention is imperative.

These children should not have to struggle. Their parents should not have to worry.

Yasmin is nine now and in second class. She has come along in every area of her physical and literacy education since her first assessment at age five. She really likes school and she is improving every day. She is starting to read really well, and I can see her catching on to maths also. Yasmin is with the same class since junior infants and they are very good to Yasmin, helping her out with finding her things, packing up her stuff or even tying shoe laces. She is also a valuable contribution to her class, as she is kind and gentle. She never squabbles with anyone or shouts at anybody, as her nature is that she likes to please. She takes her allocated play position appreciatively and loves playing with her classmates and fitting in. She's happy in school!

Yasmin has to live with her disability. Her disability doesn't go away. Her planning and organization and social skills are at the age of a four year old, but I have no doubt that they will develop as she gets older, maybe when she's a late teen, I'm in no rush to force her to be where she's not ready for.

It is difficult for her to sustain six hours in school in a confined space. I know at home she can't sit still for two minutes. I have explained to Yasmin that she has a difficulty with a few things, rather than a disability. Yasmin knows there are disabled people in the world, but she hasn't got all the language to express her feelings on the issue at the moment, but I can see her wondering is she the same as them.

I thought the Para Olympics was a great way to show Yasmin other people's different level of disabilities and also their amazing achievements.

Yasmin really enjoyed watching it, although she felt very sad for the people without arms and legs and she thought how lucky she was to have her arms and legs and that she could see also.

I explained to Yasmin that these people had to work really hard to overcome their disabilities to achieve their dreams in the Olympics and look how happy they were. I told her, that she is blessed to have all her arms and legs and her hearing and her sight and her voice, so that she can run and play and sing.

I told her, everybody in life has a challenge or a difficulty, it might not be obvious but it's still something that they have to work hard on.

I told Yasmin, 'You inspire me so much, with all your difficulties. You work so hard and it makes me want to work so hard too. I'm so proud of you.'

Every child should have the same chance, not just people who can pay for it.

It took a lot of emotional energy during these years. I had come off medication again, when Yasmin was nearly six in 2010, after being on it another 18 months. I was really busy physically and mentally, taking care of Sarah's and Yasmin's needs.

I was working at mobile hairdressing, helping out in my husband's office also. Doing my house work. I had stopped taking care of myself. I was eating on the run. I was only swimming once a week, and I wasn't taking time for my walks.

My husband and myself went off on a weekend trip to New York for a break. My Ma moved into my house to mind the kids, and it was the second time only in my life to leave them.

I was delighted to be in New York and search through the Outlets for great bargains in designer brands for my kids and for my sisters' kids. That's the way us sisters were. We'd always be thinking of the other nieces or nephews who were all similar ages to my own kids.

Delighted with my shopping, of Abercrombie sweaters, Uggs and runners, we arrived back to Dublin airport only to be stopped by Customs. The Customs girl was obviously watching too much Australia Customs on TV, because she was so rude. She took every item out of my bags, adding up figures as she went. I knew our spending limit was 495 dollars between us, and we had gone a couple of hundred over, but there was no need to be so disrespectful to us. She actually said to me, "It's people like you, shopping elsewhere that has our country in recession!"

Why do Irish people in authority think that they can just say anything that they are thinking, not even based on fact, as they don't even know you! Do I have a face that says, 'Come on, Abuse me!'

We are Tax paying citizens of Ireland. We were not smuggling anything illegal into our country. We'd buy the items in Ireland if we weren't getting robbed by the extra duty or tax on them!

If there is one thing I realize about Ireland, it's that a person is discriminated by how they look or what they wear. If a person looks rough, or a bit casually dressed, they're treated like dirt. I am not wrong.

We were standing there in public view, while the customs girl scrutinized my bags. I felt like a criminal, I was crying from exhaustion of the sleepless flight and from being treated like a nobody.

It would be only a few more months before I would break.

9

My Depression 2012

Jean age 45, 2012 Depression

The summer of July 2012, we booked a beautiful cottage in Fenore County Clare, west of Ireland, where the great Atlantic Ocean is shared with the USA. I was 45 years old and I had never been to this beautiful part of Ireland. It was very desolate. It took us hours to reach this remote beauty, but it was so worth it. The little village had one pub, one shop and one superb restaurant where the food and cakes were so delicious. There was a patio where you could sit and eat and watch this amazing ocean. I had never seen such beauty. I could even get my favourite cappuccino!

The cottage was on a hill overlooking the little Fenore beach, with the Burren Mountains at our back keeping us snuggled in. Fanore's Gaelic meaning "fainne oir" means ring of gold referring to its beautiful golden sandy beach.

I have a big family and all the kids are similar ages, so we always travel in groups. Two of my sisters, Elle and Christine and their husbands Hugo and Phil and Anto, and all our children arrived at the cottage.

We also brought my three dogs, Buster, a West Hyland Terrior who was 14, our King Charles Pongo who was six and our new dog Skye, a husky who was two years old.

The weather was typically Irish for the Summer, sometimes raining, sometimes sunny, but it didn't stop our brood of children heading to the beach and tackling those great Atlantic waves with their body boards. The water was so powerful, I was amazed at the little girls Yasmin seven, and Grace her cousin eight, having no fear, going into the water time and time again on their bodyboards with either myself or Anto.

Sarah joined in herself taking surfing lessons with the cute teenage boys on the beach, spending hours in the ocean, rain or shine. Christine and Elle packed a picnic and flasks of tea every day. It was heaven.

There are some fantastic walks in this area of the Burren and I was looking forward to walking with Sarah too, for some quality time.

One rainy morning, the family wanted to go and see the Ailwee Caves, Co Clare. I don't like Caves as I get claustrophobic. My last visit to Caves was that holiday with Anto on our own when I was I was on a week long panic attack. We had visited some caves in Majorca and as we were walking deeper and deeper into the caves, I started to sob. Anto loves things like that and he was fascinated with the rest of the tour. He had asked one of the guides to help me out. Instead of going back, the guide took all the way through the bloody caves as I was struggling to breath! The Ediot!

That was me finished with caves.

I was happy to let them all go off as I planned to go on a nice walk.

I vaguely looked at the map and decided on the Caher Valley Loop, it came around in a circle and it didn't look that far. I didn't notice the distance was 14.5km, about 10 miles. I didn't bring any food or water, just my phone and I set off at 10.30am. It was a grey rainy soft day, and it was very deserted, I saw one person on the road that day, going in the opposite direction to me. I was delighted. I wanted solitude.

I took my three dogs with me and followed the signs.

It was beautiful. The Caher Valley runs down to Fenore between two mountains, Slieve Elva and Gleninagh. The Caher River cuts its way down through the rock and glacial deposit heading to the sea.

I enjoyed the beauty of the powerful river bashing against the rocks as I walked. I marvelled at the horses on the top of the rock face, and how they didn't fall off. I enjoyed the beautiful environment of nature all around me. I breathed in the smells. I enjoyed the peace. I was thanking God.

I came to the bottom of a little mountain, I thought I'd just keep going. As I climbed higher with my dogs, my poor little Buster was staying by my heels the whole time. I was worried about his age, could he keep up.

The beauty surrounding me was breath-taking. Even on this rainy morning I could see all around the hills and valleys and the different shades of green all around me. I decided to let Skye off the lead, as she's a bigger dog, she'd enjoy a bit of a run.

She was running ahead all excited, loving this walk, loving that she was with us on holidays. I was nearly at the top running after Skye. I didn't notice the mist coming in at first. I saw some animals in the distance, I thought they were Deer. Sarah later told me they were mountain goats. I wanted Skye back on the lead, I knew if she saw the Deer she would go after them. She saw them, she ran fast into the distance. I ran after her over the bumps and ditches, trying to keep her in my sight but she was too fast for me. I could see the animals shadows in the distance. The mist and fog had come in fast, all of a sudden I couldn't see a thing.

Skye was gone. There wasn't a sound anywhere except the gentle trickle of rain drops. I couldn't see my hand in front of me. Oh My God. I started to panic. I knew I had better try find the path and keep going for my own safety, I kept calling Skye.

Skye? Skye? My voice was hoarse. I was worried sick for Yasmin. She loved the dogs and if I didn't find Skye. She would be devastated. She was a very anxious child because of her difficulties. This would really affect her.

I kept walking, I found a path, but I didn't know it was the right one as I couldn't see any signs. I was crying and crying. The rain was coming down fast. I was soaked through my rain jacket. I thought of my phone. Thank God. I'd ring for help. I got my phone from my inside pocket and dialled 999.

No Network! No Network! Seriously, I was so mad. I screamed so loud. I screamed and screamed with only the cows looking on, wondering what was this strange person doing.

I shouted at God, Why am I so thick? Why am I so stupid? Is there something seriously wrong with me? Why do I keep doing this?

I was very scared at this point. This is what happens when you hear about women who go missing. They do something stupid like this, and they fall down a hole never to be found again! I kept walking and crying, calling Skye in between sobs.

Where was I? I was walking three hours now with no end to this bloody mountain. I was at the top, but the top is bumpy and wide, not peaked. It was probably four miles over the top. I was sure I had the wrong path. I kept looking at my phone for network, at last! Network. I called 999. A nice lady answered. I asked her for air and rescue, I knew I was mad at this moment.

I told them I was lost in the mountains and I had lost my dog. I was upset, but human voices helped me calm down a little.

She was asking me where I was, and I didn't know. I told her where I started out. She said I must be within range as I now had network, to keep walking on the path. She held me on the phone till I saw a sign. I was still on the loop. I told her this, and she was assured I was ok. She told me to go to the nearest Garda Station in Ennis and ask about Skye when I got down.

My poor dog Skye, Where was she? How would I go back without her?

I eventually started to see signs of life. Houses on the mountain. I knocked at the doors for help. They were deserted. Nobody in.

I found one old man in a cottage. I told him what happened and he said he'd pass the word to his daughter. "It's a small place," he said. "We'll find your dog!" He could see how upset I was.

I met another lady as I was coming back into Fenore, five hours later. I could barely speak, I was so upset. I asked her to look out for my dog. She reassured me and said the word would be out everywhere. They'd find my dog.

What was I like?

I was so happy to get back to the cottage. I put the two little dogs in the shed with some food and water. I needed a cup of tea. I was emotionally drained. Isn't it amazing? A glass of wine or a beer wouldn't suffice at that moment. It had to be tea!

The family came home not too long behind me. I hoped Anto and Sarah wouldn't kill me about the dog. I looked at Anto, he knew something happened. I told him.

Thankfully he didn't slag me about it. I was too upset. I gave him details of where I went and where I thought Skye went missing. He and Sarah went straight out to look for Skye. Yasmin had no idea yet what happened. She always asked after the dogs and I told her they were in the shed asleep.

I didn't think they'd find Skye. If she hadn't hurt herself, I was sure someone would keep her for themselves. She was such a beautiful Husky dog with piercing blue eyes.

An hour later, Anto came back with our dog! I couldn't believe it!

Sarah told me they had drove all over the place and then went back to where I started my assent onto the mountain. Anto was whistling for Skye.

She always obeys his whistle. There was a busy road near there and they couldn't believe it when Skye jumped out from the trees! The dog was quite traumatized, after six hours running around by herself, lost.

She knew she was lucky to be found.

When I saw her, I said, "Aren't you a bold girl?" She knew she was as I hugged her and cuddled her.

We brought Buster and Pongo into the house with Skye that November night in the middle of July!

It was cold and damp. Yasmin was none the wiser.

That evening we all had a laugh at my madness.

There was a time in my life that I was cocky and confident.

I was running my own hair salon, I was about 24 then, in 1991.

The Clients were ladies of 50/60 year olds. I loved those people, They liked me too. They liked to see a young woman doing well. I suppose when they were my age, they couldn't work as they had to stay at home and raise their children, and look after their men.

Did they know when they took on a husband then, that it meant a sacrifice of their own one life? That they would inevitably get the worse end of the stick, that they would have to work harder, share everything and reluctantly give into selfish demands of their husbands? These women encouraged me, supported me, and congratulated me. I truly enjoyed my job.

In those days I was their confidante. They told me all their joys, their sadness, their worries, their fears. I did my best to reassure them, encourage them. We always had cake and tea for my clients at Christmas and a glass of wine.

Although I had witnessed my fair share of life at this point, I was still optimistic. I had Hope.

Who knew 20 years on, my hope was disappearing. I was finding life hard. It was a chore. I functioned. I wasn't enjoying it. I kept up to date and retrained continuously in education throughout my life. I knew that being educated and knowing what I was talking about would give me confidence. I always felt education was the key to freedom in life.

I enrolled in Crumlin College of further education to retrain in hairdressing in 2007. The recession was looming in fast and I wanted to start mobile hairdressing to bring in some extra money. It was a two year part time course and I was proud of myself when I passed all my exams again at age 42.

One night as I was coming home from Crumlin College at about 9.45pm. I was driving my husband's fancy Silver Chrysler 300 car. I was tired that night. I was wearing an old tracksuit and my hair was in a ponytail. I had no makeup on. Coming from Crumlin towards Island Bridge, where the Hilton hotel is on my left, there are about three or four sets of traffic lights there. I hated getting stuck at those lights. The car in front of me was going through an orange light so I sneaked in behind him. He had stopped in front of me again, waiting on the next lights to change.

It was a small boxy red car, maybe a Fiat and there were two big guys sitting in the back seat. They turned around to look at me. I was just observing them tiredly, while I waited for my turn to go. I proceeded into the lane going straight and they were in my left inside lane.

The driver rolled down his window to say something to me. I rolled down mine, thinking he must be looking for directions. He said in an angry voice, "You know, you went through an orange light!"

I wasn't in the best of form and said to myself, 'Why does everybody have to be so interfering?' To him, I said, "What's it to you?"

He said, "I'm a Guard, pull over!"

Oh feck, I thought. He didn't look like a guard. I pulled over and he approached my car.

He was really angry and started shouting at me about the way I spoke to him. I said, "I'm sorry you don't look like a guard, have you any identity?" This really pissed him off and he demanded my driving license. I was feeling really scared and said, "I'm sorry, I don't like the way you're shouting at me and I still haven't seen ID. 'I have a friend who's a policeman and I'm going to phone him for assistance,' I reached across the seat for my phone.

He shouted, "Take your hand away from that phone now, or I'll pull you out of the car so fast, handcuff you and have you locked up for the night! Give me your driving license now!" he shouted. I tell no lie.

I was terrified. I gave it to him. I started to cry. I didn't know what was going on.

The funny thing is, as he walked back to his car to look up my details, a proper police car had pulled up right beside me to proceed through the lights. He looked in at me, he saw I was crying and he drove off and I was too afraid to ask for his help!

The guard came back to my car. He saw me crying and said, "For fuck's sake! What are you crying for?" Truly.

Couldn't he see he had terrified me? I'm claustrophobic, I couldn't be locked up. The car was registered under my husband's company name and as a Director, my name was on there too. Everything was legal and above board, even the tax was up to date. He asked me to confirm my name.

He couldn't believe it that I wasn't a drug dealer's wife! I had the car, I had the tracksuit and of course I had the Dublin accent. He quickly sent me on my way without an apology. I did try to report the incident and I guess they knew who the guy was but they told me they couldn't do anything without a name. Apparently, because of the area I was in, it's very common for unmarked police cars with plain clothes detectives to be driving around as there is still a huge drug problem in Dublin city.

I was really shaken by the incident and didn't see the funny side of it till a few days later.

I silently cursed my husband for liking flash cars. My husband was in the construction industry, and in the days of the Celtic Tiger, the company had grown to 30 employees and many more sub-contractors. When the recession hit in 2007, the company was badly hit. The company was still able to survive with his small crew down to his six original lads; Tony Hawkins (Hawkeye) my brother-in-law and our son Anthony were also on board at this stage. Anto was good at doing figures; he knew how much money came in and how much money could get paid out.

I started working as a mobile hairdresser in 2009. I wasn't a bad hairdresser, but I had lost a lot of confidence in myself, because of my depression.

I was the one now, crying to my clients, telling them my fears, my worries. I felt like the old Chinese person, (no offence meant to Chinese people, they're lovely!) full of gratitude for a small fee, and a huge sweat and cost to deliver my service. I had never charged enough. I never covered my costs.

My God! How did this happen?

The day I decided I couldn't do hairdressing anymore came at Debs Season in 2011. The Debs is a huge event for 17 year old girls. The parents go all out for their debutantes, spending a fortune on beautiful gowns, fabulous shoes and gorgeous accessories. Hair and makeup is planned well in advance and tan and nails are done the day before. The style of the Irish girls could gloss any magazine.

At this point in my life, I was under huge pressure with appointments, finance, my home life, my marriage, kids, and housework. I was running around like crazy, somehow getting things done, but at a cost to my health, physical and mental. I wasn't eating right; I was living on tea and biscuits.

I had three appointments that day. Styling debs' hairs can go anyway on the day. Mostly because it relies on raw talent to do something really extravagant.

Everything seemed to go wrong that day. I was struggling to perform.

During the time I was doing the hairs, I was actually having panic attacks. I wanted to down tools and run away and never do hair again. I had become to hate my trade. I felt very faint. I had to try to breathe deeply and slowly. I was trying to hold back the tears. I was mortified. I couldn't very well leave the girls stuck. My heart was racing. I thought I was having a heart attack and would probably die soon. I didn't know what was wrong with me.

I then went through an out of body experience. It's the only way I can describe it. I was aware that I had to go home and cook for my kids. My niece Shauna was at home with Sarah and Yasmin, and I had a Spanish student staying with me also. I was feeling very weak.

I remembered my friend Caroline had invited me down to see off her daughter Amy, going to her debs. I collected the four kids and took them with me to Caroline's house.

I looked a mess, I wasn't even clean.

Caroline welcomed us all in. She had lots of food for the kids. She fed them and they had desert. I was able to eat a wholesome salad with beautiful brown bread. I had a glass of wine. I was minded. I started to relax.

Caroline didn't even know the importance of what she did that evening. She took care of my kids and she took care of me.

I was able to go home and continue my function as a Mam, but I was very shaky, very weak. I had to stop this madness. This fear. The fear that was ingrained in me as a child, everything that was going on for me, different knocks I received throughout my life: Rejection.

The recession, the financial worries, my marriage, my parenting skills, it was surfacing. Fear of failure.

I had failed in my job. Everything I had tried in my life, I felt I had failed. I wasn't good enough. It was engulfing me. It had to come out eventually. It was fear.

I had to give up work. Whatever was going on for me, work wasn't helping. There were a lot of things going on in my marriage during this time too. My husband didn't agree with me working the way I was. He knew I was killing myself for very little money.

Anto couldn't get through to me. I could only see that he wasn't supporting me when I was just trying to help our finances.

I started to resent him. We were ignoring each other, not communicating and letting our marriage suffer.

When I finished early enough at the weekends, I arrived home and poured myself a glass of wine. Soon I was having three glasses, and if we were with company, having a meal, I could drink a bottle of wine no problem, going into the second bottle.

The wine was starting to have an effect on my behaviour. I was nasty to my husband.

One time after going out for dinner with my sisters, I came home, I remember my daughter Sarah hadn't bought me something I'd asked for, I turned on her. I was so mean to her, I said horrible things to her, and I will never forget that little hurt look in her eyes.

Oh My God. To hurt my child, my beautiful innocent child. What kind of Mother was I? She didn't deserve my drunken tongue. I never drank wine again. I was turning into a horrible person. I hated myself.

I apologized to my beautiful daughter, telling her my behaviour was so wrong, unacceptable. I begged God for help. I begged God for forgiveness. I asked for help in forgiving myself. I tormented myself in my wrong doings.

I gave up work and tried to focus on my health and my nutrition. I went back to my swimming and did yoga. I tried mindfulness, which is extremely good. It's based on living in the moment and focusing on every breath you take.

I was just functioning though and everything felt like a huge effort. I didn't want to read emails. I was afraid. I didn't want to hear what people had to say. I didn't know I was withdrawing from people.

February and March, I was looking after my family and getting the kids to their activities, but I found it a huge effort. I could sit beside Yasmin and do her homework with my cup of coffee.

I remember during this time, I was walking somewhere with Yasmin and with Yasmin's disability, she can be loud, excitable, touch me a lot, grab me, hug me spontaneously.

When I held her hand, she'd let it go, run on, run back, grab my hand.

I love Yasmin completely, but this day I found it was like electric shocks to my ears and my body, every time she shouted or grabbed me. I just thought I was tired. I wasn't sleeping too well. I knew I didn't look well.

My husband booked a holiday in October 2012. We were going to visit Marcy and Joe and the kids, Christopher and Emma in Florida. Anto had also booked a three day cruise for a surprise to the Bahamas from Cape Canaveral. My sister Sharon and her two teenagers, who had just lost their dad, Myles Graham to cancer in July 2012, came with us also. Ryan and Shauna were going through a tough time and Sharon thought the break would do them good.

We never thought to check the weather as we boarded the cruise ship on Thursday 25th October 2012.

There was great excitement among us. There was singing and dancing on board, it was great fun. All the teenagers wanted to look at their staterooms. Yasmin wanted to go swimming straight away in the lovely Mickey Mouse Pool.

I let her go into the kids' pool beside me while everybody got organized. I was standing at the side of the pool taking in the atmosphere. It was beautiful, although it was a grey cloudy day, unusual for sunny Florida; the weather was calm, nice and warm.

The ship pulled out of port with everyone cheering.

Then the scariest thing happened! The wind came out of nowhere. It looked like a twister! It was howling and roaring, hard rain hurtling from the sky.

I looked for Yasmin, she was gone from the pool!

Oh my God! Everybody was running and screaming, I couldn't see anybody to help me. The sky grew dark, I looked frantically for Yasmin, I heard her scream. I looked up to see her on the top steps of the super duper water slide, Jesus, she seemed close to the side barriers!

I started to run to her, the force was immense. I truly struggled to put one foot in front of another. I was calling to Yasmin to hold onto a rail. Yasmin was frozen to the spot holding her ears. The noise level was thunderous. I was screaming for help. The stewards seemed to be running everywhere, trying to catch flying deck chairs and tie them down.

I noticed my niece Shauna up on the steps. She had grabbed Yasmin and picked her up, Yasmin clung on to Shauna's little body. She was 15 years old but tiny, Yasmin was nearly as big as her! Shauna had been on the top steps of the slide and she had seen Yasmin coming up the steps when the twister hit. As a safety measure, all gates are closed automatically on the steps up to the slide and Shauna couldn't get to Yasmin at first.

This little skinny girl had clung to Yasmin and carried her down the steps to me. The second in command Captain finally got to the girls and took them to safety. They were both traumatized. I was shaking like a leaf in shock.

We went under deck to recover and dry off. In a few minutes, the twister was gone from the ship but the Captain had to continue his journey as Hurricane Sandy had hit Cape Canaveral and he couldn't return back as it wouldn't be safe.

The Captain spent the next three days trying to keep us afloat. He was within a mile of the eye of the storm at any one time. We couldn't dock anywhere, as everywhere in the Bahamas was being ravaged by the storm racing at 150 miles an hour. We were rocking and rolling all over the Ocean. We couldn't go on deck because of the winds and rain belting down. Everyone one of us had motion sickness. It was so funny at dinner. We were all dressed really nice and the food being served was delicious. Yasmin had been doing well to not throw up, but it didn't last. As her face turned green, I knew what was coming. I grabbed the nearest thing to me and that was a Chrystal cut glass. Yasmin threw up into the glass. It was filling up fast! I grabbed another one and she filled that too. It started all the other kids off and it was an epidemic!

The ship made Titanic sounds that night. As we rolled back and forwards in our beds.

I prayed for our survival.

Amazingly we did survive. I thanked God and the Captain. It was a huge task they had to keep 4,500 passengers alive and safe. We docked back at Cape Canaveral on Sunday 28th October 2012 to a beautiful calm day, leaving the devastation and destruction of Hurricane Sandy behind us.

On my road of recovery:

2013 was a challenging year for me. It's when I discovered me again and what's important to me. Although I had no learning difficulties as a child, none of my emotional needs were met. How come I wasn't needy? How come I didn't want attention? How come I wasn't jealous of what others got?

I associated attention with severe trouble. I learned early on to keep any little worry or problem to myself to avoid any trouble between my mam and dad, or trouble for me. Although

I hadn't witnessed violence till I was about eight years old, I sensed very early on the connection between attention and trouble. Dad panicked very quickly when anything happened. Everything was a drama. Every drama was trouble.

I wasn't jealous of the attention others got, because that attention could turn to trouble very fast and I didn't want trouble. I couldn't trust that things would be ok with my dad, because they never were.

I had no faith in men. I couldn't trust them. When I was a child, I learned that men's needs were more important than women's. I felt the unfairness of that. I felt all men were selfish, only thinking of themselves first.

Burying problems have the adverse effect of coming out eventually, in the guise of physical or mental illness.

Others develop Obsessive Compulsive disorders, leading them to be socially unacceptable and reclusive.

Not learning how to deal with depression at that young stage or getting the right treatment can lead into bipolar depression, experiencing huge highs and unexplained lows.

I believe that some children with severe learning difficulties growing up in a home where their emotional needs aren't met develop Schizophrenia as young as 15. They experience hallucinations, muddled thinking, loss of interest in daily activities, difficulty concentrating and reduced motivation.

I started suffering with depression at age 11, because of the constant battering to my personality from my Dad, I already hated myself at that age. I struggled with emotions and relationships all my life.

When a child is criticised and judged throughout their growing years, they become secretive and defensive. They don't feel worthy or important.

I never treated myself as an important person. I always put myself last throughout my life, which of course meant, others could treat me last too. I had a huge difficulty being completely open in my relationship with my husband, never trusting completely. My husband had his own issues as his emotional needs weren't met as a child. Losing his father and mother in his important growing years left him needing someone to take care of him all his life. I found his needs an added pressure with trying to be a good mother to my children with huge learning difficulties and social difficulties. I hated myself, for not being a good enough wife, never feeling a good enough mother, not good enough with money, not good enough at my job.

I hated myself when I lost my head at people over incidences with my children, or something that I'd find out was my fault after I lost my head. Why couldn't I just be normal like everyone else? How come I never see people making a fool of themselves? My dislike for myself was confirmed by others rejections of me during my life.

I had to start by learning to like myself.

Dad

Just putting the pieces together from the bits I got from Dad and his brothers, I know his mother was hard and it caused him to resent his mother. I think he felt really guilty, maybe from not being good enough in his own head, or maybe from being a 'Divil' when he was a boy. I do know he used to torture himself while drunk, and cry and cry, "I'm sorry Mammy! I'm sorry Mammy!"

A child's relationship with their mother is detrimental in their rearing as she is mostly the sole carer.

Dad was the last child born to Granny aged 42. Instead of learning more about child rearing as each son came along, Granny was more disillusioned, negative and depressed. She would never have received counselling or help when her little boy Noel died. Maybe she had also wanted a girl to help her around the house. So Dad grew up with a depressed mother, with blame, anger and resentment part of his everyday life.

Children grow to think that it's their fault when their mam or dad is unhappy at home. Dad carried that guilt throughout his life. He was never able to unscramble the mess or confusion in his head. He witnessed severe violence and abuse of alcohol in his first ten years growing up in the Dublin city houses

Children had no value in the tenements. His teachers, The Christian Brothers were wicked to Dad and the other boys and gave him harsh punishments, by beating him violently for any wrong. He grew to hate them and resent the church and everything it stood for.

As a child, Granny knocked Dad for any failure, but I also think that she couldn't control him and he got away with a lot of bad behaviour serving no consequence.

As a Husband, when stress and troubles arrived at his door, he didn't know how to cope, so he panicked and threw tantrums. He also suffered no consequence, releasing him from any form of responsibility for his actions. He didn't have to change his ways. He had nothing to lose.

Granny's constant battering to Dad's self-esteem was to have a huge effect on him when he got older. As he was met with life's challenges and disappointments he started to have angry and violent outbursts himself, expressing his anger, resentments, negativities at his children. Little did he know that each of his children's emotional growth was going to be severely damaged

He became dependent on alcohol and suffered inevitable depression, trapped in a need to escape. He really did want to end his life, but he was afraid. He was sad and angry and blamed God, blamed everybody, not knowing that he had the key to his own freedom. He was never positive,. He had no gratitude, so he could never find happiness.

None of Dad's emotional needs were met, leading him to feel inadequate in life. He depended on Mam for everything, expecting her to fill the voids that were left from his mother. He childishly demanded she be there to meet his needs. He was jealous of her attentions going elsewhere.

It was the kind of behaviour only normal for young children, when a mammy's attention goes to another sibling. Jealously feelings are normal from a child when the other child seems to be getting more attention than he. Most children grow out of this behaviour when the Mother gives them much needed love and reassurance consistently.

He had never matured properly.

There's no doubt in my mind that if Dad's emotional needs were met as a child, he would not have been needy in his adult life: Jealous that others were happier than he, always thinking that others got more than he; always watching others suspiciously. He began early on to be resentful and blameful when things didn't go his way. He disliked himself. He never learned to look at his own behaviour and take responsibility for his difficulties.

Unfortunately for him, he was surrounded by poverty and negative behaviour.. Nobody knew how to be positive..

Although proven that children with learning difficulties and behavioural problems often suffer with depression from a young age when their educational and emotional needs aren't met. Receiving continued mental abuse or even mild 'put downs' on regular occasions can also cause depression and worthlessness in children. Living with negativity is also very contagious. It keeps the mood low.

Dad's sense of worthlessness was always present as long as I knew him. I believe he hated himself more than anyone else. He alienated himself from other people and friends. He knew he treated his wife and children badly, so he felt he didn't deserve friends. He chose to be alone.

God rest Dad on his deathbed, he was talking about his Mother, "Ah Molly, Molly, she'd hit you hard if you answered her back. She moved us all over Dublin to different tenements, one worse than the other. No rest. No peace. There she is now, waiting for me."

And I looked to the end of the bed to see if she was there...

Mam

Ma was also the youngest in her family. They were also extremely poor with a basic house with little possessions. There were a lot of older sisters in Ma's family and she felt minded and cared for, so her emotional needs were met.

Most important, there was a lot of positivity around Ma when she was growing up. Her family were content and accepting. Ma didn't hear critical comments. There was no blame or accusations.

Don't get me wrong, Ma's family wasn't the Brady bunch. They weren't lovey dovey and everything wonderful. They were simple and practical.

Granny Kelly was a kind woman, even while suffering depression at the loss of her sons., she kept her pain to herself .Ma learned this also. Her life was simple. She had great faith in God and prayed to him to guide her.

Ma didn't want much in life. She just wanted her family to be healthy. She knew her children were important in life. She would feed them, educate them, give advice when asked and she never judged. She loved us completely without having to pamper us.

She felt that God had given her this path to follow. She would do it to the best of ability, with grace. She was the difference in our family that made us fight the evils of life.

Me!

So here I was age 46.

I had been living my life up till now in negatives and resentment. After each knock of bullying in the workplace, accusations, suspicions towards me, negative put downs, I became very afraid. I knew what the term, suffering with your nerves were because my nerves were gone!

Fear controlled me.

I had become reclusive of people. People hurt.

How was I going to do it? I had to start trying to focus on the positive. I had been lost.. Now, I had to look at life with new eyes. I had to try to enjoy each moment, take pleasure from simple things of beauty. To Focus on gratitude.

I always had a relationship with God, whether I was angry at him, or praying to him.

I started by being thankful.

So, every morning before I got out of bed, I'd say:

God grant me peace, patience, serenity, forgiveness and acceptance of myself.

Dear Lord God, I hand my day and my will over to you, please guide me in your path for me.

Thank you for the gift of life and thank you for putting food on our table. Thank you for keeping my family safe and healthy and free from all evil and harm. Please guide them in your path for them.

I needed to accept my wrong doings to others and even to myself. I had to try to forgive myself. I had to try to love myself. I had to apologise for my wrong doings because if I didn't apologise I would carry guilt. I had to change my bad behaviour for good.

Through my bad times, I could say this prayer a hundred times a day. My family's health and happiness were important to me. I needed to focus on this, but I needed to be healthy to do this. I needed to point out to my Husband and children, that my needs were also very important. I had to explain my depression to my husband, tell him when I wasn't feeling well. He wasn't a mind reader! I had to remind them also, that I was a good Mother and Wife and I was doing the best I could. I decided I wouldn't accept any bad behaviour or disrespect from them from there on. I deserved respect, like they deserved it also from me. I needed to put myself first, this was going to be a challenge since I had got so used to putting myself last for the longest time. I had allowed myself to be put last!

I craved the freedom to be myself. I needed to do things that were important to me.

I took my first trip to America on my own with Yasmin in August 2013 to see my sister in law, Marcy and the kids. Anto and Sarah were following a week later but Anto was reluctant for me to go on my own with Yasmin. It was important to me to have this independence. It would be fun if I could take little trips with Yasmin when she wasn't in school.

Emma eight and Christopher nine, were adopted by Marcy and Joe as babies, and are Mexican by origin, they are always delighted to see Yasmin.

Christopher was named after my dad, and he has lots of difficulties because his birth mother was on drugs while she was pregnant. He was only four pounds born. He's a nice lad and sensitive. Emma is a year younger than Yasmin and really smart.

Yasmin, Christopher and Emma are some of the youngest cousins on Anto's side of the family and I like them to see each other as much as they can, which is mostly once a year. Christopher knows me now and looks forward to seeing me and Emma loves having her cousin Yasmin coming to stay and playing all the dress up games they love.

After a few days together, I took a day trip with Yasmin by ourselves, to have some Mammy and daughter time. I reassured Joe, Anto's brother, I knew where I was going. What could go wrong at 46 years old?

I headed to Legoland, 50 minutes south of Orlando. It was a beautiful hot day, and as the sun was beaming down from the sky, Legoland was easy to find. I had hired a car, that didn't have a satellite navigator available but I thought the roads were fairly simple to follow. I would be fine and I had a map. I didn't want to put my data roaming on my phone, as the last time I was in America, I came home with a 660 euro bill.

We arrived at Legoland, it's a really new park and it's located in Winter Haven. It's expensive at $200 for the two of us, but, had we known, there are various vouchers from McDonald's available and other restaurants, for free children's tickets.

We headed straight to the water park at the back of the park, because it was so hot. I was very impressed with the walk-through of the park as it's set beside a lake and the scenery is beautiful. There are also various water shows that go on at the lake.

The water park was a water wonderland with slides and buckets of water pouring down on top of us at every moment. Yasmin loved climbing the water drenched steps, it was hard to get her to leave the water area in scorching temperatures of 30 degrees at 5pm, but we had only two hours left to see the rest of the park. The crowds had left at this time, so we didn't have to queue for any of the rides and it was surprisingly good after the water park.

The model cities were amazing with every capital city in the world. The park also had a couple of really good roller coasters and a learn-to-drive centre for kids, with a driving license on completion. Yasmin really enjoyed the park and didn't want to leave, which is a great sign for any park!

By 7pm, at closing time, we headed back on the road to Sarasota, where Joe and Marcy live. It's a handy two hour drive from Orlando, but we could be there by dark at 8.30pm.

It was a beautiful evening, and I chose to go on a country road from just outside Orlando to Sarasota, as the tour guide on leaving Legoland gave me good directions. The countryside wasn't unlike Ireland's country, with farm houses and fields stretching for miles, surprisingly green in Florida's heat. It was beautifully clean.

My map finished on entering Sarasota's back road, Bee Ridge. The road went on for endless miles and unusual for America, I didn't see frequent signs telling me where I was. As it turned out, I was driving around in circles and got lost. It was dark and 10pm at this stage. This is where I got confused. We came to a crossing with Beneva road, I knew I was close, but I just couldn't find Joe and Marcy's road, Antigua Place. I completely lost my sense of direction and had no idea where I was at this stage. My phone was dead, and I had no way of contacting Joe. Yasmin was getting really scared of being in the dark this long.

I was trying to reassure her, but I was getting worried. I stopped in a busy housing area and asked for help, but nobody wanted to help. That is the thing about America, people are scared to get involved with people that aren't where they should be. I also looked wrecked; I had a little sun top on, with shorts, my hair was fuzzy, maybe I looked a bit like trailer trash in my rental car. I was also exhausted looking. I started to look for the beach directions to Siesta Key, as I remembered the area and I could find my sense of direction from there.

I finally found a sign directing me to the beaches and then Yasmin spotted a McDonald's. Yey!

I'm not normally this dopey, but areas seem different in the dark, and I really wanted to find it myself. I was so close. We went into McDonald's and Yasmin was delighted we had found proper food! I asked the Manager could I use his phone, as there were no pay phones anywhere. He was really helpful and got me a cup of well-deserved tea and Yasmin a Happy Meal. I finally phoned Joe to come and meet me at the McDonald's to take us to his house.

Joe and Marcy had been worried sick, wondering where we were. He was concerned about my behaviour. I was stressed and I was losing my head at Joe over directions, which I am really sorry Joe and Marcy. I obviously wasn't as well as I thought I was.

In the back of my mind, I was aware that I had brought my little girl on one of my unknown journey's. I could have put her at risk to danger. I felt stupid. I panicked. What if something had happened to us?

I felt a huge sense of failure each time I went backward in my quest for a better me. This was the core of my depression. I couldn't get rid of that thought. I felt so distorted as a human being.

I had to start to believe in myself. I had to make myself believe I had a good soul. God created my soul. He gave me this path in life. He is guiding me. I will learn. I will succeed.

The crazy walks and lone journeys I had taken throughout my life was my fight for freedom: Freedom from control. I was controlled by fear.

My son came home in January 2013, he was away from home five years. He's back together with his lovely girlfriend

Sally after a year break up, she's so good for him. I am so grateful I have a chance to be a mother to him again.

I can't explain the feeling of giving birth to a son that I loved completely but losing him because of my bad parenting.

Why were all my relationships with the men in my life so difficult?

My father; my husband; my son: my God; Was the damage that great when I was a child?

I am grateful that I have a new daughter in Sally. She is just like one of my girls..

I take joy in having coffee with Sarah and going shopping with her. The recession has given me a different budget, but it's good for us, we don't need bags of stuff. A shared coffee and cake is precious.

My beautiful flower Yasmin, always blossoming, innocent colour, always giving love. She forces me to go on, to keep trying.

I am so grateful for these children; they have taught me so much.

I now live with depression in my life, coming and going. I have learned to recognize those anguish feelings when they arrive and follow the instructions of my body to take care of myself.

With life's usual challenges, I worry, I keep busy, I don't sleep well and I don't eat well. Even on medication, it won't protect me from a relapse. It's really important for anyone with depression to eat well, sleep well and rest. Ask for help. But of course, if you're like me, you won't. A friend told me to 'Bite the bullet' and that is such a great description!

Having the symptoms of depression is like catching that bullet in your mouth and holding on tight to it, so that it doesn't explode. Trying to perform your everyday duty's is really difficult when you're depressed, but if you keep on going slowly but steady, you will get there.

Although, I am working every day to be positive, I am still on medication and have no wish to come off it.

I hope families of suicide victims may take some comfort in the knowledge that it was their own feelings of worthlessness and self-hatred of themselves and not the people they left behind.

I'm not pinning this on my father; I believe he had no idea of the damage he was causing. He had no idea of how to parent from his own experience of childhood, but when a child's vision of life is so distorted in their growing years, by fear, it causes a lot of emotional damage.

I learned very young not to express feelings of worry or fear or sadness or love and happiness. I taught myself not to feel. I could never comfort others with hugs or cuddles, until my children came along. I wasn't really good at playing games with the kids. I wasn't a fun person. I guess I could never relax.

My poor son. I think I cuddled him a lot till he was at least six and then I thought he was grown, because he was so independent and capable.

Sarah was so happy in herself. She played really well by herself and didn't need too much attention from me. She loved to hug and cuddle, a typical little girl!

When Yasmin came along with all her difficulties, she needed a mother in top shape. When I shouted, she cringed in fright, I had to speak quietly. If I was hysterical over any little thing, Yasmin became hysterical and panicked. I had to be calm. If I was impatient dealing with her needs, I got nowhere. I had to learn patience. I had to give her hugs and cuddles, she demanded them every minute!

I found the greatest love inside myself! You must love yourself first to enable you to love others. Just like Whitney Houston sang. It's all about the children. Children can teach us so much. Doesn't this look like God's intervention to help me?

I was a lost cause, and he sent Yasmin to help me, to teach me. I've learned I am a sensitive person, but I've been masking myself with a tough exterior for over 40 years.

As a young woman, I could never relate to other's sadness and cry with them. I could never relate to other's happiness and laugh truly.

I never knew I was important in my sex life. I enjoyed our sex life, we matched well, but when my husband likes something, he wants it all the time, another addiction! Who knew I had the same problem as Catherine Zeta Jones? Even with her beauty, she must've got tired of the sex!

I remember when I was 27; Myself and Anto went to see a sex therapist in the 'Well Woman' centre, Cathal Bruagh Street, Dublin. I felt I only wanted to have sex twice or three times a week, and Anto loved sex every night, or more. I thought I had a low sex drive. I wanted to know how I could improve my libido. The therapist should've sent me on my way and told me and Anto that I was perfectly normal!

Instead, she gave me work to do on myself, including thinking happy sex thoughts and reading romantic novels!

I wasn't confident enough to say, feck off Anto! I don't need that much sex! I thought a woman had to keep her man happy. It made me so confused.

Of course Anto just thought he was a very normal, virile male, instead of a sex addict! Acknowledged, I'm sure, by all the male population of Ireland.

What did I want? Where did I go? The damage I had done to myself, hiding my personality, not being truly myself, was the cause of my depression. I felt guilty all the time when I didn't conform to the perfect woman.

Eventually I had to learn to rediscover myself. My husband and I both had the same goals in life. We loved our children completely, we wanted to recover from our past and we wanted to provide a better life for ourselves and our kids.

Now I was becoming a different person. I had to try to find me and live freely being me. Was I strong enough to just be me?

I'm in Dublin city every Saturday now as I drop Yasmin into drama in the Gaiety school of acting at the end of Temple Bar. Basically, it's old-fashioned play therapy. The kids can pretend to be anything they want, a tree, a dog, a poster. They pretend and use their imagination. It teaches the kids to express themselves and I think it will really help Yasmin in her social skills. I love going into the city.

There are lots of tourists around this area and I like the animosity of it. While Yasmin is in her class, I go into the

Starbucks at the end of Dame Street. I park just outside the wax museum. There are loads of homeless people sleeping in this area. I often just sit in my car and watch these poor young people sleeping on the ground.

I don't have to wonder how they got there.

Painful lives. Parents given up on them. Learning difficulties. Depression. Abuse. Damaged.

There are so many young people homeless in Dublin, it amazes me. It must be tough on the young girls with no privacy or dignity. I pray for these young people. I don't judge them. It is not their fault that they are homeless. There are not enough resources in the HSE to provide nutrition, education and emotional support for these kids.

These young people are on their lonely journey through life.
They have been alienated from their families, their homes.
They didn't choose the path they're on.
They fell into it, through their own weakness.
They can't get out now.
They will die young, but, at least in oblivion.
Who will break their cycle of abuse?

God? Are you watching over them?

I wrote this poem on this morning,
13th October 2013

'Under The Great Gates of the Bank of Ireland'
by Jean Murray
(off Dame street Dublin)

What age are those feet under that blanket?
They look so young
And the stench of urine that surrounds them.
It sickens my stomach.
I should stay here to feel what real pain is.
Real loss.
Real dysfunction.
The ground must be cold and hard even with an extra sleeping
bag underneath him, and boxes to sleep on.
Whose child is this?
No Mother to care?
Only the others like him.
They bring the hot tea, a sandwich to share.
Then the other stuff and tin foil.
All their faces weathered red and sleepy heads.
Teeth not good.
Faces so young so old.
So grateful for anything.
The boy loves hot chocolate with five spoons of sugar.
"Thanks Love,
God Bless You"

20th November 2013

It's just a year since my breakdown. It's not been an easy road. I have been struggling with my depression these past couple of weeks and this morning as I went walking with my dogs I was asking God to help me, to guide me, to send me his wisdom. I have been trying to focus on the positives and stay away from the negatives, but sometimes the weariness is in my bones.

It was a beautiful morning and I was focusing on the beauty and breathing in the cold air. I decided to go down the Glas Cairn route as it's a beautiful back road surrounded by fields, it's a good long walk at five kilometres long. I take my neighbour's Golden retriever also with my two Husky's. I'm tired this morning and they're pulling strongly against me. I'm talking to God, asking for help and guidance as I walk, taking in and appreciating the beauty that surrounds me.

I feel fragile and weak.

As I come back towards the village on the main Kilbride road now, I see a gate leading into the fields. I can see St Paul's school in the distance and I think, 'I'll take the dogs through that way and let them off their leads and give them a bit of a run. I looked all around to check for other animals, purposely taking in the beauty of the blue clear sky and breathing deeply in the cold fresh air. The beauty of the vast fields, spotlessly clean surrounding me. I walked across the first field, it seemed about two kilometres long. It was a little bit mucky but it had grass and the dogs were running around with glee. There were bushes up ahead dividing the next field, I was hoping there wasn't a gully filled with water to cross. There was. It also had bushes of wild thorns and briar. The dogs even doubted going through. I didn't fancy going back so I decided to get through it. I pulled the thorns away from the dogs and they scampered through and then I slid down the five-foot ditch on my bum and hoped it wasn't deep water.

Thankfully, it was only a foot deep and I prayed I could get up the steep climb on the other side. I thought, 'Here I go again, not checking things out, just jumping straight into things'. I did think for a moment I would get stuck in the thorns and a bull would come along and eat me, or at least poke holes in me with his horns like they do in Spain. Yes I'm still crazy!

But I got through it and up the gully. I was a little impressed with myself. I am 46 years of age!

I started through the next field. It had just been turned over, so it was all muck. Beautiful fields in your eye's vision are full of difficulty in reality. I had to keep my eyes on the ups and downs of the upturned muck. One slip and I could've twisted my ankle. I looked ahead, 'Maybe two kilometres?' I thought to myself.

I kept an eye on the dogs also as they scrambled across. I came to the back of the school. I'm sure my nephew Finn was looking through his classroom window, saying 'That's my aunty Jean and her dogs, she's crazy!' All the kids in that school know me and my dogs well now.

I looked back over the distance I had come. It was unknown terrain. It was scary at times. I had my doubts about making it through the rough fields.

The sun was shining down over the land I had walked. It looked beautiful now, not threatening.

And I felt God say to me, 'It will be ok'.

Conclusion

16th July 2014

There are always going to be some tough days in my life, because every day in my life is different. Each new day brings its own new challenges. It's how I deal with these challenges that will determine the outcome.

These last few months I have been really well. I have started my day with gratitude. I have stopped looking at the things negatively. I ignore the things that annoy me.

In my head I am saying to God, 'Thank you for this new day of life. I will walk in your footsteps of kindness and compassion. Free my mind of worries, negatives and resentments. Fill my mind with positives and gratitude.'

I am focusing on everything I have instead of things I want. I have everything I need today.

Thank you God.

I listen to other people who know, Rosena a Psychiatric nurse, a friend, teaching me, leading me, helping me on my journey.

My friend Josie, going through her own challenge in life with her son Thomas's battle with terminal cancer. Spiritually guiding me. Telling me it'll be ok.

Two Jehovah Witness ladies, Bernie and her friend had been calling to me once a month for a few years. I brought them in and made them tea. Sometimes they had younger girls with them, from different countries. Bernie would then talk about God and his work, gently, not pushy. At one point I said to Bernie, 'I'm a Catholic Bernie, and I'm not going to convert!

My dad would kill me if he was alive!'

I know the Catholic Church itself was full of corruptness and lies, but the newer priests like Father Gerry in Ratoath parish and our friend Father Madden, are talking the language that people want to hear: Importance of family, importance of faith, of living life without resentment, in God's footsteps.

Bernie said 'I'm not here to convert you Jean'. And then I understood. She had seen that I was a woman in distress and she came to help and guide me.

These people whom we were always warned against, are only talking about God and family importance. There are a few things I don't get about their religion, but we do have a common interest in that we need God and we need to have a faith: Something to believe in, to aspire to.

I have to walk my dogs each day. It's good for me as it takes me out of the house and I breathe the fresh air of the beautiful days. It's Summer now and I love the longs days and the warm breezes. In fact, I love all the seasons. I love every day of life.

It's a gift.

I'm very grateful for the positives in my life right now.

I will never go back to that place where I had gone.

I am grateful for the solitude of this walk, so I can remember the gift of Life. I breathe deeply. I am at peace. I look up to the skies and the wonders of life. I used to walk looking down at the ground, seeing nothing but grey, achieving nothing.

As I arrive back to my home, I wish I have a magic wand to wave around my house and magic it clean, a mundane job that I don't relish doing every day. (Hey! I have a sense of humour!)

I think of my children. Their beauty. I have these three great kids who know that working hard is their only way forward in life. I taught them that. I've got to be proud of myself.

I think of my husband. He has worked so hard to be a good husband. He is a good father and a good provider. He has come a long way and I'm grateful for his strength.

I am grateful my children are nourished and warm, my bills are paid and my family are healthy today.

It's that simple.

A few weeks ago, I met a lovely young man in the Aquatic centre. I was having a coffee before going for my swim. This young man was approaching my table. I knew he was blind as he walked towards me. I said, 'Hi' just to let him know I was there in case he wanted to sit at another table. He was happy to join me.

He was a tall lad, way over 6 feet I think, and about 26 years maybe.

I asked him, 'Was he always blind?' and he said no, it had happened when he was 19 years old. He started to fall over things and he was sent for tests. It took six months to confirm degenerative eye disease. He was totally blind before he reached 21.

I asked him how he coped and he said he started swimming. He arrives at the Aquatic centre at 6am and leaves it at 10am. He's training for the Rio Para Olympics. He said he just missed the London Para Olympics, he didn't qualify. He said his only worries were for his mam and dad who were getting on in years and he didn't want them they worrying about him, the youngest of five children.

I was really impressed by this young man, his courage, his strength: His selflessness.

I look for positive influences. When I think, 'I can't do this,' I quickly erase it from my brain and I say, 'Well, I won't know till I try!'

Anto and I are 28 years together this December 2014.

I have learned a lot about myself while I was writing this story. It was difficult for both of us to stay together on this journey. I was so rigid and controlled and he was so easy going. Anto wasn't aware of my depression and didn't know how to handle it.

Anto was really insecure because of all the personal loss he suffered as a young child. He tried controlling situations because he thought he could keep them from changing,

keep them from negative outcomes. Inevitably causing negative outcomes himself.

He turned to alcohol at such a young age because it helped him feel better, give him confidence, help him feel tough. He then became dependent on alcohol to mask his own feelings of weakness. He then became addicted to it and he couldn't think at all. When he gave up alcohol at age 35, he had to learn how to live again, without a crutch. It was really tough for him. Living with sobriety was even more difficult if you can understand that.

Was the work worth it? All of the stress we endured.?

It was of course, if nothing else, we would be stronger people.

My strict regime of getting things done, my desire for wanting it better, why couldn't I just settle for what was instead of tirelessly pushing?

That might seem a great tribute for someone, but I kept making mistakes. Maybe my way was wrong. Anto's laissez-faire attitude to everything annoyed me.

You might wonder how we lasted so long together.

Having a child with a disability or learning difficulties or indeed any other difficulty, takes up all of a mother's emotional and physical energy. It's not surprising that most couples don't make it.

Sarah also had learning difficulties and she needed me a lot to make sure all her stuff was in the right place.

It drives me crazy when my husband is surprised that the chemist doesn't stay open just for him on Sunday evening, after he has remembered he has forgotten to get his medication for blood pressure three days ago! It's like having triplets with dyspraxia!

I knew because of my emotional dysfunctions, I was attracted to someone just like me, who had lots of issues. I don't mean to knock my husband in any way by saying this, but I felt I got what I deserved. I didn't deserve a non-dysfunctional person, as I was so messed up myself. I also knew if I didn't resolve my own personality defects within my relationship that I would be attracted to dysfunction again. I would certainly be attracted to the same look as my husband, as I like that rugged look and his day old stubble, so why didn't I just work it out with him?

When I said my marriage vows, I took them seriously, 'For better for worse, through sickness and health.' At times, those words were like a prison sentence.

Marriage is not an easy path, but as the initial lust slinks away, it's then about your marriage vows. It's about loyalty and commitment; supporting each other when times are tough. That's what my marriage is now. We are learning to pick each other up when each of us are suffering. It's not lovey dovey, like you see on the telly. It's constructive. We both work hard at our bit. I run the home and the kids and my husband runs the business and provides for his family.

I see in the last few months the difference our 'grown up' behaviour has on our kids. They're assured.

Women in their 40s start going through 'The Change'. Their body is changing. First, the mind changes. Women start to look back at how they lived their first 40 years. What had they learned? For their future, they want to do it better. They know they are on the other side of the ladder of life.

I had to start to live as myself; I couldn't continue being the wimpy woman I had become in life and in my relationship.

With my change, I let go of all the resentment of the past. With encouragement for the future, our relationship has started to mature. I know when we raise our last child Yasmin, educated and secure, that Anto and I will be a young couple again! Please God!

It won't matter about the wrinkles or age. When I was younger, I used to look at old craggy couples in their 50's and wonder how were they still in love? Surely, they couldn't be doing the business still?

Yasmin

It was the week before Christmas 2013 and it was nearly the school holidays. Yasmin had made a mistake. She gets really mad with herself when she makes a mistake. She hits herself or pinches herself. I calmly, but firmly tell her not to hit herself, "Everybody makes mistakes! That's how we learn, Yasmin!" She's upset. She's tired and cranky. I hug her.

She asks me a question.

"Mammy, Does God make mistakes?"

I am so impressed with Yasmin little personality that I want to share with you a little insight to what she is like. These are some of the conversations Yasmin has with me while I'm taking her to school in the car.

Yasmin talking to her cousin Elle July 2013 aged 8:

Yasmin: "Elle, when I grow up, I'm going to drink wine, it's made from grapes and it's really healthy, isn't that right, Mam?"

Yasmin aged 6:

"Mammy, what does God do in Heaven? Is He dead?"

"Granddad's in Heaven too, isn't he, Mam?"

"And he's dead?"

Yasmin figuring out Christmas age 7:

"Mam, why does Santa come?" She asks.

"Well, I think it's because of the three wise men bringing presents to Jesus when he was born, then a kind old man took on the tradition and used to make toys for children and give them for free. He then became Saint Nicolas!" I explain wisely, proud of myself!

"Is He dead?" asks Yasmin.

"No ... He's a saint," I answer, phew!

"I love Christmas, Mammy!" She giggles excitedly.

"Mammy, do reindeers die?" she asks.

"Deer die, yes honey," I say, I'm beginning to see where this is all going!

"No, reindeer, mammy, Santa's reindeers, do they die?" she asks.

"Hmm, no, they don't die"... (well, what can I say?)

"Ahh, they're saints too, Mammy? And the elves? Are they saints too?"... (Somebody should have thought of all this when inventing Santa!)

"Yes Yasmin, I suppose so ... ." I answer.

"Mammy, in the olden days, Saint Nicolas just had a small factory, didn't he, Mammy?" Yasmin asks.

"Kind of, he made the toys in his house," I say.

"Now he has a big huge factory, Mammy, in the North Pole!" She says knowledgeably.

"Yes honey" I say.

"You know, Mam, Rudolf grabbed me and Pluto (our King Charles) in my dreams last night and flew me up to the sky to see all the other reindeers!" She giggles. "And Pluto was barking like crazy!" She giggles hysterically.

"Wow! I'd love to be in your dreams!" I say.

Yasmin age 7:
"Mam, do you know? If we were minding a dolphin, we would need lots of fish to feed him!"

Yasmin aged 7:
"Mam, if we had to spend Christmas in a hotel with a balcony, we could put lights all over the balcony and a big sign with lights on it too, saying 'Santa! Yasmin is in here!' That way he'll know where I am. Is that ok, Mammy?"

Yasmin aged 6:
One Day on our way home from school, Yasmin is looking at her mouth in the mirror.

"Mam, What's your tongue made of?"

"It's a muscle," I say.

"Ugh, why?"

"Cos it needs to be able to help you swallow," I say.

"What's that thing under it?" she asks.

"It holds your tongue in your mouth," I answer.

"Mam, What does it look like down my throat?"

"Kind of like your mouth, but darker," I say.

'Mam, I know what it's like for the food getting swallowed!" She exclaims. "It's like being on a roller coaster going, Agh! Agh! Agh! as they go down and down!" She giggles.

Yasmin aged 7:

"Mam, why is Cupid called Cupid?" (as in the little cherub) "Oh I know!" She answers her own question, "He's called after The Love Angel on The love Planet Cupid!" She says assuredly.

Yasmin 9th October 2013 Getting ready for school:

"Mammy, Why is God's birthday on Christmas?"

Me, "Mmm, I suppose it's the day he was born, it's his birthday."

Yasmin, "Does he get older every year in Heaven, Mammy?"

Me, "No honey, He stays the same age."

Yasmin, "Oh that's cool Mammy! That means that your friend Karen is still age 11! She is so much younger than you, Mammy!"

Yasmin and her cousin Isabella talking in the back of the car, 13th October 2013:

Yasmin: "My godmother lives in Cabra…"

Isabella: "So does mine, it's Maria, my Ma's friend…"

Yasmin: "My godmother is Aunty Pauline…"

Isabella: "My godmother gave me 20 euro for my birthday…"

Yasmin: "My godmother bought me a 'One Direction Mug' with my name on it!"

Yasmin: "Godmothers are great, aren't they, Isabella?"

Isabella: "Yeah …"

Yasmin: "I think they're called Godmothers because God sent them to us, do you think so too Isabella?

Isabella: "Yeah Yasmin ... ."

6th November 2013 5am in the morning:
Yasmin: "Mam, I know what Rudolf is doing in the North Pole right now!"

Me: "What, Yasmin?" As I sleepily get into her bed beside her.

Yasmin: "He's so excited about Christmas, he's jumping up and down in the snow, saying Christmas! Christmas! Christmas!"

Yasmin questions the Tooth Fairy: 5th December 2013
Yasmin: "Mammy, why did the tooth fairy leave me money and not take my tooth?"

3rd February 2014: Yasmin 9 1/2
"Mammy, I can skip!"

This is the letter I wrote to my husband in my diary in 2012.
(I still have it)

Anto

If I die before my time, make sure that Yasmin continues her weekly sessions with Andrea for her dyslexia; and every second week with Emir, her OT. Constantly, all through primary school!!!!!

Encourage her love of animals and her weekly pony lessons.

Encourage her to follow her dreams.

Anthony and Sarah;

Work hard for the things you want; and you shall get them.

Look after your sisters and brother and Dad.

Listen to each other and have patience, kindness and love in your lives.

I love you all and am so proud of you all.

Mam